ENGAGING THE SPIRIT WORLD

Popular Beliefs and Practices in Modern Southeast Asia

Edited by
Kirsten W. Endres and Andrea Lauser

Berghahn Books
New York • Oxford

First published in 2011 by
Berghahn Books
www.berghahnbooks.com
© 2011 Kirsten W. Endres and Andrea Lauser

Library of Congress Cataloging-in-Publication Data

Engaging the spirit world in modern Southeast Asia / edited by Kirsten W. Endres,
Andrea Lauser.
   p. cm. – (Asian anthropologies ; v. 5)
   Includes bibliographical references and index.
   ISBN 978-0-85745-358-7 (hardcover : alk. paper) – ISBN 978-0-85745-359-4 (ebook)
1. Spiritualism–Southeast Asia. 2. Southeast Asia–Religious life and customs. 3. Religion
and culture–Southeast Asia. I. Lauser, Andrea. II. Endres, Kirsten W. III. Series: Asian
anthropologies; v. 5.
   BF1242.S644E54 2011   133.90959–dc23

                                                                        2011037633

British Library Cataloguing in Publication Data

A catalogue record for this book is available from the British Library
Printed in the United States on acid-free paper

ISBN 978-0-85745-358-7 (hardback)
ISBN 978-0-85745-359-4 (ebook)

Contents

❦

LIST OF FIGURES

☙❧

PREFACE

Like many scholarly projects that extend from personal interests into larger issues shared by other colleagues, this collection of articles arises from the editors' own anthropological interests and research on the revitalization of religious and ritual practices in late socialist Vietnam. The cultural and religious landscape of Vietnam has undergone striking transformations in the last two decades. In the course of the economic and political reforms known as "renovation" (đổi mới), Vietnam has experienced a multifaceted resurgence of religion. In tandem with the intensification of beliefs and practices in institutional religions, there has been a sharp increase in non-institutionalized religious activities, ranging from household rites and individual propitiation at neighbourhood shrines to local and national religious festivals and pilgrimages across the country. Popular beliefs and rituals that once had been banned as backward and superstitious remnants of the old society are flourishing again and continue to adapt to the realities and challenges of contemporary urban and rural life. Whereas Kirsten Endres focused on the flourishing of Vietnamese urban spirit mediumship, Andrea Lauser's research addressed ritual practices such as the worship of ancestors, heroes, and local deities venerated during festivals and pilgrimages. A major theme was investigating the relationship between "religion" and "politics" by questioning what is accepted by whom, for what purpose, in which circumstances and under what political conditions as "religion" or as legitimate belief.

With the intention of illuminating the wider context of the contemporary dynamics of religion in Southeast Asia, we invited the contributors to this volume to explore how different factors (market relations, economic opportunity, social change, political power struggles, and so on) contribute to the reconfiguration of local spirit worlds, and how these processes in turn (re)shape discourses about cultural identity, morality, power relations, and interpretative control. By examining contemporary engagements with the world of spirits, ghosts, and ancestors in various parts of Southeast Asia, this collection of essays offers manifold insights and fresh interpretations that seek to contribute to the broader (theoretical) discussion of the relationship between religion and modernity. Furthermore this volume aims to bring fresh perspectives to ongoing debates about the anthropological critique of rationality.

This volume grew out of the contributions presented at two different conferences and workshops. At the fifth conference of the European Association for South East Asian Studies (EuroSEAS) held in Naples in September 2007, the editors put together a panel on "Spirited Modernities: Prosperity, Religions, and the Politics of Cultural Identity in Contemporary Asia." In September 2010, Andrea Lauser, with the assistance of Paul Christensen, organized a workshop at the Lichtenberg-Kolleg, a newly established Institute for Advanced Study at the University of Göttingen, that dealt with "Spirits in Modern Asia: Challenges for Societies and Scientists." The Lichtenberg-Kolleg also provided generous and vital funding in support of this book project. Early versions of the chapters in this book were originally presented at one or the other of these two occasions, and we would like to extend our thanks to all participants, including those whose contributions are not included in this volume. In particular, we would like to thank Peter J. Bräunlein, Annette Hornbacher, Brigitta Hauser-Schäublin, and Mu-chou Poo for their insightful contributions that helped expand our ideas. Parts of our own research have been conducted under the auspices of the Max Planck Institute for Social Anthropology (Halle/S. Germany), and we most sincerely express our gratitude to Chris Hann for his support and advice. We are grateful to the two anonymous reviewers of Berghahn Books for their careful reading of the manuscript and suggestions for improvement. The encouragement of the editors at Berghahn is much appreciated. Finally, we are grateful for the invaluable assistance of Jelana Vajen and Jelka Günther in preparing the manuscript and the index.

Andrea Lauser, Göttingen, Germany
Kirsten W. Endres, Halle/Saale, Germany

Introduction

MULTIVOCAL ARENAS OF MODERN ENCHANTMENT IN SOUTHEAST ASIA

Kirsten W. Endres and Andrea Lauser

Spirits have haunted the human imagination since times immemorial. Conceptualized in countless human and non-human forms, they may appear as the disembodied souls of the dead, as fiery demons with drooling fangs, as seductive heavenly fairies, or as uncanny creatures that can assume any shape. They may be envisioned as an anonymous mass of hungry ghosts or spirit soldiers, or as clearly defined personalities with noble moral qualities.[1] Some are identified as ancestral beings, mythological heroes, or saintly guardians. Spiritual entities inhabit the landscape, including forests, fields, rivers, and mountains; they reside at the margins of human habitation, in abandoned spaces, cemeteries, or in shrines erected for them in various spaces, including bustling urban centers. As dwellers of the invisible world, they may manifest themselves as dreamlike apparitions, as bodiless, ethereal voices, or, spontaneously or summoned at will, in the bodies of human beings. Spirits depend on human care and need to be propitiated with offerings and rites lest they cause misfortune, illness, and disaster. For either good or evil, they may interfere in worldly affairs, local politics, and matters of morality. Tylor's classic minimum definition of religion as "the belief in spiritual beings" (Tylor 1871: I, 424) may be semantically debatable, but it speaks to the immutability of spirit conceptions throughout the world and thus still serves as a useful starting point for a discussion of spirits in and of modernity.

Scientific Enlightenment Meets "Superstition"

In East and Southeast Asia, the advent of modernity as an epochal concept was closely tied to the colonial project of exercising power and "enlightened control" over non-Western peoples who appeared to be prone to magic, sorcery, and other

---

Endnotes for this chapter begin on page 13

"primitive" beliefs, and therefore incapable of responsible self-government (Styers 2004: 14; cf. Watson-Andaya 1997). Whether or not their countries had been colonized, the emergence of Western science and scientific rationality as prime markers of European superiority thus became a key issue for native political and intellectual elites of the late nineteenth and early twentieth century. Their deliberations entailed a critical rethinking of popular religious beliefs and practices. The modernizers of the Japanese Meiji era unleashed a torrent of attacks against "irrational" beliefs in order to recast the people as enlightened, knowledgeable subjects (Fujitani 1993). Korean progressives of the early twentieth century faulted Confucian ritualism for Korea's humiliation at the hands of foreign powers and criticized popular forms of Korean folk religion as unscientific (Kendall 2001, 2009). Reformers in Republican China saw popular spirit cults as a major factor blocking the way of modern progress (Duara 1991; Anagnost 1994). French-educated intellectuals in colonial Vietnam blamed traditional customs and beliefs for the weakness and "backwardness" of the country (Phan Kế Bính 1995[1915]; Endres 2007).[2] Among the new vocabulary that emerged to express modern ideas and their opposites was "superstition." Coined as a neologism by Meiji-era Japanese modernizers, the term was subsequently adapted by other Asian languages as *mixin* (China), *misin* (Korea) and *mê tín* (Vietnam). As in the West, at least since the Enlightenment, it implied an irrational belief or action that was based on a premodern, unscientific worldview. In the modernizing agendas of these emerging nation-states, superstition would come to serve "as modernity's dark alter ego, the realm of unacceptable practices, of things irrational, invalid, and consequently harmful" (Kendall 2001: 29). Subsequently, both communist and non-communist authoritarian regimes launched vigorous anti-superstition campaigns that denied the existence of supernatural powers considered to influence human lives and banned all practices involving the invocation of the spirit world.

Other "new" Southeast Asian nation-states were somewhat less explicit in rejecting popular religious practices as undesirable remnants of the pre-modern era.[3] Thai Buddhism, for example, was "modernized" by establishing a national *Sangha* organization under the control of the monarchy. King Chulalongkorn's reforms primarily aimed at incorporating all regions of the periphery into the emergent nation-state of Thailand and sought to eliminate unorthodox regional variants that were considered dangerous to the project of national integration (Tambiah 1976; Kitiarsa 2009; cf. Keyes 1971). Local spirit cults, though not expressly prohibited, were seen as remnants of irrationality and subordinated to Theravada Buddhism (Kitiarsa 1999; White 2005). This was also the case in Malaysia, where folk religious and hybrid Indian Hindu elements of Malay culture were deemed as premodern and un-Islamic by the postcolonial ruling elites (Willford 2005). For the Indonesian independence movement, the heterogeneity of local cultural systems, cosmologies, and beliefs across the archipelago posed a big challenge to the project of building a unitary, modern nation-state. The five tenets of the "national statement of purpose" (McVey 1999), the *Pancasila*, included the belief in a supreme God (*Ketuhanan Yang Maha Esa*), and the right to freedom of religious belief and conviction was enshrined in the 1949 constitution. Orthodox Muslim influence in the Ministry of Religion contributed to the institutionalization of a nuanced distinction between religion (*agama*) and current of belief (*aliran keper-cayaan*) that would play a crucial role under the *Orde Baru* (New Order) regime of Suharto, when adherence to a religion became a requirement of citizenship. While religion was understood as a monotheistic faith based on a holy scripture, a current of belief was defined as "a dogmatic opinion, which is closely connected to the living tradition of several tribes, especially of those tribes that are still backward" (Ramstedt 2004: 9).[4] Adherents of local beliefs were consequently classified as *belum beragama*, or "not yet having religion." Converts to one of the five acknowledged "world religions" could nevertheless retain some of their indigenous religious practices, tolerated as traditional custom (*adat*) and part of culture (*kebudayaan*).[5]

Despite their different ideological underpinnings, the marginalization of indigenous religious belief systems constituted an important element in the modernizing projects of the emerging Southeast Asian nation-states. Local spirit cults, even if not explicitly outlawed, came to be looked upon as epitomizing irrationality and backwardness and obsolete remnants of premodern thinking by the enlightened subjects of the postcolonial era. Even those who did not subscribe to Marxist thinking would certainly not have defined religion in Tylorean terms as "belief in spiritual beings."

Modernity and (Re)Enchantment

For many decades, any effort to think about the relationship between religion (or magic) and modernity in the social sciences has been haunted by the spirit of Max Weber (Weller 2008). Weber saw the inevitable disenchantment of the world as part of an all-encompassing process of modernization that would gradually marginalize, and ultimately replace, religion as a major source of meaning and moral guidance. In the past few decades, however, the tenability of the secularization thesis has been called into question (Asad 2003; see also Hefner 1998a), not only by the (almost universal) pervasiveness and persistence of religion, but also by "the fact that religious traditions throughout the world are refusing to accept the marginal and privatized role which theories of modernity as well as theories of secularization had reserved for them," a process Casanova (1994: 5) characterizes as deprivatization. The current proliferation of scholarly publications dealing with modernity and re-enchantment indicates that spirits, too, have refused to lurk in the gloomy shadows of the enlightened world of reason to which they were relegated and from where they have continued to fulfill their "traditional" roles. Around the globe, they have returned (if they had ever disappeared) with a venge-

ance to address the risks and opportunities of economic restructuring and neolib-
eral globalization, social tensions, political insecurities, and the more mundane,
everyday manifestations of modernity's malcontents.[6]

Southeast Asia is no exception. In Vietnam, the reforms of the 1980s, known
as "renovation" *(đổi mới),* triggered an explosion of religious activity that led to a
gradual change in state attitudes toward popular religious practices as part of national cultural identity (Malarney 2003; Endres 2011). While public discourse still
retains a somewhat critical stance vis-à-vis "superstitions," temples dedicated to
the worship of ancestors and efficacious deities are teeming with worshipers, and
spirit mediums no longer have to hold their possession rituals in secluded privacy.
Although the situation in Laos is influenced by a different religious landscape, the
politics of religion there have largely been modeled after the Vietnamese example.
Despite many years of repression under socialism and the current state-supported
dominance of Buddhism over spirit cults (Ladwig 2007), here we can also observe
a shift towards a greater acceptance and openness toward the performances of
female spirit mediums (Evans 1998). In Thailand, spirit mediumship has likewise
"enjoyed a comeback from the shadows of Thai public life" (George and Willford
2005: 18) and enhances the multiplicity of "Thailand's boom-time religions of
prosperity" (Jackson 1999b). In Indonesia, since the 1980s, several indigenous
religions have been re-molded as varieties of Hinduism and acknowledged by
the state in response to local campaigns striving for official recognition of traditional belief systems as *agama* (Schiller 2002; Ramstedt 2004). Although the New
Order considered the belief in ancestral spirits as antithetical to progress, politicians have continued to commune with and seek the blessings of potent ancestors
(Chambert-Loir and Reid 2002). Moreover, the political and economic insecurity
of the post-Suharto era has led to a proliferation of witchcraft idioms (Bubandt
2006; Siegel 2006).

The myriad ways in which devotees transact with the spirit world in dealing
with the discontinuities of their lives reveals that spirit beliefs and practices possess a tremendous creative potential and easily adapt to changing circumstances.
Moreover, the fleeting, amorphous nature of spirit beings allows them to constantly
hybridize and "reinvent themselves in novel situations" (Moore and Sanders 2001:
3). It is precisely the fact that they have (re)entered the public sphere to engage with
the complexities and ambiguities of the contemporary world that has led to calls for
a (re)conceptualization of spirit beliefs and practices as eminently modern.

This book contributes to the re-enchantment debate by providing ethnographic
evidence from various Southeast Asian societies. A key assumption of the authors is
that local traditions of engaging supernatural entities are important arenas in which
the dynamics of political, economic and social change are confronted and negotiated. Accordingly, the contributions investigate the role and impact of different
dynamics (market relations, economic opportunity, social change, political power
struggles, and so on) in the reconfiguration of local spirit worlds, and how these

dynamics have in turn (re)shaped discourses on cultural identity, morality, power relations, and interpretative control. The spirited modernities that have emerged in the process defy the conventional dichotomies of modern/traditional, rational/irrational, religious/secular, scientific/indigenous, progressive/backward, global/local—and thus they invite a critical rethinking of the concept of modernity itself.

Southeast Asian Spiritscapes of the Alternatively Modern

Modernity is a problematic term. As Gaonkar has aptly pointed out, "Western discourse on modernity is a shifting, hybrid configuration consisting of different, often conflicting, theories, norms, historical experiences, utopic fantasies, and ideological commitments" (Gaonkar 2001: 15). It goes beyond the scope of this introduction to reiterate the different perspectives and theoretical positions on "modernity" (and "postmodernity") in Western sociology.[7] What many of the classic approaches shared was the assumption that modernization and modernity—construed as nation-building, rational, technological progress, economic development and institutional differentiation—would ultimately result in cultural homogenization on a global scale. These theories conceived of modernity as a set of cognitive and social transformations which each and every culture would be (eventually) forced to undergo. Such a view is essentially acultural, inasmuch as it assumes that these transformations are culturally neutral processes that operate in the same way across the globe (Gaonkar 2001; Taylor 2001).

In recent shifts away from these acultural notions of a homogenizing force, modernity has been reconceptualized in the plural rather than the singular. Concepts of multiple, vernacular, alternative, or hybrid modernities have drawn significant attention to the fact that "modernity always unfolds within specific cultures or civilizations" (Gaonkar 2001: 17; see also Randeria 2006; Raffin 2008). Different societies (or cultures) may thus bring forth "other" forms of modernity that diverge from the Western model—a model that, in fact, has also been revealed as an imaginary, ideological construct. Whereas Eisenstadt's focus is on "culturally specific forms of modernity shaped by distinct cultural heritages" (Eisenstadt, Reidel, and Sachsenmaier 2002: 1; see also Eisenstadt 2000), the alternative modernities perspective provided by Gaonkar focuses on site-specific creative adaptations as expressions of an active and critical engagement with modernity. Timothy Mitchell describes modernity as a "complex rearrangement of social practices driven by a series of different and intersecting logics" (Mitchell 2002: 14). Knauft, meanwhile, suggests that alternative modernities "happen" in a multivocal arena that is delimited and framed by local cultural and subjective dispositions on one side, and by global political economies (and their possibilities and limitations) on the other (Knauft 2002). His conception emphasizes the hybridity and interwovenness of local and global processes through which political, economic, societal, and cultural interests are articulated and negotiated. At the same time, it underscores the dialectical relationship between past and present, or tradition and modernity, and thus allows modernity to become "spirited"—a feature once thought of as modernity's very antithesis.

Southeast Asia offers a particularly rich field of inquiry into the dynamics and processualities of multiple, alternative modernities, as these have produced and (re)shaped a wide variety of religious phenomena. Arjun Appadurai has suggested conceptualizing alternative modernities and the global flows that link them through a variety of "-scapes": ethnoscapes, mediascapes, technoscapes, financescapes, and ideoscapes, composed of ideas, terms and images. The suffix -scape emphasizes the "fluid, irregular shapes of these landscapes" and indicates that they are "deeply perspectival constructs, inflected by the historical, linguistic, and political situatedness of different sorts of actors" (Appadurai 1996: 33). By ethnoscapes Appadurai means "the landscape of persons who constitute the shifting world in which we live: tourists, immigrants, refugees, exiles ... and other moving groups and individuals" (ibid.: 33). Similarly, the spiritscapes of Southeast Asia consist of transworldly, transreligious, and transethnic beings who move freely in and out of the permeable boundaries between material and metaphysical realms, between different religions and ethnicities, and between historical pasts and political presents (Lauser and Weisskoppel 2008; Huwelmeier and Krause 2010).

The various manifestations of spirits and ghosts in possession cults, popular rituals, and the media in different parts of Asia include Philippine Christian spirits and faith healers who express their devotion by having themselves crucified (Braunlein 2010), vengeful spirits of aborted fetuses in Taiwan and Japan who need to be placated (Hardacre 1997; Moskowitz 2001), spirits of resistance to the capitalist mode of production who possess Malay factory workers (Ong 1987), spirits of prosperity who are believed to support those facing risks associated with the modern market economy (e.g., Jackson 1999a, 1999b), hungry ghosts who haunt the memories of the living and demand their share in consuming their new-found wealth (Kwon 2006, 2008; Kendall 2008, 2009; Ladwig, this volume), and melodramatic ghosts that appear on movie screens to entertain a young, educated and upwardly mobile pan-Asian audience (see McRoy 2006; Kitiarsa, this volume). The themes that emerge from the ethnographic encounters with these entities and their human hosts underscore the entangledness of local worlds and global flows and reflect the "hybrid or composite character of much of what one recognizes as modern" (Venn and Featherstone 2006: 461).

One recurrent issue in the literature is that spirits have always been closely associated with the implementation of power. As potent and efficacious supernatural beings, they may exercise power over human bodies and make them bend to their will. On the other hand, mortals may acquire certain techniques that enable them to tap into the powers of the spirit world and enhance their own potency. Kari Telle (this volume) describes how the Hindu minority on the island of Lombok responded to a prevailing sense of ontological insecurity by creating their own security force of Dharma Wisesa, or "spirited warriors," a civilian defense group that is understood as being backed by an invisible spirit army. Lee Wilson (this volume), in contrast, looks at the relationship between knowledge and power in Indonesia through the West Javanese martial art Pencak Silat. He notes that traditional knowledge practices of invulnerability entailed mediating relations with the denizens of the unseen world, whereas contemporary institutionalized forms of invulnerability practices are defined by rational scientific explanations.

In many places, spirits play an essential role in bringing the past into the present (Kramer 1993; Stoller 1995; Levy, Mageo and Howard 1996; Lambek 2010). Their historical dimension intimately ties certain spirits to issues of legitimacy and authority, and thus also enables them to act politically in this world (Bubandt 2009). Spirits and politics, in fact, have at all times gone hand in hand in many parts of Southeast Asia (Chambert-Loir and Reid 2002; Willford and George 2005; Platenkamp 2007). The civilian defense force established on the island of Lombok, described by Kari Telle (this volume), derives its strength from the same protective supernatural powers that once backed the last Balinese king to rule Lombok. Lee Wilson (this volume) characterizes the knowledge of invulnerability in the Indonesian martial art of Pencak Silat, be it conceptualized as a transmission of spiritual potency or as a chemical reaction in the body, as a "state-forming knowledge." Claire Chauvet (this volume) mentions that in an attempt to bring their spirits in line with an official state ideology that celebrates patriotism and heroic sacrifice for the good of the nation, Vietnamese spirit mediums emphasize the historicity and meritoriousness of their spirits. Kirsten Endres and Andrea Lauser (this volume) illustrate how the glorious dead of the Vietnam War may become efficacious spirits that mediate between the needs and requests of the living and the deceased. These ghosts thus actively engage the living in the project of challenging official state commemorative practices. On the Indonesian island of Ternate, the souls of past rulers possess human mediums in order to debate proper procedures in the re-establishment of the sultanate in the Moluccas (Bubandt 2009). Spirits, ghosts and ancestors thus deal with contemporary political processes, power relations, and moral values by bringing "the authority of the past to bear in the present" (Lambek 1996: 239).

Another central theme in recent anthropological scholarship on modern enchantment is the dynamic interplay between spirit phenomena and market forces (e.g., Kendall 1996, 2009; Weller 1994). In Southeast Asia, as elsewhere, the onslaught of unbridled global capitalism has resulted both in substantially greater (though unequally distributed) wealth and in increased economic insecurity. The "sacred canopies" of the region have been deeply impacted by these dynamics (Kitiarsa 2008). Not only has the emergence of "market cultures" (Hefner 1998b) spurred processes of religious commodification, it has also propelled the rise of "prosperity cults" and "occult economies" that promise wealth and riches mediated by supernatural forces (Comaroff and Comaroff 1999). Vietnamese spirit mediums, as well as Korean shamans, conceptualize some of their spirits as particularly responsive to the material needs of their adherents. On the other hand, spirits and ancestors also demand a share of their devotees' and descendants' accrued wealth in the form of lavish rituals and modern consumer goods as offerings, as can be seen in the chapters by Chauvet, Endres and Lauser, and Kendall. As Laurel Kendall shows (this volume), this enhanced religious materiality has also resulted in a renegotiation of the term "superstition" as part of modernity talk among thoroughly modern spirit mediums and devotees in contemporary Vietnam. Patrice Ladwig (this volume) addresses the relation between the material and the immaterial from yet another angle. Based on ethnographic examples from Laos, he explores the ontological status of ghosts and spirits through the traces of their presence left in the material world.

In comparison to other spirits in the region, the Malay Muslim *keramat* demand rather little from the Chinese property developers who encroach on the land they guard. Beng-Lan Goh (this volume) traces the movement of *keramat* from their hybrid Islamic origins to their adoption by middle-class Chinese and Indian communities in contemporary urban Malaysia. In transcending these religious and ethnic divides, *keramat* challenge Malaysian nationalist discourses about ethnic and religious identity and remind us that both tradition and modernity must be seen as "hybrid assemblages in a state of flux" (Venn and Featherstone 2006: 457). In a related vein, Bénédicte Brac de la Perrière (this volume) interprets the interaction between the normatively separate spheres of Burmese spirit worship and Buddhist-oriented practices as part of an ongoing dialogical process of defining the boundaries between different religious practices, a process she describes as the autonomization of spirit possession. A separation of (formerly) multi-religious spaces into separate spheres also seems to take place in southern Thailand. Alexander Horstmann (this volume) looks at the *manora rongkru* as a hybrid, multi-religious spirit possession ritual-cum-performance art that can be traced back to a shared ancestry of *manora* teachers. Formerly rejected by Theravada Buddhism, the recent proliferation of the *manora* has contributed to the re-enchantment of popular Buddhism, while at the same time losing its footing in Muslim communities.

The Presence of Spirits: Voice and Agency

Spirits are essentially characterized by their "coming into presence" (Lambek 2010). In doing so, they do not depend so much on human beliefs as on their practices. As Chakrabarty puts it, "They are parts of the different ways of being through which we make the present manifold" (Chakrabarty 2000: 111). The most common form in which spirits come into presence is through the mediating body of a human host. This may happen unexpectedly, even involuntarily, in the sense of an affliction, or in rather controlled ways of deliberately summoning a spiritual being into the body of a medium. Scholars have attempted to classify and theorize spirit possession in many ways (see Boddy 1994). Ioan Lewis's interpretation of spirit possession as a strategy of the weak and marginalized to command attention, voice their grievances, and achieve their goals (Lewis 1989[1971]) has been influential and spawned numerous anthropological studies in this vein. Although illness and human suffering is often at the core of spirit possession, recent scholarship proposes that possession phenomena must not be taken as an index of social deviance or psychological pathology. Ethnographic evidence from various parts of the world instead suggests that, rather than being peripheral, spirit possession phenomena are central to cultural production and may serve as important strategies of self-empowerment (e.g., Boddy 1989; Sharp 1993; Kapferer 1997; Carrin 1999; Phạm Quỳnh Phương 2007, 2009; Kendall 2009).

Possession practices are widespread in Southeast Asia. Many of them are strongly, but not solely, associated with healing, such as the ritual possessions of the Vietnamese *bà đồng* and *ông đồng* (Nguyễn Thị Hiền 2002; Chauvet, this volume; Kendall, this volume), the seances of the Malay *bomoh* (Laderman 1991), or the numerous "shamanic" practices of ethnic minority groups in the interior or upland areas of Southeast Asia (Neumann Fridman and Walter 2004). Other possession practices are instrumental in communicating with spirit entities for divination purposes and establishing contact with the ancestors. Several of the contributions to this volume focus on spirit possession in one form or another (Brac de la Perrière; Chauvet; Endres and Lauser; Horstmann; Kendall). The Burmese *natkádaw* of the Thirty-seven Lords conceive of themselves as married to one of the spirits in the pantheon and couch their experience of trance-like states during ritual possession in metaphors of erotic love (Brac de la Perrière, this volume). Possessed by their ancestors, the spirit-mediums of the *manora* in southern Thailand seem not to be their human selves until after the ancestral souls have left their bodies (Horstmann, this volume). The spirits of the Vietnamese cult of the Four Palaces are said to descend on, or mount, their hosts who often claim they have no control over their actions and utterances during possession (Chauvet, this volume). Many possession idioms in fact construe possession as the displacement of the host's agency by the agency of the possessing spirit. The spirit medium, taken over by the spirit, deity, or ancestor, is perceived as a mere vessel for the expression of the supernatural entity's will. As such, the possession idiom stands in stark contrast to the image of the human individual advanced by modernity— that is, a bounded, rational, autonomous agent that is not to be seen as acted upon by cosmic forces or divine will. Despite the apparent displacement of their human agency, however, spirit mediums generally feel empowered by the experience of possession. In many cultures, possession practices have real therapeutic effects on mental health and overall well-being and provide a forum for social networking and mutual support. Possession practices may also enable spirit mediums to exert effective social influence and accumulate material wealth (Boddy 1994; Behrend and Luig 1999; Keller 2002; Johnson and Keller 2006; Cohen 2008). How, then, does this apparent paradox relate to the question of agency?

Over the past few decades, "agency" has become a prominent topic of debate in the social sciences, particularly in the fields of feminist and subaltern studies. Most commonly, agency refers to the capacity of individual persons to act independently and pursue their interests within (or despite) the constraints of structure. With regard to (female) spirit possession, Mary Keller has theorized an "instrumental agency" in which "possessed bodies share the same paradoxical agency in that the body is not speaking, it is spoken through; the body is not hammering, it is being used to hammer; the body is not mounting, it is being mounted" (Keller 2002: 82). This emphasis on the instrumental dynamics of possession highlights the subject/agency aspect in a different way: It is the apparent "passivity" of the subject that is wielded like a hammer or played like a musical instrument that actually endows the possessed body with the special authority accorded him (or her) by the community in the context of the ritual.[8] Rather than conceptualizing this agency as "instrumental," however, it seems more apt to speak of a distributed, relational agency, as it is in the interrelationship between the spirit or deity who needs the human body in order to come into presence, the possessed body that is worked on by a supernatural power, and the ritual community for whom the spirits have an ontological reality that agency resides. This emphasis on the relational aspect of agency also resonates with anthropological perspectives on selfhood that challenge the idea of an autonomous individual as "simply another local model" (Moore 1994: 30)— that is, a Western construct that does not necessarily apply to other cultures where people do not think of selves and persons as indivisible and bounded, but as unbounded and dividual (Marriott 1976; Strathern 1988; Smith 2006). Moreover, it indicates that agency is not essentially a property unique to human beings. A broader definition of agency that can include both human and non-human entities is, for example, suggested by the proponents of Actor-Network Theory (ANT). One of its key progenitors, Bruno Latour, defines an actor or actant as: "something that acts or to which activity is granted by others. It implies no special motivation of human individual actors, or of humans in general. An actant can literally be anything provided it is granted to be such a source of an action" (Latour 1996: 373). From this perspective we can discern that agency is not limited to human beings but may also be found in material objects, works of art, landscapes, or rituals (Gell 1998; Tilley 2004; Sax 2006; Allerton 2009). It is not so much a matter of intentionality and free will as it is one of the ability to bring about transformations in the external world. From this assumption it is only a small, but radical, step to the claim that spirits and deities, too, have agency and are "part of the agentive network" (Sax 2009: 133; see also Ladwig, this volume; Kendall, this volume).

Keller's notion of the medium as being acted upon also draws attention to the other side of agency, namely "patiency." A key text for understanding the concept of patiency in the context of spirit beliefs and practices is Godfrey Lienhardt's study of the religion of the Dinka (Lienhardt 1961; see also Kramer 1993). Lienhardt argues that in contrast to the interpretation of such phenomena in modern Western thinking, the Dinka of Southern Sudan do not conceive of their dreams and memories as inner processes of an autonomous individual's remembering or imagining mind. Rather, certain dreams are seen as personal encounters with divine powers—spirits, deities, and ancestors—that are held to influence human lives "for good or evil" (Lienhardt 1961: 147). While we, as Westerners, construe ourselves as active agents in many situations, the Dinka see themselves as passive objects, or patients, of actions initiated by spiritual powers that work on them and, at times, even enter the human body. Lienhardt chose the Latin word *passio/ passiones* because it describes the opposite of action not as mere passivity or as non-action, but as the experience of being acted upon.

Building on this notion of *passiones*, Schnepel (2008, 2009) urges us to pay more attention to the dialectics of agency and patiency. He illustrates his point with the example of the East Indian *Dando Nato* ("dance of punishment"), a ritual dance dedicated to the deities Kali and Shiva. During the time of the festival, which lasts for fourteen days, the male dancers have to renounce their worldly lives and fully devote themselves to divine worship. The constant sound of drumming, the wafting smell of incense, the physical exertion of dancing in the heat of the day, and the spiritually charged atmosphere may cause the participants to experience trance and even spirit possession. Schnepel argues that the way in which the devotees take on their roles during the ritual dances must not be understood as an active process. Rather, the dancers understand themselves as acted upon by external powers that take possession of their bodies and inscribe them with divine wisdom and knowledge. The encounter with the divine thus imbues the devotees with an agency that is effective "not although, but exactly because it is embedded into and encompassed by the (actively sought) experience of 'patiency' or *passio*" (Schnepel 2006: 125).

From the above it should have become clear that a focus on alternative modernities also calls for a recognition of alternative subjectivities and of multiple forms of agency beyond that of a bounded, autonomous self. Moreover, for the people whose cultures we study, the spirits may be as real as any material object or living being. In contrast, as anthropologists we generally do not share this ontological certainty and instead tend to think of spirits as metaphors, symbols, and collective imaginaries (Ladwig, this volume; cf. Turner 2003). Personal convictions and uncanny encounters notwithstanding, a conventional social-science perspective does not allow us to presume otherwise, lest we risk the ridicule and consternation of our peers. The ethnographic examples presented in this book, however, buttress Dipesh Chakrabarty's claim that gods and spirits are "existentially coeval with the human" and "that the question of being human involves the question of being with gods and spirits" (Chakrabarty 2000: 16; see also Kendall, this volume). Conceiving of spirits as authentic social and political actors/agents in networks of distributed agency (Sax

2009) also brings us nearer to the point of view of the devotees, for whom spirit phenomena represent powerful encounters with the ontological reality of a supernatural presence. As Kendall shows (this volume), the deployment of material things as gifts and enticements serves to secure their positive presence in the here and now. This presence, in turn, also drives the expanding and diverse market in ritual goods: new intricate costumes, better-produced statues, and more elaborate and luxurious offerings are felt to cause the deities to be more responsive, and thus more present, in the contemporary human world. In this regard, Nils Bubandt suggests understanding spirits as "methodologically real," and treating them as "key informants who can be engaged, interviewed and analysed very much like the conventional key informant technique suggests" (Bubandt 2009: 298, 296).

Closing Remarks

Neither the Western conception of modernity, nor the notion of the modern individual as a bounded, rational subject applies uniformly throughout the world. In most Southeast Asian societies that are the focus of this book, the self is experienced as a radically relational entity. The networks of such relational selves may even transcend the boundaries of the human world and include close exchange relationships with gods, spirits, and ancestors. Cosmologies and belief systems shape and are shaped by powerful social structural and political forces; they are models of and models for the world. From an anthropological point of view, then, it does indeed make a difference whether a jealous god reigns or a multitude of spirits needs to be propitiated, because these conceptions also have an impact on how individual agency and subjectivity are perceived in different cultures. In theorizing spirit phenomena in modernity, we thus need to be sensitive to local concepts of self, personhood, and agency. A focus on networks of distributed, relational agency may enhance our understanding of how processes of global integration, social fragmentation, political alienation, cultural commodification, and various other transformations associated with modernity are experienced and resolved in different cultural contexts.

The project of modernity not only promises happiness and material well-being, but also produces tensions, ambivalences, and anxieties. "Religious capital" in Bourdieu's sense can be both an asset for prosperity and a resource against the unsettling disquiet fostered by modernity. The upsurge of spirit religions in times of economic prosperity and social transformation is not just a recent phenomenon, however. Neither does it represent a retreat to archaic traditions as a response or solution to the uncertainties of life in times of political, economic, and social change. On the contrary, the various spirit beliefs and practices discussed in this book have effectively engaged with the actual historical and political contexts of their times. In doing so, they have been continuously recreated and reinvented into creative strategies of confronting the existential uncertainties, economic opportunities, and political upheavals that many Southeast Asian societies face today. Hence, in connecting local and global flows, past and present meanings, human and spirit worlds, the Southeast Asian spiritscapes discussed in this volume not only embody a distinct feature of the contemporary moment, but also challenge the grand narrative of a unitary, globalized secular modernity.

Notes

1. In this Introduction, we do not wish to draw a clear line between different categories of spiritual beings (for an overview of typical categorizations, see Levy, Mageo, and Howard 1996). In many societies, the most relevant distinction seems to be the one between "spirit" and "ghost." Pattana Kitiarsa (this volume) distinguishes between the two categories by associating "spirit(s)" with the sphere of religious belief or cult and reserving the term "ghost(s)" for the malevolent and revengeful dead. In contrast, Mu-Chou Poo defines "ghost" in far more general terms as "a kind of post-earthly existence of a dead individual, which can be perceived by those still alive in a variety of different forms" (Poo 2009: 4). Yet he also points out that the application of the term "ghost" in the familiar Western sense is likely to distort other meanings associated with "ghosts" and "spirits" in different parts of the world. We therefore leave it to the individual authors to define and draw lines, if necessary, between different categories of spiritual/ghostly existences within the cultural context of their research.

2. Popular forms of spirit worship had of course also been attacked in precolonial times. Confucian rules of propriety, for example, prescribed other forms of ritual than those practiced by sorcerers and spirit mediums. In Vietnam, popular religious practices such as spirit possession, fortune telling and sorcery were expressly prohibited by the Lê Code, a law code enacted in the fifteenth century under the Lê dynasty (Dror 2007: 165). Yet the repressive stance towards such practices, characterized as superstition only in the twentieth century, had not been continued in an unbroken line by imperial successors (ibid.: 166), nor was it rigidly enforced at the grassroots level of Vietnamese society.

3. By Southeast Asia, we shall primarily cover the following countries in the region: Myanmar (Burma), Malaysia, Thailand, Laos, Vietnam and Indonesia. For critical discussions of Southeast Asia as a regional construct, see Chou and Houben (2006).

4. For a wider regional perspective, see DuBois (2009).

5. In 2006, Confucianism (again) joined Islam, Protestantism, Catholicism, Buddhism and Hinduism as the sixth formally recognized faith of Indonesia. While Confucianism had originally been recognized during the Sukarno era, after 1965 all open displays of Chinese religiosity were prohibited.

6. See, e.g., Comaroff and Comaroff (1993), Geschiere (1997), Behrend and Luig (1999), Morris (2000), Moore and Sanders (2001), Meyer and Pels (2003), West and Sanders (2003), Fjelstad and Nguyễn Thị Hiền (2006, 2011), Willford and George (2005), Taylor (2007), Kendall (2008, 2009), Kitiarsa (2008), Taylor (2008), and Hüwelmeier and Krause (2010).

7. For overviews, see Gaonkar (2001), Eisenstadt, Riedel, and Sachsenmaier (2002), Friedman (2002), Knauft (2002), and Pels (2003).

8. With this argument we do not wish to imply that spirit mediums merely serve as unconscious or passive vehicles of the possessing spirit. Ample ethnographic evidence has shown that this is clearly not generally the case. However, Keller's analogy of the hammer and the flute resonates with the fact that spirit mediums typically deny their capacity to act willfully during possession and ascribe agency, intentionality, and authority to the ancestors, spirits, and divinities that possess them.

References

Allerton, Catherine. 2009. "Introduction: Spiritual Landscapes of Southeast Asia," *Anthropological Forum* 19: 235–51.

Anagnost, Ann S. 1994. "The Politics of Ritual Displacement," in *Asian Visions of Authority: Religion and the Modern States of East and Southeast Asia*, eds. C.F. Keyes, L. Kendall, and H. Hardacre. Honolulu: University of Hawaii Press, pp.221–54.

Appadurai, Arjun. 1996. *Modernity at Large: Cultural Dimensions of Globalization*. Minneapolis: University of Minnesota Press.

Asad, Talal. 2003. *Formations of the Secular: Christianity, Islam, Modernity*. Stanford, CA: Stanford University Press.

Behrend, Heike, and Ute Luig, eds. 1999. *Spirit Possession, Modernity and Power in Africa*. Madison: University of Wisconsin Press.

Boddy, Janice. 1989. *Wombs and Alien Spirits: Women, Men, and the Zar Cult in Northern Sudan*. Madison: University of Wisconsin Press.

———. 1994. "Spirit Possession Revisited: Beyond Instrumentality," *Annual Review of Anthropology* 23: 407–34.

Bräunlein, Peter. 2010. *Passion/Pasyon: Rituale des Schmerzes im europäischen und philippinischen Christentum*. Stuttgart: Wilhelm Fink Verlag.

Bubandt, Nils. 2006. "Sorcery, Corruption, and the Dangers of Democracy in Indonesia," *Journal of the Royal Anthropological Institute* 12: 413–31.

———. 2009. "Interview with an Ancestor: Spirits as Informants and the Politics of Possession in North Maluku," *Ethnography* 10: 291–316.

Carrin, Marine, ed. 1999. *Managing Distress: Possession and Therapeutic Cults in South Asia*. New Delhi: Manohar.

Casanova, José. 1994. *Public Religions in the Modern World*. Chicago: University of Chicago Press.

Chakrabarty, Dipesh. 2000. *Provincializing Europe: Postcolonial Thought and Historical Difference*. Princeton, NJ: Princeton University Press.

Chambert-Loir, Henri, and Anthony Reid, eds. 2002. *The Potent Dead: Ancestors, Saints and Heroes in Contemporary Indonesia*. Honolulu: University of Hawaii Press.

Chou, Cynthia, and Vincent Houben, eds. 2006. *Southeast Asian Studies: Debates and New Directions*. Singapore: ISEAS.

Cohen, Emma. 2008. "What Is Spirit Possession? Defining, Comparing, and Explaining Two Possession Forms," *Ethnos* 73: 101–26.

Comaroff, Jean, and John L. Comaroff. 1999. "Occult Economies and the Violence of Abstraction: Notes from the South African Postcolony," *American Ethnologist* 26: 279–303.

———. eds. 1993. *Modernity and its Malcontents: Ritual and Power in Postcolonial Africa*. Chicago: University of Chicago Press.

Dror, Olga. 2007. *Cult, Culture, and Authority: Princess Liễu Hạnh in Vietnamese History*. Honolulu: University of Hawaii Press.

Duara, Prasenjit. 1991. "Knowledge and Power in the Discourse of Modernity: The Campaigns against Popular Religion in Early Twentieth-century China," *Journal of Asian Studies* 50: 67–83.

DuBois, Thomas, ed. 2009. *Casting Faiths: Imperialism and the Transformation of Religion in East and Southeast Asia*. New York: Palgrave Macmillan.

Eisenstadt, Shmuel N. 2000. "Multiple Modernities," *Daedalus* 129: 1–29.

Eisenstadt, Shmuel N., Jens Riedel, and Dominic Sachsenmaier. 2002. "The Context of the Multiple Modernities Paradigm," in *Reflections on Multiple Modernities*, eds. D. Sachsenmaier and J. Riedel. Leiden: Brill, pp.1–23

Endres, Kirsten W. 2007. "Spirited Modernities: Mediumship and Ritual Performativity in

Late Socialist Vietnam," in *Modernity and Re-Enchantment: Religion in Post-revolutionary Vietnam*, ed. P. Taylor. Singapore: ISEAS, pp.194–220.

———. 2011. *Performing the Divine: Mediums, Markets and Modernity in Urban Vietnam*. Copenhagen: NIAS Press.

Evans, Grant. 1998. *The Politics of Ritual and Remembrance: Laos Since 1975*. Honolulu: University of Hawaii Press.

Fjelstad, Karen, and Nguyễn Thị Hiền, eds. 2006. *Possessed by the Spirits: Mediumship in Contemporary Vietnamese Communities*. Ithaca, NY: Southeast Asia Program, Cornell University.

———. eds. 2011. *Spirits Without Borders: Vietnamese Spirit Mediums in a Transnational Age*. New York: Palgrave Macmillan.

Friedman, Jonathan. 2002. "Modernity and Other Traditions," in *Critically Modern: Alternatives, Alterities, Anthropologies*, ed. B.M. Knauft. Bloomington: Indiana University Press, pp.287–314.

Fujitani, Takashi. 1993. "Inventing, Forgetting, Remembering: Toward a Historical Ethnography of the Nation-State," in *Cultural Nationalism in East Asia: Representation and Identity*, ed. H. Befu. Berkeley: University of California Press, pp.77–106.

Gaonkar, Dilip Parameshwar. 2001. "On Alternative Modernities," in *Alternative Modernities*, ed. D.P. Gaonkar. Durham, NC: Duke University Press, pp.1–23.

Gell, Alfred. 1998. *Art and Agency: An Anthropological Theory*. Oxford: Clarendon Press.

George, Kenneth M. and Andrew C. Willford. 2005. "Introduction: Religion, the Nation, and the Predicaments of Public Life in Southeast Asia," in *Spirited Politics: Religion and Public Life in Contemporary Southeast Asia,* eds. A.C. Willford and K.M. George. Ithaca, NY: Southeast Asia Program, Cornell University, pp.9–22.

Geschiere, Peter. 1997. *The Modernity of Witchcraft: Politics and the Occult in Postcolonial Africa*. Charlottesville: University Press of Virginia.

Hardacre, Helen. 1997. *Marketing the Menacing Fetus in Japan*. Berkeley: University of California Press.

Hefner, Robert W. 1998a. "Multiple Modernities: Christianity, Islam, and Hinduism in a Globalizing Age," *Annual Review of Anthropology* 27: 83–104.

———. ed. 1998b. *Market Cultures: Society and Values in the New Asian Capitalisms*. Singapore: Institute of Southeast Asian Studies.

Hüwelmeier, Gertrud, and Kristine Krause, eds. 2010. *Traveling Spirits: Migrants, Markets and Mobilities*. London: Routledge.

Jackson, Peter A. 1999a. "The Enchanting Spirit of Thai Capitalism: The Cult of Luang Phor Khoon and the Post-modernization of Thai Buddhism," *South East Asia Research* 7(1): 5–60.

———. 1999b. "Royal Spirits, Chinese Gods, and Magic Monks: Thailand's Boom-time Religions of Prosperity," *South East Asia Research* 7(3): 245–320.

Johnson, Paul Christopher, and Mary Keller. 2006. "The Work of Possession(s)," *Culture and Religion* 2: 112–22

Kapferer, Bruce. 1997. *The Feast of the Sorcerer: Practices of Consciousness and Power*. Chicago: University of Chicago Press.

Keller, Mary. 2002. *The Hammer and the Flute: Women, Power and Spirit Possession*. Baltimore, MD: Johns Hopkins University Press.

Kendall, Laurel. 1996. "Korean Shamans and the Spirits of Capitalism," *American Anthropologist* 98(3): 512–27.

———. 2001. "The Cultural Politics of 'Superstition' in the Korean Shaman World: Modernity Constructs its Other," in *Healing Powers and Modernity: Traditional Medicine, Shamanism, and Science In Asian Societies*, eds. L.H. Connor and G. Samuel. Westport, CT: Bergin and Garvey, pp.25–41.

———. 2008. "Of Hungry Ghosts and Other Matters of Consumption," *American Ethnologist* 35(1): 154–70.

———. 2009. *Shamans, Nostalgias, and the IMF: South Korean Popular Religion in Motion*. Honolulu: University of Hawaii Press.

Keyes, Charles F. 1971. "Buddhism and National Integration in Thailand," *Journal of Asian Studies* 30: 551–67.

Kitiarsa, Pattana. 1999. "You May Not Believe, But Never Offend the Spirits: Spirit-medium Cult Discourses and the Postmodernization of Thai Religion," Ph.D. dissertation. Seattle: University of Washington.

———. 2009. "Beyond the Weberian Trails: An Essay on the Anthropology of Southeast Asian Buddhism," *Religion Compass* 3: 201–24.

———. ed. 2008. *Religious Commodifications in Asia: Marketing Gods*. New York: Routledge.

Knauft, Bruce M. 2002. "Critically Modern: An Introduction," in *Critically Modern. Alternatives, Alterities, Anthropologies*, ed. B.M. Knauft. Bloomington: Indiana University Press, pp.1–54.

Kramer, Fritz. 1993. *The Red Fez: Art and Spirit Possession in Africa*. London: Verso.

Kwon, Heonik. 2006. *After the Massacre: Commemoration and Consolation in Ha My and My Lai*. Berkeley: University of California Press.

———. 2008. *Ghosts of War in Vietnam*. Cambridge: Cambridge University Press.

Laderman, Carol. 1991. *Taming the Wind of Desire: Psychology, Medicine, and Aesthetics in Malay Shamanistic Performance*. Berkeley: University of California Press.

Ladwig, Patrice. 2007. "From Revolution to Reform: Ethics, Gift Giving and Sangha–State Relationships in Lao Buddhism," Ph.D. dissertation. Cambridge: University of Cambridge.

Lambek, Michael. 1996. "Afterword: Spirits and their Histories," in *Spirits in Culture, History, and Mind*, eds. J.M. Mageo and A. Howard. New York: Routledge, pp.237–49.

———. 2010. "Traveling Spirits: Unconcealment and Displacement," in *Traveling Spirits: Migrants, Markets and Mobility*, eds. G. Hüwelmeier and K. Krause. New York: Routledge, pp.17–35.

Latour, Bruno. 1996. "On Actor-Network Theory: A Few Clarifications," *Soziale Welt* 47: 367, 369–81.

Lauser, Andrea, and Cordula Weissköppel, eds. 2008. *Migration und Religiöse Dynamik: Ethnologische Religionsforschung im transnationalen Kontext*. Bielefeld: Transcript.

Levy, Robert I., Jeannette Marie Mageo, and Alan Howard. 1996. "Gods, Spirits, and History: A Theoretical Perspective," in *Spirits in Culture, History, and Mind*, eds. J.M. Mageo and A. Howard. New York: Routledge, pp.11–29.

Lewis, I.M. 1989[1971]. *Ecstatic Religion: A Study of Shamanism and Spirit Possession*. London: Routledge.

Lienhardt, Godfrey. 1961. *Divinity and Experience: The Religion of the Dinka*. Oxford: Clarendon Press.

McRoy, Jay, ed. 2006. *Japanese Horror Cinema*. Edinburgh: Edinburgh University Press.

McVey, Ruth. 1999. *Redesigning the Cosmos: Belief Systems and State Power in Indonesia*. Copenhagen: Nordic Institute of Asian Studies.

Malarney, Shaun K. 2003. "Return to the Past? The Dynamics of Contemporary Religious and Ritual Transformation," in *Postwar Vietnam: Dynamics of a Transforming Society*, ed. H.V. Luong. Boulder, CO: Rowman and Littlefield, pp.225–56.

Marriott, Mckim. 1976. "Hindu Transactions: Diversity without Dualism," in *Transactions and Meaning: Directions in the Anthropology of Exchange and Symbolic Behavior*, ed. B. Kapferer. Philadelphia: Institute for the Study of Human Issues, pp.109–42.

Meyer, Birgit, and Peter Pels. 2003. *Magic and Modernity: Interfaces of Revelation and Concealment*. Stanford, CA: Stanford University Press.

Mitchell, Timothy. 2002. *Rule of Experts: Egypt, Techno-politics, Modernity*. Berkeley: University of California Press.

Moore, Henrietta L. 1994. *A Passion for Difference: Essays in Anthropology and Gender*. Cambridge: Polity Press.

Moore, Henrietta L., and Todd Sanders, eds. 2001. *Magical Interpretations, Material Realities: Modernity, Witchcraft and the Occult in Postcolonial Africa*. London: Routledge.

Morris, Rosalind C. 2000. *In the Place of Origins: Modernity and its Mediums in Northern Thailand*. Durham, NC: Duke University Press.

Moskowitz, Marc L. 2001. *The Haunting Fetus: Abortion, Sexuality and the Spirit World in Taiwan*. Honolulu: University of Hawaii Press.

Neumann Fridman, Eva Jane, and Mariko Namba Walter, eds. 2004. *Shamanism: An Encyclopedia of World Beliefs, Practices, and Culture*. Santa Barbara, CA: ABC Clio.

Nguyễn Thị Hiền. 2002. "The Religion of The Four Palaces: Mediumship and Therapy in Viet Culture," Ph.D. dissertation. Bloomington: Indiana University.

Ong, Aihwa. 1987. *Spirits of Resistance and Capitalist Discipline*. New York: SUNY Press.

Pels, Peter. 2003. "Introduction: Magic and Modernity," in *Magic and Modernity: Interfaces of Revelation and Concealment*, eds. B. Meyer and P. Pels. Stanford, CA: Stanford University Press, pp.1–38.

Phạm Quỳnh Phương. 2007. "Empowerment and Innovation among Saint Tran's Female Mediums," in *Modernity and Re-Enchantment: Religion in Post-revolutionary Vietnam*, ed. Philip Taylor. Singapore: ISEAS, pp.221–49.

———. 2009. *Hero and Deity: Tran Hung Dao and the Resurgence of Popular Religion in Vietnam*. Chiang Mai: Mekong Press.

Phan Kế Bính. 1995[1915]. *Việt Nam Phong Tục* ['Vietnamese customs']. Ho Chi Minh City: NXB Thành Phố Hồ Chí Minh.

Platenkamp, Jos D.M. 2007. "Spirit Representations in Southeast Asia: A Comparative View," in *La Nature des Esprits dans les Cosmologies Autochtones*, ed. F.B. Laugrand. Quebec: Presses de l'Université Laval, pp.99–129.

Poo, Mu-Chou, ed. 2009. *Rethinking Ghosts in World Religions*. Leiden: Brill.

Raffin, Anne. 2008. "Postcolonial Vietnam: Hybrid Modernity," *Postcolonial Studies* 11: 329–44.

Ramstedt, Martin. 2004. "Negotiating Identities: Indonesian 'Hindus' between Local, National, and Global Interests," in *Hinduism in Modern Indonesia: A Minority Religion between Local, National, and Global Interests*, ed. M. Ramstedt. London: Routledge Curzon, pp.1–34.

Randeria, Shalini. 2006. "Entangled Histories of Uneven Modernities: Civil Society, Caste Councils and Family Law in India," in *Unraveling Ties: From Social Cohesion to New Practices*, eds. Y. Elkana, I. Krastev, E. Macamo, and S. Randeria. New York: St Martin's Press, pp.284–311.

Sax, William S. 2006. "Agency," in *Theorizing Rituals, Vol 1: Issues, Topics, Approaches, Concepts*, eds. J. Kreinath, J. Snoek, and M. Strausberg. Leiden: Brill, pp.473–81.

———. 2009. *God of Justice: Ritual Healing and Social Justice in the Central Himalayas*. Oxford: Oxford University Press.

Schiller, Anne. 2002. "How to Hold a Tiwah: The Potency of the Dead and Deathways among Ngaju Dayaks," in *The Potent Dead: Ancestors, Saints and Heroes in Contemporary Indonesia*, eds. H. Chambert-Loir and A. Reid. Honolulu: University of Hawaii Press, pp.17–31.

Schnepel, Burkhard. 2006. "The 'Dance of Punishment': Transgression and Punishment in an East Indian Ritual," in *Celebrating Transgression: Method and Politics in Anthropological Studies of Culture*, eds. U. Rao and J. Hutnyk. Oxford: Berghahn, pp.115–28.

———. 2008. *Tanzen für Kali: Ethnographie eines Ostindischen Ritualtheaters*. Berlin: Reimer.

———. 2009. "Zur Dialektik von *Agency* und *Patiency*," *Paragrana* 20: 15–22.

Sharp, Lesley A. 1993. *The Possessed and the Dispossessed: Spirits, Identity, and Power in a Madagascar Migrant Town*. Berkeley: University of California Press.

Siegel, James. 2006. *Naming the Witch*. Stanford, CA: Stanford University Press.

Smith, Frederick M. 2006. *The Self Possessed: Deity and Spirit Possession in South Asian Literature and Civilization*. New York: Columbia University Press.

Stoller, Paul. 1995. *Embodying Colonial Memories: Spirit Possession, Power, and the Hauka in West Africa*. New York: Routledge.

Strathern, Marilyn. 1988. *The Gender of the Gift: Problems with Women and Problems with Society in Melanesia*. Berkeley: University of California Press.

Styers, Randall. 2004. *Making Magic: Religion, Magic, and Science in the Modern World*. New York: Oxford University Press.

Tambiah, Stanley J. 1976. *World Conqueror and World Renouncer: A Study of Religion and Polity in Thailand against a Historical Background*. Cambridge: Cambridge University Press.

Taylor, Charles. 2001. "Two Theories of Modernity", in *Alternative Modernities*, ed. D.P. Gaonkar. Durham, NC: Duke University Press, pp.172–96.

Taylor, James. 2008. *Buddhism and Postmodern Imaginings in Thailand: The Religiosity of Urban Space*. Farnham: Ashgate.

Taylor, Philip, ed. 2007. *Modernity and Re-Enchantment: Religion in Post-revolutionary Vietnam*. Singapore: ISEAS.

Tilley, Christopher. 2004. *The Materiality of Stone: Explorations in Landscape Phenomenology*. Oxford: Berg.

Turner, Edith. 2003. "The Reality of Spirits," in *Shamanism: A Reader*, ed. G. Harvey. London: Routledge: pp.145–52.

Tylor, Edward B. 1871. *Primitive Culture*. London: John Murray.

Venn, Couze, and Mike Featherstone. 2006. "Modernity," *Theory, Culture and Society* 23: 457–76.

Watson-Andaya, Barbara. 1997. "Historicizing 'Modernity' in Southeast Asia," *Journal of the Economic and Social History of the Orient* 40: 391–409.

Weller, Robert P. 1994 "Capitalism, Community, and the Rise of Amoral Cults in Taiwan," in *Asian Visions of Authority: Religion and the Modern States of East and Southeast Asia*, ed. C.F. Keyes and H. Hardacre. Honolulu: University of Hawaii Press, pp.141–64.

———. 2008. "Asia and the Global Economics of Charisma," in *Religious Commodification in Asia: Marketing Gods*, ed. P. Kitiarsa. London: Routledge, pp.15–30.

West, Harry G., and Todd Sanders, eds. 2003. *Transparency and Conspiracy: Ethnographies of Suspicion in the New World Order*. Durham, NC: Duke University Press.

White, Erick. 2005. "Fraudulent and Dangerous Popular Religiosity in the Public Sphere: Moral Campaigns to Prohibit, Reform, and Demystify Thai Spirit Mediums," in *Spirited Politics: Religion and Public Life in Contemporary Southeast Asia*, eds. A.C. Willford and K.M. George. Ithaca, NY: Southeast Asia Program, Cornell University, pp.69–91.

Willford, Andrew C. 2005. "The Modernist Vision from Below: Malaysian Hinduism and the 'Way of Prayers'," in *Spirited Politics: Religion and Public Life in Contemporary Southeast Asia*, eds. A.C. Willford and K.M. George. Ithaca, NY: Southeast Asia Program, Cornell University, pp.45 68.

Willford, Andrew C., and Kenneth M. George, eds. 2005. *Spirited Politics: Religion and Public Life in Contemporary Southeast Asia*. Ithaca, NY: Southeast Asia Program, Cornell University.

1

CAN THINGS REACH THE DEAD? THE ONTOLOGICAL STATUS OF OBJECTS AND THE STUDY OF LAO BUDDHIST RITUALS FOR THE SPIRITS OF THE DECEASED

Patrice Ladwig

Introduction

During my fieldwork in one of the Buddhist monasteries in Vientiane,[1] I witnessed several cases of lay people coming to a monk and handing him an object. Often it was an umbrella, a shirt, a cooking pot or another item of everyday use. I was told that most of these lay people had had a dream in which one of their deceased kin appeared. Often the deceased person was lacking something in this dream. In the understanding of the lay person, the monk then ritually "transferred" the object to the deceased. The ritual transfer of objects to the spirits of the deceased also plays a crucial role in larger rituals that are part of the Lao ritual cycle such as *boun khau salak*, the festival of baskets drawn by lot.[2] Moreover, family rituals for honoring a deceased person, sometimes performed many years after their death, follow a similar pattern. In a ritual I observed in Luang Prabang in 2007, family and friends bought a small model house (*huean pa*) and filled it with items of everyday use. The monks then transferred the house to the deceased so that they could profit from it in the afterlife. In both cases, the transfer of objects to non-human beings plays a crucial role in establishing a link between humans and the spirits of the dead. Although the "reality" of this transfer is rarely discussed among the Lao themselves, more orthodox Buddhist monks and some lay people see these practices as "folk Buddhism" and deny the transferability of the object itself. Instead, they argue, it is only the merit (*boun*, Pali: *punna*) from this karmically skilful act of generosity that is transferred to the deceased. In this interpretation, the gifts remain in this world and are actually intended for the monks.

Endnotes for this chapter begin on page 36

Over the last two decades, some of the major trends in social anthropology have focused on two concepts, which I would like to employ in order to explore some methodological and theoretical issues relevant to studying the ritual transfer of objects to the deceased among the ethnic Lao, and contextualize them in terms of Buddhist practice. The first concept, ontology, entered the subject in the early 1990s largely via Bruno Latour's (1993) exchanges with anthropologists such as Eduardo Viveiros de Castro (1998) and Philippe Descola (1998).[3] Both have applied the notion of ontology to the study of spirits (Descola 2007; Viveiros de Castro 2007). The second concept, materiality, is linked to the first one. The return of the material derives from the critique of allegedly anthropocentric, subject-oriented understanding in the social sciences. Actor-Network Theory and other critiques of the nature/culture divide look at the wider interactions of humans with non-humans and the material world. Here, it is not exclusively the human subject that molds the material world through its agency, or projects meaning onto the object, thereby making it a representation or symbol. Instead, there are efforts to restore the role of objects and non-human entities beyond dead matter, fetishism, or representations and symbols (Gell 1998; Miller 2005; Keane 2005, 2006). A recent volume by Henare, Holbraad, and Wastell (2007), on which I draw, connects ontology and materiality. All these approaches in their own way aim at a wider understanding of objects, leaving space for their agency, power, and mediating capacities.

Instead of seeing spirits solely as objects of study, I would like to propose that a look at their ontological status and their involvement with materiality might enhance an understanding of spirits as social beings that are in dialogue with humans. In the first part of this chapter I suggest that despite their invisibility, the "traces" spirits leave in the material domain are important for understanding their needs, desires, and interactions with humans. I do not reject understandings of spirits and ghosts as representations, symbols, or symptoms of something else, but taking the materiality and ontological status of these beings seriously is—beyond all the theoretical apparatus to be used—also a methodological question. I then develop this theoretical discussion with regard to the two ethnographic examples from Laos I mentioned in the opening paragraph. Here I look at the transfer of objects (baskets and model houses) between the living and the dead with Buddhist monks acting in both cases as ritual mediators. I will then discuss differences in ideas regarding the ontological status of these spirits held by orthodox Buddhist monks and "modern Buddhists" on the one hand, and elderly lay people on the other. Some monks (and more rarely lay people) deny the transferability of objects, whereas more "traditional" lay people understand the objects as actually reaching the dead. I will argue that this modern understanding of communication with the ancestors can be understood as a result of what Latour has called "purification" (Latour 1993: 10), an ontological separation of and distinction made between humans and non-humans. I argue that this process is grounded in a rationalization of Buddhism through socialist politics and the influence of Buddhist modernism and doctrinal orthodoxy. Throughout this chapter, my emphasis will be more on the theoretical and methodological aspects of the issues, and the ethnography will remain focused on specific ritual events without referring to the role of spirits of the deceased in other parts of the Lao ritual cycle.

Taking Ontology and Materiality Seriously

Most of us have encountered situations in the field in which certain "things" are imbued with special qualities, in which objects in specific contexts and events become living beings or take on roles that are beyond their everyday use. There are numerous examples of what could be called "ontological shifts": people slipping from one form of being into another, passing from one sphere to another, or subjects becoming objects. In Amazonia, people are said to have "unstable bodies" and can transform themselves into animals (Vilaça 2005); among the Nuer, birds are sometimes regarded as being human twins (Evans Pritchard 1966); or certain gods in Nepal are ritually invited and then "live" in a statue (Ortner 1975). In the region I work in, statues of the Buddha made out of concrete are endowed with life in extremely elaborate consecration rituals and are regarded afterwards as living entities (Swearer 2004).

Anthropologists of different generations have usually followed one of the following ways of understanding these phenomena: either there is a purpose connected to these transformations (functionalism), they show how the brain works (cognitivism), they have to be interpreted (interpretivism), or these transformations have a metaphorical nature (symbolism) (GDAT 2010: 183). Early anthropology understood these phenomena of non-distinction as a *mentalité primitive* (Lévy-Bruhl 1975), in which a sort of prelogical confusion produces an inability to delineate between dream and reality, between subject and object. Other accounts have described these cases for Melanesia as being founded on socio-cosmic principles, in which humans and non-humans share certain substances that are the basis of their transformations (Leenhardt 1979). Some of these heavily criticized accounts of "primitive thinking" could in my opinion undergo a fruitful revision.[4] More widely accepted and rehearsed has been the contribution of Mauss (1990), whose ideas about exchange are based on a participation of a certain principle or substance related to persons *and* things.

Focusing here only on objects that are used to connect human and non-human entities, the most widely accepted ideas about "explaining" these phenomena are related to the concept of representation. In the Durkheimian tradition,[5] these objects are primarily of interest because they "materialize and express otherwise immaterial or abstract entities, organizing subjects' perpetual experiences and clarifying their cognitions. The very materiality of objects, their availability to the senses, is of interest primarily as the condition for the knowability of otherwise abstract or otherwise invisible structure" (Keane 2005: 198). Webb Keane and other proponents of the ontological turn in anthropology argue that this understanding reduces objects to our modern way of thinking in which the material world becomes a passive matrix of projection. According to Eduardo Viveiros de Castro, the conditions of knowability (using Keane's words) are also questions regarding epistemology and representation. He states that with modernity we witness a "massive conversion of ontological into epistemological questions—that is, questions of representation [in which] *objects* or things have been *pacified— retreating* to the *exterior, silent, and uniform world* of nature" (Viveiros de Castro 2004: 480). He then outlines the significance of the concept of ontology for going beyond this approach:

> I think that the language of ontology is important for one specific and, one might say, tactical reason. It acts as a counter-measure to a de-realizing trick frequently played against natives' thinking, which turns their thought into a sustained fantasy by reducing it to the dimensions of a form of knowledge or representation—that is, to an "epistemology" or a "world-view." (Viveiros de Castro 2003: 18)

At a recent discussion of the ontological turn held in Manchester (GDAT 2010), some participants stated that the study of culture is in many ways merely the study of meaning and interpretation of peoples' epistemes, and neglects ontological questions. Quoting Tim Ingold, some participants argued that in this sense, culture is "conceived to hover over the material world, but not to permeate it" (Ingold 2000: 349). Another contributor said that "by contrast, ontology is an attempt to take others and their real difference seriously" (GDAT 2010: 175). At the same event, the claim was made that "an ontological approach, more than any other within anthropology, takes things encountered in the field 'seriously'" (ibid.: 154). Henare, Holbraad, and Wastell, referring to the link between ontology and materiality, argue in the same vein for taking a fresh look at objects: "The aim of this method is to take 'things' encountered in the field as they present themselves, rather than immediately assuming that they signify, represent or stand for something else" (Henare, Holbraad, and Wastell 2007: 2). How can materiality and its connection to ontology then be taken "seriously" as a method? How can we understand objects and the way they present themselves without directly launching a project of symbolization and representation? And how can this illuminate the ways in which ghosts, spirits, and other non-human entities are studied?

When we stick to the claims made above, one could say that in anthropological analysis spirits, ghosts, and the material objects attached to their apparition and worship often have suffered the fate of too quickly becoming representations and symbols. Heonik Kwon, examining the ghosts of war in Vietnam, argues that apparitions also continue to play a role in the "modern" world, but that "their enduring existence is often unrecognized in modern societies because its domain of existence has changed from the natural to the symbolic" (Kwon 2008: 16). Again, then, spirits only "symbolize" and stand for something else. To make myself clear: I think there is essentially nothing wrong with interpreting spirits, ghosts, and the objects surrounding them as symbols or representations of something else. Our job as anthropologists demands such work, and the most illuminating studies of spirits and ghosts have followed this method in various forms. Aihwa Ong's study of the possession of female factory workers in Malaysia takes spirits to be a sign of resistance to industrial discipline (Ong 1987). Janet Carsten argues that spectral apparitions are often linked to loss and memory and proposes that "excesses of grief cause these ghosts to appear" (Carsten 2007: 7). Heonik Kwon sees ghosts and their haunting as expressions of traumatic events, violence, and socially un-processed deaths (Kwon 2008). Ghosts, on a larger comparative level, often stand for something that cannot be expressed otherwise; one could say that the "ghost embodies the disruption and alienation of that other which resists assimilation" (Buse and Stott 1999: 137).

However, I think that before we undertake an analysis of more abstracted rep-resentations and interpretations, it is worth keeping in mind that the first encounter with ghosts and other spirit entities in the field should be guided by taking their ontological status seriously. Ghosts can be beings with desires, with taste, with biographies. They appear in specific ways, at certain places at a certain time; they slip into objects, they live in them, they consume things and demand a certain treatment as social beings. A detailed and multifaceted interpretation or analysis of their representative qualities, their symptomatic nature, and their "meaning" can only be carried out with these things in mind. I think that the place for an on-tological approach to spirits, and of their involvement with the material world, is the point from which we have to start understanding them, before we write about what they stand for and symbolize.

Invisibility, Traces, and Materiality.
Lao Spirits of the Deceased

The problem we very often have is that the encounters with beings subsumed under the category of spirits or ghosts are marked by non-visibility and non-ma-teriality, at least for most people and anthropologists. Some of our informants might regularly see ghosts and spirits, get possessed by them, talk to them, or even marry them. Unfortunately, this hasn't happened to me yet. While working on a research project at the University of Bristol concerned with Buddhist funeral cul-tures of Southeast Asia and China, my colleagues and I at one point realized that the main actors of our research were never present in the conventional sense. The deceased, ancestors, ghosts, or the spirits of people who died a bad death were in some sense omnipresent because all the things we researched (rituals, narratives, offerings, prayers, and so on) happened because of them, but they were not to be seen. This is a paradox that marks every religion to a more or less intense degree: "Humanity constantly returns to projects devoted to immateriality, whether as religion, philosophy ... But all of these rest upon the same paradox: that immateriality can only be expressed through materiality ... The more humanity reaches toward the conceptualization of the immaterial, the more important the specific forms of materialization" (Miller 2005: 28).

One way to study immaterial beings and take their apparitions seriously would be to analyze under which circumstances they appear to which people, or how images of them are, for example, caught on media. Gregory Delaplace has developed this idea in relation to spirits in Mongolia and has proposed a notion he labels "regimes of communicability."[6] Regarding the materiality of these invisible beings, I would like to use the idea of the "trace," which I also take as being part of a regime of communicability. Ghosts and spirits leave material traces in this world. A trace might indicate the places where they appear, the materiality of the ritual items to deal with them, or with the offerings they receive. The trace is in a sense a track, a footprint, or an imprint—a sign left in the material domain of something that by its nature is not graspable for those people not endowed with the special capacities to do so. The trace is never a "direct" reference to the being in question. The trace as I use it as a concept is only partial, never revealing the whole being, but nevertheless pointing to certain features of the entity and its way of being.[7]

In the context of the above-mentioned project on death rituals, we decided to look at the materiality surrounding the apparition of non-human entities. However immaterial these beings might be, they must find expression in the material world. In my own research, I explored one Buddhist festival for the deceased that marks the end of a period of two weeks (usually in September) in which an intensified communication between the living and the dead takes place: the aforementioned *boun khau salak*. In this ritual, food, but also other objects of exchange, are constitutive of the communication between the living and the dead. In addition, I also looked at a ritual I researched in Luang Prabang in 2007 that aims at honoring a deceased ancestor by providing a small model house filled with items for daily use. I will here only present the basic structure of the rituals, briefly introduce the beings addressed, and point to the similar mechanisms at work there; namely, the transfer of objects and/or merit to the deceased with the help of Buddhist monks. After that, I will return to the question of ontology and materiality.

The Lao festival *boun khau salak* usually takes place in September and closes the period of the dead, which is opened two weeks before by a festival called *boun khua padab din* (the festival or rice packets decorating the earth). The festivals have to be understood as one ritual complex, but I shall here focus only on *boun khau salak* as the question of the transfer of objects is most apparent here.[8] This ritual focuses on ancestors that are labeled either generally in Lao as *phu day* (dead person), *phi* or in Buddhist terms as *vinyan* (Pali: *vinnana*, conscience).[9]

In the case of *boun khau salak*, the category primarily refers to recently deceased relatives who are still known by name. *Boun khau salak* is a yearly ritual; it occurs in a temple, and involves baskets labeled with the names of the donor (sender) and deceased relatives (recipient). On the day of the festival, family members bring their baskets to the temple early in the morning. The baskets contain mostly

Figure 1.1: Basket for the deceased presented at *boun khau salak*. The paper indicates the receiver and the donor of the basket. Photograph by Patrice Ladwig, 2007.

food, with some of the items being chosen according to the taste of the deceased. Moreover, there are also items for everyday use: cigarettes, umbrellas, pencils, or a comb (the latter object will be crucial in the analysis below). In a large public ritual, an elaborate system of gift allotment distributes the items equally among the monks. Each basket gets a number, which is passed on to the owner of the basket. Then the monks draw lots from a pot, written on small paper slips; on these slips are written the numbers of the baskets. This practice gives the ritual its name (*salak* signifies lottery). Then, over the space of an hour or more, each person is called to the front where the monks sit, and gives the basket to the monk who has drawn the number of their basket from the pot. Each monk usually ends up with several baskets. After all the baskets have been distributed, they are assembled in front of the main statue of the Buddha. The monks chant a dedication prayer and transfer them to the dead. This transfer is understood by most lay people, and more so by monks, as a simultaneous transfer of merit (*boun*), as the skilful act of presenting a gift to a deceased relative through a monk. The "fruits" (Pali: *phala*) of this karmically positive act are then also transferred to the deceased. After the ritual, the monks collect the baskets, empty them, and use their contents.

In the second ritual, *boun huean pa* (festival of the cloth house), we observe a very similar mechanism, but the rite is based on kinship groups and the neighborhood of the family initiating it. The ritual is rarely seen in Vientiane, but seems to be a local tradition found in the northern provinces of Laos like Luang Prabang, Oudomsay, Luang Namtha and Sayabouli.[10] To my knowledge, there is no ethnographic account of this rite in the older literature on Lao Buddhism. The rite is sometimes performed one week after the death of a family member, but in many cases years after death has occurred. In both cases, the family prepares a wooden model house (usually bought in a shop), which gives the ritual its name. *Huean* signifies house while *pa* refers to the roof of the house that is sometimes made out of white cloth, probably due to the widespread use of white cloth in Buddhist funerary culture. Several informants in Luang Prabang pointed out that this also refers to the purity (*khwambolisut*) of the intentions of the donors.

The house, measuring approximately 1.5m in height, is elaborately decorated with bank notes hanging from the roof, and it is filled with items intended for daily use such as clothing, cooking pots, fans, food, sleeping mats, and so on. It also has a small ladder leading into it, and sometimes even has windows. Several monks enter the house, are ritually fed, and then perform a chant of auspiciousness (Pali: *mangala sutta*) and finally a chant of dedication. The latter signifies the transfer of the house to the deceased. The house is sometimes so heavy that it has to be carried by several men who then bring it to the temple by car, where it is disassembled. Like the baskets at *boun khau salak*, the house is labeled with a sign that lists the name of the deceased (the receiver), the donors (usually his family), and a short phrase of dedication containing the wish that the *vinyan* (consciousness, soul) of the deceased finds the right way to paradise (*sukhadi*).

Figure 1.2: *Boun huean pa*: House with items and some couture for the spirit of the deceased. Photograph by Patrice Ladwig, 2007.

An elderly woman I met in the temple compound while observing the transport of the house pointed to the sign above its entrance and explained the ritual to me like this:

> This is for the father of the family. He has died many years ago. The children and other relatives get together; they miss the deceased. They are afraid that the deceased does not have a place to stay after his death. Here, see, there is a sleeping mattress; they put all the things into the house that one needs for living. Then today they performed the ritual. They pray to Buddha and the monks come to the house and chant. The *vinyan* descends from heaven. It receives the house and can take it with it. Then they [the lay people] pour water (*yad nam*) and transfer the merit to the deceased.[11]

Then, as in *boun khau salak*, the house is transferred or dedicated (*uthid*)[12] to the deceased. Both rites use signs to label the gift, the receiver, and the sender. Again, the monks are supposed to act as intermediaries transferring the object to the spirit of the deceased, but they "keep" the items intended for the dead and use most of them. The point that they use *most of them* will later become crucial in the analysis: in both the rites, most of the items presented to the deceased can actually be used by monks, but the baskets and the houses often also contain objects which are of no use to monks. Due to their special lifestyle as renouncers or because of the meticulous code of conduct for monks laid down in the *vinayapitaka* ("basket of discipline" – one of the three parts of the Buddhist canon), not all of them can be used.

Ontologies in Competition: Objects for the Use of the Dead or the Veneration of Monks?

I now turn to aspects of materiality in the ethnography and use these for exploring the ontological status of the spirits of the deceased. With reference to both rituals, I refer to differing and conflicting ideas about the ontological status of the dead. I shall describe cases in which the objects provided for the deceased point to a potential conflict between a "modern" form of the ontology of the dead advanced, for example, by orthodox monks and a more "traditional" one proposed by elderly lay people. This rift is also related to a wider field of discussion about rationality, superstition, and the modernization of Buddhism in Laos, but also reflects a discussion that is already apparent in some early Buddhist textual sources.

As I have already noted, *boun khau salak* mainly addresses the spirits of the recently deceased. Despite the Buddhist doctrine of reincarnation, Lao Buddhists continue to feed these spirits long after they have died. This is done especially with deceased parents or siblings, but can theoretically be extended to anyone. I described above how the offerings are labeled: lay people put a stick with a paper into their basket, which states the name of the recipient (*khun hab*) and the sender (*khun song*). Many informants compared this to sending a letter, or making a telephone call. Without a correct address, the basket will not reach its intended recipient. Several informants told me that there is also an administration in the "other world" where the ancestors live and therefore an address must be attached to the basket. This transfer to the spirits of the dead—whereby an object passes from one ontological sphere (the world of the living) to another (the world of ancestral spirits)—is usually not an act of dispute among Lao Buddhists.[13] Rituals are mainly performed and few think about the "reality" of the acts. Moreover, discourse may say one thing, whereas in practice people might still perform these acts despite denying their reality. As among Buddhists in Chiang Mai, most Lao Buddhists in Vientiane generally believe that "although the offerings are given to monks, they are thought to be used by the deceased as well" (Davis 1984: 193).

However, more orthodox monks in the urban setting of Vientiane whom I interviewed about *boun khau salak* stated that this belief is only "peasant Buddhism" (*phutasasana khong sauna*) or "false belief" (*khwamsuea pit*), adding that the deceased obviously cannot receive gifts. The gifts were, they claimed, only "symbols" (*sanyalak*), and they denied that a real transfer of the objects occurred. One of them told me in an interview: "You are an educated man from Germany and you know that most Lao people are peasants that have not yet understood that the dead cannot receive things. It is their wishful thinking." He advanced a Buddhist interpretation and said that the gifts are given to, and intended for, the monks, honoring their discipline during the three-month rain retreat (Buddhist lent; Pali: *vassa*). Giving this an additional Buddhist spin, he stated that the merit generated through this karmically skillful act is then transferred to the dead. This is also congruent with the interpretation of many Lao lay people, but they expect both things to happen: a transfer of the object *and* the transfer of merit generated through the act of giving. This difference in interpretation became most apparent when one monk insisted that the gifts are chosen, even by lay people, according to the needs of the monk, and are intended for them and not for the dead. He said that this kind of superstition only survives in the countryside, but not in Vientiane. I told him about the umbrellas in the baskets, and he replied that monks also need umbrellas. Then I remembered the comb a friend of mine had found in one of the baskets: monks shave their hair and do not need combs, I pointed out. The monk gave me an annoyed look and brushed off my remark. The conversation had come to its end.

With regard to the *huean pa* it was harder for orthodox monks to advance a coherent interpretation referring to certain sources of doctrinal Buddhism. Although monks can use most of the items placed within the house, they often contain things that monks cannot use, such as shirts. Most monks in Luang Prabang were less orthodox in that regard than their colleagues in Vientiane. I had a discussion with an abbot of one of the large monasteries in Luang Prabang regarding the house for the deceased. Asking him about the invitation addressed to the *vinyan* of the deceased to enter the house via the ladder, he did not directly deny the transferability of the object, but referred to different understandings of the rite among people of different ages:

> In our belief one is supposed to give offerings to the monks. After the monks have received them, the lay people pour water and transfer the merit generated through this act of generosity to the deceased person. The crucial thing, however, is that the *vinyan* of the deceased is made happy and that he or she has to be informed that there is a dedication being performed [referring to the invitation]. It might be possible that the things reach the dead or not—we simply don't know. Some monks and the younger people actually don't think so, but the older people who do the *boun huean pa* think that the deceased's *vinyan* really comes, receives the house and takes it away.

However, some monks also classified this practice as "folk Buddhism," denying the fact that the objects could reach the dead, but due to the kind of objects presented it was hard for them to claim that the items were actually intended for the monks. Again, as in the case of *boun khau salak*, reference was made to "wishes" (*khwambattana*) of lay people and the fact that they miss (*kid hood*) the deceased and therefore symbolically construct a house for them. Several monks answered that the items that could not be used by monks are usually distributed among poor families in the neighborhood of the temple, giving these, in some sense misplaced objects, a charity appeal.

So when we try to take ontology and the role of objects seriously, how can we understand these different attitudes toward objects in both rituals? Arjun Appadurai has proposed that instead of only looking at human actors and their intentionality, it is also valid to look at exchange from the point of view of the objects exchanged: "Even though from a theoretical point of view human actors encode things with significance, from a methodological point of view it is the things-in-motion that illuminate their human and social context" (Appadurai 1986: 5). When objects "speak," when objects are the vocabulary in which the living and spirits of the dead communicate with each other, I think that there is indeed a large difference between more orthodox Buddhist ideas about those objects and the ones that many lay people advance. In the case of the basket in the festival in Vientiane, we have a denial of the transferability of the object of some modernist monks; while regarding the house we have an open answer that involves doubt and a reference to different understandings of older and younger people. One could say that at one end of the spectrum of responses, the more orthodox monks and lay people following a more rationalized approach have adapted a modern ontology that postulates a clear distinction between subject and object, between the living and the dead. The dead are ascribed a different ontological status; they are not reachable with objects anymore.

Where do these differing views derive from? Obviously, people always have divergent views about how rituals work and a certain attitude of doubt towards certain practices is nothing unusual. Nevertheless, I think that there are some identifiable factors that have influenced the different discourses on the ontological status of the dead and communication with them via objects. I mostly carried out fieldwork in big monasteries in Vientiane, and most of the monks I worked with were highly educated, having studied either in Laos or at Buddhist universities in Thailand. The institutions in both countries have undergone thorough reforms resulting in a "rationalization" of many Buddhist doctrines.[14] While it is evident that many monks actually come from poor rural areas, and that the Buddhism practiced there might not construct such an opposition, the training they receive in urban institutions of higher Buddhist education, especially since the communist revolution of 1975, in some cases seems to alter ideas regarding these subjects. Despite the continuing existence of all kinds of "unorthodox" practices, some monasteries—like the ones I worked with in Vientiane—are propagating a reformed Buddhism that is compatible with the "scientific rationalism" that modernist Buddhists have been advocating (McMahan 2008: 63f.). The notion of "protestant Buddhism," whose main feature has been the blurring of the monk/laity distinction in reaction to Christian missionary activity in Sri Lanka, has also been described as having a more this-worldly orientation with a de-emphasis on ritual (Gombrich and Obeyesekere 1988). The conclusions that could be drawn from these developments for the efficacy of Buddhist rituals for the deceased in Laos, and the position of objects in them, cannot be discussed here in detail. However, I think that the rather heterodox Buddhist practices described, for example, by Francoise Bizot (1981) in Cambodia and Thailand in the 1960s and 1970s have been largely suppressed in Laos.[15] I do not want to paint an image of disenchantment and overall rationalization for the case of Buddhism in Laos, but in comparison to Thailand's flourishing postmodern Buddhist scene (Jackson 1999), with its "commercialized Buddhism" (*Buddha phanit*) (Kitiarsa 2008), things in Laos look different. The emergence of Buddhist charisma and magic monks has been successfully blocked by the one-party state (Ladwig 2007), and indeed the Lao monastic order (*Sangha*) remains under the strict control of the Department of Religious Affairs of the Lao National Front for Reconstruction (Ladwig 2008). On the one hand, then, Lao Buddhism has remained fairly "traditional" due to its isolation until the mid 1990s. On the other hand, the developments outlined above have—at least in urban areas and among high-ranking monks—led to changes that might also be linked to the understanding of the rituals discussed here.

In some sense this modernist approach to communication with the dead is an effect of the "rationalization" of beliefs propagated in the Buddhist education system and among lay people in the propaganda against superstitions. I think that Lao (socialist) modernity has here left its mark on the interpretation of this transfer of objects. Many monks who are in leading positions today received their education after the revolution, at a time when Buddhist doctrines and practices that were considered "irrational" were under attack. Local traditions that showed a strong intertwining of Buddhism and spirit-cults were harassed in particular (Stuart-Fox and Bucknell 1982). The *Sangha* was thoroughly restructured and ideologically cleansed after 1975. Whereas lay people often stuck to more traditional interpretations of rituals, the *Sangha* itself was exposed to higher ideological pressure and was easier to target due to its institutional structure. For the early period of Lao socialism, Lafont states, "It is interesting to note that whereas most lay followers have remained faithful to the traditional beliefs of their parents and ancestors, and do not want any change in their religion, the monks have been more prepared to accept changes imposed by the new regime in their monastic rules, sacred texts or religious practices" (Lafont 1982: 157). In a book written by one of the leading monks of the Lao Buddhist Fellowship Organization—the official association of all Lao Buddhist monks founded after the communist revolution—we still find traces of this politics of religion. Here, a secularized and rationalized explanation of the festivals for the dead such as *boun khau salak* is given. References to spirits of the deceased and ancestors, which according to lay people as well as in ritual practice are crucial elements, are not found in this rather ideological account. The solidarity of peasant culture is pointed out, and the "feeding of oneself, family, friends and society" (Buakham 2001: 44) is described, but the dead are actually completely absent. The shallow remark, "that in the old [political] system there were many things that were not practiced according to the truth" (ibid.: 44) might explain this conscious eradication of the traces of the dead, even in rituals dedicated to them. Books written before the revolution discuss these festivals in a very different manner and explicitly mention spirits (e.g., Philavong 1967: 68).

Objects, Emotions and Plastic Buckets

From the perspective of this rational, protestant Buddhism, subjects have been cut off from objects. The communication between the living and the dead has been abstracted into a pure mental concept (merit), and the material offerings circulate only in one ontological sphere, that of the living (between monks and lay people). I think that we here witness what Latour has called purification: "Purification creates two entirely distinct ontological zones: that of human beings on the one hand; that of non-humans on the other" (Latour 1993: 10). Although communication is still possible, it is now just a transfer of something invisible that poses less of a problem for modern ontology than the actual transfer of an object.

The reduction to a transfer of merit only, and the non-reachability of the dead has further implications. I think that the difference between the different ontologies goes even deeper when we take a closer look at the objects themselves and their sensual qualities. Many elderly lay people sometimes choose specific kinds of food to be put into the baskets at *boun khau salak* or into the *huean pa*. Life histories, memories of people, and emotions of care for the dead might be "materialized" in food or objects, for example. In order to understand the "emotional investment" of people in the rituals, the sensuous qualities such as smell and taste might be relevant for understanding the object as a "container" for memories of the deceased, for example,[16] or as a trace they have left in the memory of the living. In opposition to that, the simple reference to merit as understood by more orthodox monks is less tangible and not corporeal. I believe that the efficacy of rituals is also achieved through metaphors of the body and personalized objects, for example, rather than through abstract and mental concepts such as merit.[17] The care of the living for the dead (or, to put it in theoretical terms, the agency of the living on the spirits of the deceased) is often expressed through the transfer of objects. Laurent Thevenot remarks: "the autonomous intentional individual is usually regarded as a prerequisite for moral agency. But it achieves such moral agency only with the support of other elements: the functional agency of objects" (Thevenot 2002: 59). The views that I have presented as those of orthodox monks, and their modern ontology of the dead, could be said to have something in common with many earlier studies of Buddhism and Hinduism. There has been a tendency to "abstract away from the sensuous materiality of objects" (Manning and Menely 2008: 289f.) in studies of religion and the focus has often been too heavily on human agency, neglecting the material aspects of religion. Earlier scholars working on renouncer religions have often had an ambivalent relationship to materiality and sensuality. Gregory Schopen's analysis of "protestant presuppositions" in the archaeology of early Buddhism (Schopen 1991) might also apply here: scholars have often looked at sources that confirmed a certain philosophical image of Buddhism as a world-renouncing religion, but neglected the polyvocality of the textual and material sources. In the accounts of some researchers—and in the religious profiling of modernist propagators of these religions—the sensuous quality of offerings and the question of transferability plays, if at all, only a peripheral role or is denied.

The biography of the object, or what I have before labeled its trace, indicates the final receiver of the gift. The comb and the shirts in the *huean pa*, rather insignificant objects, reveal different roles for objects in two differing ideas about the ontological status of the dead. In one system, that of the orthodox monk, the dead are beyond reachability, whereas in the other—that of many elderly lay people—they can be accessed through objects. For lay people following the "older" interpretation of the rituals, the spirits of the ancestors exist somewhere where they can receive things; they can use the comb and the items in the house. Their act of giving them to the deceased is seen as a moral action; as a care for the dead that takes into account their needs. The comb and the shirt, in this sense, are not only symbols or representations of lay people's wish to establish contact with the dead and care for them. Rather, they are primarily for these lay people just what they are—objects to be put to use for the dead. Objects in this perspective have to be understood as *sui generis* meanings: "Rather than accepting that meanings are fundamentally separate from their material manifestations (signifier vs. signified, word vs. referent etc.) the aim is to explore the consequences of an apparently counter-intuitive possibility: *that things might be treated as* sui generis *meanings*" (Henare, Holbraad, and Wastell 2007: 3).

Disputes like the one I described regarding the comb in the basket are rather rare, and were probably provoked by the external intervention and presence of myself as an anthropologist.[18] Nevertheless, I think that they reveal a certain rupture. Webb Keane has observed something similar in Eastern Indonesian Christianity, where exposure to Calvinist missionary activity was supposed to "purify" Sumbanese culture. Here, discourses on religious objects could reveal the ontological insecurity caused by missionary activity among the "fetishists" who believed in the agency of bibles as objects beyond the words contained in them: "It is for reasons like this that battles over apparently minor matters such as the use of a prayer book can be taken so serious by combatants. They involve basic assumptions about what kinds of beings inhabit the world, what counts as a possible agent, and thus what are the preconditions for and the consequences of moral action" (Keane 2007: 20ff.).

I suggest that one can understand the abstraction of communication between the living and the dead as a mental concept (merit), and the mere "symbolic" role of objects in this understanding, as a form of purification, a distinction of two ontological spheres between which objects cannot circulate. Latour understands this process—together with translation—as one of the central, self-contradictory themes of the project of modernity. Current changes in the Lao Buddhist gift economy could intensify this trend, and after socialism's purifications we now witness the impact of capitalism's mass production. In recent years there has emerged a trend in Vientiane and other urban regions of Laos that more orthodox monks would certainly consider appropriate. Pre-packed plastic buckets containing gifts intended for monks are becoming more and more popular at Buddhist festivals, especially with younger people. Combs, shirts and other strange items are no longer to be found in these buckets. Despite the fact that some items in the bucket might be chosen according to the taste, need, or desire of the spirit of the dead, the pre-packaged object is less open to emotional investment than the traditional, hand-made basket with its individual food selection. The trace the spirits of the deceased leave in this world is therefore substantially modified. A good friend of mine, inspired by Buddhism as a social teaching, stated when asked about this:

> I have seen that all the baskets and even most of the food is thrown away after the ritual; the monks burn them. They can't use some of the items given to them. I went to Vat Ongtoe [a large temple in Vientiane] and presented a plastic bucket to the monks during the ancestor festival. The monks were delighted, and said that they really prefer to get the plastic buckets.

Here, questions regarding the utility of the gift seamlessly merge with that of rationality. Finally, purification has arrived in the temples of Vientiane in the form of mass-produced plastic gift buckets.

Conclusion

I began with an effort to try and take ontology and materiality "seriously" and apply them to the study of rituals dealing with Lao spirits of the deceased. I introduced the idea of trace in order to explore spirits through the fragments of their presence left in the material world. The idea of the immaterial must somehow find expression in the material domain. These traces in the material domain and the discourses surrounding them, I suggested, enable us to understand the ontological status of these beings and reveal certain features that can be attributed to them. I briefly explored critiques of the notion of representation that quickly fix meanings to objects, but also remarked that this method does not exclude ideas of representation or symbolization. My methodological suggestion was that before we embark on such a project, we could indeed follow the call of Henare, Holbraad, and Wastell (2007) to take things as they present themselves in the field, and not immediately reduce them to a "meaning." An ontological approach in this sense is "one that does not privilege epistemology or the study of other people's representations of what we know to be the real world, rather acknowledging the existence of multiple worlds" (GDAT 2010: 153).

I have contrasted the views of orthodox monks about the ontology of the dead with that of older lay people. Here, I explored the different understanding of ontology in my field sites in Vientiane and Luang Prabang and looked at differing ontological models as the basis of these diverging views. Again by looking at the trace and the biography of the objects, I showed how the circulation of things can reveal which beings are addressed in the ritual. On the one hand, orthodox monks argue that the offerings are intended for monks, and only merit is transferred to the dead. On the other hand, elderly lay people actually understood the objects such as the basket and the house as reaching the deceased. I remarked that usually no disputes arise because the objects can satisfy both proposed recipients (the monks and the dead). Objects have the capacity to take on multiple roles, and can mediate between various systems of interpretation.[19] In certain rare cases, however, these uncertainties and struggles reveal themselves. In the case of *boun khau salak*, I identified one object (the comb) that can only have been addressed to the spirits of the ancestors and not the monks. With regard to the *huean pa*, I referred to the shirts and other objects that could not be used by monks. I presented these differing views as an outcome of various modernization processes (rationalization through Buddhist education, socialism's impact on Buddhism). Whereas elderly lay people use, for example, the sensuous qualities of the object for reactivating memories of the dead, investing emotions, and expressing care through the transferred objects, modernist monks and lay people prefer an abstraction into a Buddhist concept of merit. The latter is unproblematic for the modernist ontology because the transfer of an invisible substance (merit as positive karma) is easier to legitimize than the actual transfer of an object. I proposed that this shift can be understood, following Latour (1993), as a process of purification: establishing an ontological divide between humans and spirits as non-humans. Communication between the realm of the dead and the living is still possible, but objects cannot circulate between the two spheres. The traces that the spirits of the deceased leave in the material domain actually become "thinner" the less reachable they are through objects.

Finally I mentioned that through the mass production of gift buckets for monks, the sensuous quality of the object is partially lost. I wonder about the future impact of this "purification" of the Buddhist gift economy. Many researchers including myself think that Laos, since the decline of the socialist master narrative, is going through a phase of Re-buddhification. State rituals have become more pompous, temples are being renovated, and festivals for the spirits of the deceased proliferate. Congruent with this, social scientists now proclaim the "return of religion" and the continuity, or even intensification, of ritual practices relating to spirits. But perhaps this revitalization is only possible in the context of a modern ontology. Despite the continuity and the intensification of the worship of spirits of the deceased, the way they are addressed and understood might be of a quite different nature now.

Notes

1. Initial research on which this chapter is based was carried out in Vientiane and several provinces of Laos from 2003 to 2005. I gratefully acknowledge funding by the German Academic Exchange Service (DAAD) and the University of Cambridge. A second field trip in 2007 was part of an AHRC-sponsored project, "Buddhist funeral cultures of Southeast Asia and China," hosted by the University of Bristol. Thanks to my colleagues Paul Williams and Rita Langer at the University of Bristol, and Oliver Tappe, Giovanni Da Col, and Chris Hann at the Max Planck Institute for Social Anthropology for comments and inspiration. Special thanks to Andrea Lauser and Paul Christensen for inviting me to the workshop on "Spirited Modernities" held at the Lichtenberg-Kolleg in Göttingen in September 2010. I also profited from the comments of the other participants at this workshop, especially Annette Hornbacher and Pattana Kitiarsa.
2. There is no standardized transcription system for Lao. I will use a simplified one. This is also valid for terms in Pali and Sanskrit, which appear here without diacritics.
3. The problem, as often, is that the term ontology in many of these discussions is rarely defined. I understand ontology as dealing with questions concerning what entities exist, and how these can be classified according to similarities, differences, and positions in a hierarchy of beings. Although this is a very narrow definition of ontology—which in some of its uses can be close to that of discussions of cosmology or animism in anthropology—I hope that in the course of reading the concept will become sharpened. For recent anthropological discussions of ontology, see Rio (2007), Scott (2007), and Wardle et al. (2009).
4. Despite his evolutionary tendencies, Lévy-Bruhl could be accredited with pointing out that Western ideas about rationality, and some of the oppositions mentioned above, are far from universal. Something similar is valid for Maurice Leenhardt's Melanesian anthropology, in which the socio-cosmic principles animating the body are an essential part of the concept of the person. This ontology makes it possible to transform the body and actually become another being. To my knowledge, the relationship of these older accounts to current studies of materiality and ontology has not yet been systematically explored.
5. I use this term very loosely here. In many recent writings of Latour (2005) and some of his followers in anthropology (Candea 2010), Durkheim is criticized for his very influential account of representation, while Gabriel Tarde, his largely forgotten contemporary, has found new favor.
6. This was one of the main themes of a recent conference held in Cambridge in December 2009 entitled "Figuring the Invisible: An Anthropology of Uncanny Encounters." See also Delaplace (2009) and Delaplace and Empson (2007). Looking at how apparitions are understood and described is in my opinion another way of taking ontology seriously. This idea has also been transferred to spirit apparitions in Western societies. A recent German exhibition looked at how apparitions are inscribed into the real through haunted media of TV, radio, and computers (Arns and De Ruyter 2009).
7. I borrow the term loosely from Jacques Derrida, who has made it one of the main concepts of deconstruction. In his philosophy, his anti-metaphysics of non-presence, there are no stable meanings or origins: "The trace is not only the disappearance of origin … it means that the origin did not even disappear, that it was never constituted except reciprocally by a non-origin, the trace, which thus becomes the origin of the origin" (Derrida 1976: 61). Spivak further elaborates on this rather difficult concept in her introduction to Derrida's text (Spivak 1976: 15–20). Interestingly, more than twenty

years after this work, Derrida came back to the trace, but then chose the "specter" as a figure that demonstrates the eternal slippages of meaning, of that which is not graspable and beyond dualities (Derrida 1994). See also Jameson (1999) for an interpretation of the trope of the specter in Derrida.

8. In the few ethnographies available on these festivals among the Lao, they are usually treated as one ritual, which, in my opinion, does not do justice to the rather different ritual practices observed in both rites. For a more detailed ethnographic account of the first festival and its textual backgrounds in Buddhism, see Ladwig (forthcoming b). Tambiah states that among the Lao of northeast Thailand, "the dead are allowed to visit the earth" during the period between the festivals (Tambiah 1970: 156f.). Zago refers to both rituals as being "for the favour of the dead," but additionally links them with the worship of agricultural divinities (Zago 1972: 315–18), a claim also found in Archaimbault's short account of the rites (Archaimbault 1973: 222–23). Tambiah also builds up a link to agricultural fertility and remarks that among the ethnic Lao of northeast Thailand the rituals take place "at the critical time when the rice grains are forming in the fields" (Tambiah 1970: 156). Although the link to agricultural fertility is an important feature, I cannot discuss this point here; for this, see Bouté's account of *boun khau salak* among the Phu Neuy, a Buddhist ethnic minority in Laos (Bouté 2005: 399–414). Kourilsky (2008) discusses the notion of filial piety and ideas about the reproduction of bodies in relation to ancestors.

9. Lao cosmology and understandings of life after death are based on a complex mixture of Buddhist and Tai-Kadai conceptions of the person. See Pottier (2007) for what is in my opinion the best study of Lao cosmology, and Platenkamp (2007) for a comparative examination of Lao spirits in a wider Southeast Asian context.

10. I have observed a very similar rite in a village north of Chiang Mai in northern Thailand, however. The northern regions of Laos and Thailand have long-standing cultural connections.

11. Pouring water after giving a gift to a monk is a standardized ritual action in Laos and Thailand that, one could say, approves receipt of the gift and symbolizes the flow of merit generated through the positive act of giving. The giver in this context also receives a share of the merit through his cultivation of generosity (Pali: *dana*; Lao: *thaan*). See Keyes (1983) for the Thai case.

12. The Lao term *uthid* derives from Pali *uddisati* and *ādisati,* words often used for merit transfer in the *Petavatthu*, and other Buddhist Pali sources relate to this practice. They can be translated as to make over, to transfer, to ascribe the merit or virtue of a gift to someone (Gehman 1923: 421). The important question of whether this is only a transfer of an invisible "positive karmic substance" and/or of the gift itself will be discussed below. See also Ladwig (forthcoming a) for more doctrinal and historical details on the interplay of merit and offerings.

13. The separation of these spheres could be understood as the application of an ethnocentric concept of this- and other-worldly. In the case of Lao cosmology, these ontological spheres are pretty porous and the boundary between them is at times permeable, as in the case of the festival described. In Lao one makes reference to "this world" (*look ni*) and the other world. In the context of death the latter is either described as paradise (*sawan*) or hell (*narok*), just to mention the most simplistic conceptions beyond the subtleties of Buddhist cosmology.

14. The Lao monastic education system was reformed by the French colonial regime, putting an emphasis on philology and Pali Buddhism (Kourilsky 2006). The Thai *Sangha* also underwent several reforms with a heavy emphasis on developing doctrinal Buddhism based on certain texts and a struggle against local traditions.

15. Francoise Bizot's work on Khmer and Thai Buddhism in the 1960s and 1970s (Bizot 1981) tries to uncover the heterodox and esoteric practices of the non-reformed strains

of Southeast Asian Buddhism heavily influenced by Tantric practices. Although he at times overstresses the contrast between reformed and non-reformed Buddhism, I think that many researchers have taken reformed Buddhism to be the natural state of affairs.

16. Sutton, for example, skillfully elaborates on the role of food in rituals linked to death, remembrance, and care for the dead in Greek culture: "Even the ephemeral and perishable medium of food, then, can be extended into the future through memory of the act of giving. Indeed, food may be a particularly powerful medium exactly because it internalizes the debt to the other ... Furthermore, in carefully preparing food one is once again projecting the self, in this case the caring, nurturant self, into an external object—the food—which is meant to inscribe a memorable impression on the receiver" (Sutton 2001: 46f.). This care can be expressed simply through the giving of food, but can also be intensified with a supplement deriving from the sensuality of food and the choice of food according to the taste of a deceased relative.

17. Latour therefore asks: "Why must society work through them [artifacts] to inscribe itself in something else? Why not inscribe itself directly, since the artifacts count for nothing?" (Latour 1999: 197). He thinks that the function of objects "is not to mirror, congeal, crystallize, or hide social relations, but to remake these very relations through fresh and unexpected sources of action" (ibid.: 197). Objects are needed to re-establish relationships and regenerate them.

18. When discussions about these topics occurred, it was in relation to the reality of spirits. The issue of spirits was a subject of discussion at several funerals I attended. On one occasion some monks from a rather "modernist" monastery in Vientiane ridiculed some lay people because they used the term spirit (*phi*) while talking about the deceased. The monks said that there is no such thing, there is only reincarnation, which for them is a process involving another entity based on a Buddhist concept, namely consciousness (Pali: *vinnana*).

19. Webb Keane states that "part of the power of material objects in society consists of their openness to 'external' events and their resulting potential for mediating the introduction of 'contingency'" (Keane 2005: 416). This contingency rests on the fact that: "both the value and the possible meanings of objects are underdetermined. They call for speech, interpretative practices, and political strategies. This means that they are necessarily caught up in the uncertainties of social action" (Keane 2001: 70).

References

Appadurai, Arjun. 1986. "Introduction: Commodities and the Politics of Value," in *The Social Life of Things: Commodities in Cultural Perspective*, ed. A. Appadurai. New York: Cambridge University Press, pp.3–63.

Archaimbault, Charles. 1973. *Structures Religieuses Lao (rites et mythes)*. Vientiane: Vithagna.

Arns, Inke, and Thomas De Ruyter. 2009. "Awake are Only the Spirits: On Ghosts and their Media," in *Exhibition Catalogue*, ed. I. Arns. Dortmund: Hartware Medien Kunst Verein, pp.4–9.

Bizot, Francoise. 1981. *Le Don de Soi-Même: Recherches sur le Bouddhisme Khmer, III*. Paris: Ecole Française d'Extrême-Orient.

Bouté, Vanina. 2005. *En miroir du pouvoir: Les Phounoy du Nord Laos – ethnogenèse et dynamiques d'intégration*, Ph.D. dissertation. Paris: Ecole Pratique des Hautes Etudes.

Buakham, Saribub Maha. 2001. *Preachings of 108 Anisong* [in Lao]. Vientiane: no publisher indicated.

Buse, Peter, and Andrew Stott, eds. 1999. *Ghosts: Deconstruction, Psychoanalysis, History*. Basingstoke: Macmillan.

Candea, Matei, ed. 2010. *The Social after Gabriel Tarde: Debates and Assessments*. London: Routledge.

Carsten, Janet. 2007. "Introduction: Ghosts of Memory," in *Ghosts of Memory: Essays on Remembrance and Relatedness*, ed. J. Carsten. Oxford: Blackwell, pp.1–35.

Davis, Richard. 1984. *Muang Metaphysics: A Study of Northern Thai Myth and Ritual*. Bangkok: Silkworm Press.

Delaplace, Geregory. 2009. *L'invention des morts: Sépultures, fantômes et photographie en Mongolie contemporaine*. Paris: Collection Nord-Asie.

Delaplace, Gregory, and Rebecca Empson. 2007. "The Little Human and the Daughter-in-law: Invisibles as Seen through the Eyes of Different Kinds of People," *Inner Asia* 9: 59–76.

Derrida, Jacques. 1976. *Of Grammatology*. Baltimore. MD: Johns Hopkins University Press.

———. 1994. *Specters of Marx: The State of the Debt, the Work of Mourning, and the New International*. London: Routledge.

Descola, Philippe. 1998. "Societies of Nature and the Nature of Society," in *Conceptualizing Society*, ed. A. Kuper. London: Routledge, pp.107–26.

———. 2007. "Le commerce des âmes: L'ontologie animique dans les Amériques," in *Nature of Spirits in Aboriginal Cosmologies*, eds. F. Laugrand and J. Oosten. Quebec: Presses de l'Université de Laval, pp.3–30.

Evans-Pritchard, E.E. 1966. "Twins, Birds and Vegetables," *Man* 1(3): 398–399.

GDAT. 2010. "Ontology is just Another Word for Culture," Meeting of the Group for Debates in Anthropological Theory, University of Manchester. *Critique of Anthropology* 30(2): 152–200.

Gehman, Henry. 1923. "Ādisati, Anvādisati, Anudisati, and Uddisati in the Peta-Vatthu," *Journal of the American Oriental Society* 43: 410–21.

Gell, Alfred. 1998. *Art and Agency: An Anthropological Theory*. Oxford: Oxford University Press.

Gombrich, Richard, and Gananath Obeyesekere. 1988. *Buddhism Transformed: Religious Change in Sri Lanka*. Princeton, NJ: Princeton University Press.

Henare, Amiria, Martin Holbraad, and Sari Wastell, eds. 2007. *Thinking Through Things: Theorising Artefacts Ethnographically*. London: Routledge.

Ingold, Tim. 2000. *The Perception of the Environment: Essays in Livelihood, Dwelling and Skill*. London: Routledge.

Jackson, Peter. 1999. "The Enchanting Spirit of Thai Capitalism: The Cult of Luang Phor Khoon and the Post-modernization of Thai Buddhism," *South East Asia Research* 7: 5–60.

Jameson, Frederic. 1999. "Marx's Purloined Letter," in *Ghostly Demarcations: A Symposium on Jacques Derrida's Specters of Marx*, ed. M. Sprinkler. London: Verso, pp.26–67.

Keane, Webb. 2001. "Money is no Object: Materiality, Desire, and Modernity in an Indonesian Society," in *The Empire of Things: Regimes of Value and Material Culture*, ed. F. Myers. Santa Fee, NM: School of American Research Press, pp.65–90.

———. 2005. "Signs are not the Garb of Meaning: On the Social Analysis of Material Things," in *Materiality*, ed. D. Miller. Durham, NC: Duke University Press, pp.182–205.

———. 2006. "Subject and Object," in *Handbook of Material Culture*, eds. C. Tilley et al. London: Sage, pp.197–202.

———. 2007. *Christian Moderns: Freedom and Fetish in the Mission Encounter*. Berkeley: University of California Press.

Keyes, Charles. 1983. "Merit Transference in the Karmic Theory of Popular Theravada Buddhism," in *Karma: An Anthropological Inquiry*, eds. C. Keyes and E.V. Valentine. Berkeley: University of California Press, pp.261–86.

Kitiarsa, Pattana. 2008. "Buddha Phanit: Thailand's Prosperity Religion and its Commodifying Tactics," in *Religious Commodifications in Asia: Marketing Gods*, ed. P. Kitiarsa. London: Routledge, pp.120–43.

Kourilsky, Gregory. 2006. *Recherches sur l'institut Bouddhique au Laos (1930–1949): Les circonstances de sa création, son action, son échec*, Master's dissertation. Paris: Ecole Pratique des Hautes Etudes.

———. 2008."Note sur la piété filiale en Asie du Sud-Est theravādin: la notion de gu□" *Aséanie: Sciences humaines en Asie du Sud-Est* 20: 27–54.

Kwon, Heonik. 2008. *Ghosts of War in Vietnam*. Cambridge: Cambridge University Press.

Ladwig, Patrice. 2007. "Die Störung des Staats-Effekts: Kulturelle Überreste und die spukenden Geister des Spätsozialismus in Laos," in *Ordnungen im Wandel: Globale und lokale Wirklichkeiten im Spiegel transdisziplinärer Analysen*, eds. M. Meyer and F. Arndt. Berlin: Transcript Verlag, pp.57–80.

———. 2008. "Between Cultural Preservation and This-worldly Commitment: Modernization, Social Activism and the Lao Buddhist Sangha," in *Nouvelles recherches sur le Laos*, eds. Y. Goudineau and M. Lorillard. Paris: Ecole Française d'Extrême-Orient, pp.465–90.

———. Forthcoming a. "Feeding the Dead: Ghosts, Materiality and Merit in a Lao Buddhist Festival," in *Buddhist Funeral Cultures of Southeast Asia and China,* eds. P. Ladwig and P. Williams. Cambridge: Cambridge University Press.

———. Forthcoming b. "Visitors from Hell: Hospitality to Ghosts in a Lao Buddhist Festival," *Journal of the Royal Anthropological Institute.*

Lafont, Pierre. 1982. "Buddhism in Contemporary Laos," in *Contemporary Laos*, ed. M. Stuart-Fox. New York: St. Martin's Press, pp.148–62.

Latour, Bruno. 1993. *We Have Never Been Modern*. Cambridge, MA: Harvard University Press.

———. 1999. *Pandora's Hope: Essays on the Reality of Science Studies*. Cambridge, MA: Harvard University Press.

———. 2005. *Reassembling the Social: An Introduction to Actor-Network Theory.* Oxford: Oxford University Press.

Leenhardt, Maurice. 1979. *Do Kamo: Person and Myth in the Melanesian World.* Chicago: University of Chicago Press.

Lévy-Bruhl, Lucien. 1975. *The Notebooks on Primitive Mentality*. Oxford: Blackwell.

McMahan, David. 2008. *The Making of Buddhist Modernism*. New York: Oxford University Press.

Manning, Paul, and Anne Meneley. 2008. "Material Objects in Cosmological Worlds: An Introduction," *Ethnos* 73: 285–302.

Mauss, Marcel. 1990. *The Gift: The Form and Reason for Exchange in Archaic Societies*. New York: Norton.

Miller, Daniel, ed. 2005. *Materiality*. Durham, NC: Duke University Press.

Ong, Aihwa. 1987. *Spirits of Resistance and Capitalist Discipline: Factory Women in Malaysia*. Albany: State University of New York Press.

Ortner, Sherry. 1975. "God's Bodies, God's Food: A Symbolic Analysis of a Sherpa Ritual," in *The Interpretation of Symbols*, ed. R. Willis. New York: Wiley, pp.133–69.

Philavong, Pha Maha. 1967. *Costumes, Rites and Worthy Traditions of the Lao People* [in Lao]. Vientiane: no publisher.

Platenkamp, Jos D.M. 2007. "Spirit Representations in Southeast Asia: A Comparative View," in *Nature of Spirits in Aboriginal Cosmologies*, eds. F. Laugrand and J. Oosten. Quebec: Presses de l'Université de Laval, pp.99–129.

Pottier, Richard. 2007. *Yû dî mî hèng, Etre bien, avoir de la force: Essai sur les pratiques thérapeutiques Lao*. Paris: Ecole Française de l'Extrême Oriente.

Rio, Knut Mikjel. 2007. *The Power of Perspective: Social Ontology and Agency on Ambrym Island, Vanuatu*. Oxford: Berghahn.

Schopen, Gregory. 1991. "Archaeology and Protestant Presuppositions in the Study of Indian Buddhism," *History of Religions* 31: 1–23.
Scott, Michael W. 2007. *The Severed Snake: Matrilineages, Making Place, and Melanesian Christianity in the Southeast Solomon Islands*. Durham, NC: Carolina Academic Press.
Spivak, Gayatri. 1976. "Translator's Preface," in J. Derrida, *Of Grammatology*. Baltimore, MD: Johns Hopkins University Press, pp.ix–lxxxvii.
Stuart-Fox, Martin, and Rod Bucknell. 1982. "Politicization of the Buddhist Sangha in Laos," *Journal of Southeast Asian Studies* 13: 60–80.
Sutton, David. 2001. *Remembrance of Repasts: An Anthropology of Food and Memory*. New York: Berg.
Swearer, Donald. 2004. *Becoming the Buddha: The Ritual of Image Consecration in Thailand*. Princeton, NJ: Princeton University Press.
Tambiah, Stanley. 1970. *Buddhism and Spirit Cults in North-East Thailand*. Cambridge: Cambridge University Press.
Thevenot, Laurent. 2002. "Which Road to Follow? The Moral Complexity of an 'Equipped' Humanity," in *Complexities: Social Studies of Knowledge Practices*, eds. J. Law and A. Mol. Durham, NC: Duke University Press, pp.53–87.
Vilaça, Aparecida. 2005. "Chronically Unstable Bodies: Reflections on Amazonian Corporalities," *Journal of the Royal Anthropological Institute* 11: 445–64.
Viveiros de Castro, E. 1998. "Cosmological Deixis and Amerindian Perspectivism," *Journal of the Royal Anthropological Institute* 4: 469–88.
———. 2003. (anthropology) AND (science). *Manchester Papers in Social Anthropology*, Vol. 7.
———. 2004. "Exchanging Perspectives: The Transformation of Objects into Subjects in Amerindian Ontologies," *Common Knowledge* 10: 463–84.
———. 2007. "La forêt des miroirs: Quelques notes sur l'ontologie des esprits amazoniens," in *Nature of Spirits in Aboriginal Cosmologies*, eds. F. Laugrand and J. Oosten. Quebec: Presses de l'Université de Laval, pp.45–74.
Wardle, Huan, et al. 2009. "Comparative Ontologies and Cosmologies," *Open Anthropology Cooperative*. Retrieved 15 December 2010 from: http://openanthcoop.ning.com/group/philosophicalanthropologyanthropologyofphilosophy/forum/topics/comparative-ontologies-and.
Zago, Marcel. 1972. *Rites et cérémonies en milieu bouddhiste lao*. Rome: Università Gregoriana.

2

SPIRITED WARRIORS:
CONSPIRACY AND PROTECTION ON LOMBOK

Kari Telle

Introduction

Returning to the island of Lombok in 2001, I could not fail to notice that a security post had been put up next to Pura Meru, the largest Hindu temple in Cakranegara, the island's commercial centre. With its brightly painted façade made up of red, black, and white stripes, ceremonial umbrellas, and engraved golden plaques, the headquarters of Dharma Wisesa, a Hindu-oriented civilian security group, stood out from the rather drab urban surroundings. Bold letters made plain that the converted storefront served as a "command centre" (*pos komando pusat*). Waving above the entrance was a flag depicting Siwa, the main deity of the Hindu Balinese pantheon, meditating on a lotus throne inside a ring of fire surrounded by magical weapons. Facing east, west, north, and south, these eternally spinning weapons (*cakra*) intercept and ward off dangers from all directions. Steeped in religious imagery yet replete with the language of the state's military apparatus, the headquarters projected an image of power culled from different domains.[1]

My first reaction was to see the headquarters as an example of the militarization of religious identities in post-New Order Indonesia. But closer investigation suggests that Dharma Wisesa and similar movements are recasting the modern discourse and practice of security by infusing it with spiritual force. Drawing on fieldwork carried out among the Balinese community on Lombok, I argue that popular spirit beliefs have gained renewed salience in the Reformasi era that was ushered in after the collapse of the military-dominated New Order regime (1966–1998).[2] Spirit beliefs and the "occult cosmology" (West and Sanders 2003: 6) in

Endnotes for this chapter begin on page 59

which they are embedded have become important resources for dealing with the uncertainties arising in the new political landscape of decentralization, regional autonomy, and democratic reforms. The renewed importance attached to securing spiritual protection testifies to the creative potential of local traditions of engaging supernatural entities in adapting to and addressing new circumstances. As I will show, such traditions also nurture contemporary myth-making.

This chapter explores how members of the Balinese minority on Lombok responded to a pervasive sense of insecurity by forming their own civilian security force. Ten years after the New Order regime proved to be vulnerable, the country is awash with popular initiatives with the claimed mission of fighting "crime" and enhancing security. This process was well underway before the sprawling archipelago nation was jolted into the frontline of the "war on terror" after the devastating bomb attacks on the island of Bali in October 2002. If under the New Order the state had a near monopoly on the "securitization" (Wæver 1995) of society, in recent years the role of all kinds of private organizations in providing protection has become more prominent. What is taking place is not simply a privatization of the public order but a parallel trend characterized by an informalization of security arrangements. These intertwined developments have, as I will demonstrate, fueled the religious imagination and given renewed impetus to engage spirit forces in the quest to achieve what might be called ontological certainty.[3]

Formed in a context of upheaval and sectarian violence, Dharma Wisesa is a quasi-corporate civilian security force organized by members of the Balinese minority on Lombok. While this civilian security force bears the distinct imprint of New Order militarism, another notable aspect is the emphasis on infusing this movement with religious and spiritual power. Dharma Wisesa is located within a broader Hindu Balinese religious imaginary and has the moral support of prominent Brahmana priests (*pedanda*). What is less apparent, though of no less importance, is the fact that this movement is aligned with spiritual forces associated with the Balinese Karangasem dynasty that controlled Lombok until 1894 when the island was incorporated into the Dutch colonial empire. Both the leadership and lay guards understand themselves to be "backed" by a spirit army (*bale samar*) which engages in a form of spiritual warfare on behalf of the Lombok Balinese when their collective interests and well-being are threatened. However fleeting the glimpses of these spirits may be, they bring assurance that supernatural protection is close by. The availability of these spirit forces also suggests that what Tony Day calls the "magic of the cosmological state in Southeast Asia" (Day 2002: 164) has not been eclipsed by modern bureaucratic state formations, whether colonial or postcolonial.

The current interest in cultivating relations with invisible forces, including those associated with seemingly defunct forms of political authority, should not be seen as a residual traditionalism nor dismissed as a pure "invention of tradition" (Hobsbawm and Ranger 1983). Rather, I will argue that these practices of "imagining

Figure 2.1: The Dharma Wisesa headquarters in Cakranegara. Photograph by Kari Telle, 2006.

continuity" (Lambek 2002: 4) are potent expressions of Lombok Balinese historical consciousness which entail a continuous crafting of the past in the present and of the present in respect to the past. Techniques of remembrance and disclosure, including narrative and ritual practice, render aspects of the past available. Certain figures and events of the past continue to have active relevance in the present. As products of the religious imagination, the spirits who figure in myths and historical narratives sometimes irrupt in and confront the present, and this perhaps especially so in moments of crisis. The uncertainties of the Reformasi era have, if anything, reinforced the assumption that personal and collective well-being hinges on the ability to navigate the interpenetrating realms populated by humans and a range of invisible non-human forces, which may become a resource in times of danger.

Rioting and Conspiratorial Fears

Located just east of Bali, the island of Lombok and the neighboring island of Sumbawa form the Indonesian province of Nusa Tenggara Barat. The Sasak people, most of whom are Muslims, constitute more than 90 per cent of the island's population of 2.6 million, with Balinese, Chinese, Arabs, Buginese, and Javanese making up the remainder. Balinese Hindus, numbering approximately 120,000 people, form the largest ethnic and religious minority. Having lived here for many generations, and sometimes inter-married with the Sasak, they have a strong sense of identity as Lombok Balinese. Most Balinese trace their origin to the Karangasem area in east Bali. Between 1740 and 1894, a branch of the Karangasem dynasty acquired control over Lombok and a Balinese population moved into the western part of the island (Kraan 1980). Much effort was put into the construction of irrigation works and temple building, and the king presided over state rituals promoting human as well as agricultural fertility. Balinese performing arts and courtly traditions were firmly established on Lombok in the nineteenth century (Harnish 2006).

Balinese rule ended in 1894 when they were defeated by Dutch forces fighting alongside Sasak aristocrats from east Lombok who rebelled against the Balinese overlords and their Sasak allies. At the time of the Dutch conquest, the supreme ruler on Lombok was Anak Agung Ngurah Karangasem, who was among the wealthiest indigenous rulers in the archipelago. The royal palace was destroyed, numerous treasures were brought to the Netherlands (Vanvugt 1995), and the king and his two sons were exiled to the island of Java. But members of the small court of Singasari refused to accept the humiliation of defeat and perished in a ritualized *puputan*, which may be glossed as a "fight to the end" or "the finishing" (Wiener 1995: 315–30). The Dutch quickly established themselves as the new colonial power and thus began a harsh colonial reign. Though the Balinese were henceforth reduced to the status of a religious minority with little political influence, collective memories of the "golden era" of Balinese rule have been nurtured through oral traditions and annual temple festivals. During the turbulent transition to the Reformasi era, these narratives gained renewed salience and became wedded to a militant defence of Hindu Balinese culture.

The fact that the Lombok Balinese have become preoccupied with security is directly related to the "mood of profound uncertainty that swept Indonesia" (Reuter 2003: 1) after thirty-two years of enforced stability ended with President Suharto's resignation from power in 1998. The collapse of his iron-fisted regime was accompanied by a sense of euphoria about the new possibilities for political participation, but this euphoria was rather short-lived. Not only was Indonesia badly affected by the Asian monetary crisis in the late 1990s, the first three years of the Reformasi era saw a variety of collective violence across the archipelago.[4] In many cases the violence was cast in religious terms, pitting members of one religious community against another, as was the case during the anti-Christian rioting on Lombok in January 2000. Although the rioting was over in a week, the violence has cast a long shadow of suspicion over relations between religious communities. Religious minorities produced their own narratives of suspicion. They also responded by re-actualizing ancestral connections and harnessing dormant spiritual forces and their associated spiritual territories (MacDougall 2005: 275–98). For many Lombok Balinese, the riot and the conspiratorial fears generated in its wake convinced them of the need to empower themselves by forming a security force.

The riot began immediately after an Islamic rally (*tabliq akbar*) held on 17 January 2000 in Mataram, the provincial capital. The rally was organized in support of the

Muslim victims of the violence in the Malukan islands in eastern Indonesia where ethno-religious clashes between Christians and Muslims had occurred since January 1999. Drawing close to six thousand participants, the rally was one of a series organized in different parts of Indonesia to express sympathy and raise money for Muslims in Maluku. Churches, shops, businesses, and homes belonging to Christians, often but by no means exclusively of Sino-Indonesian descent, were looted and burned. The rioting spread rapidly from the urban areas of Mataram and Cakranegara into the tourist destinations along the coast and into the hinterland of west and north Lombok, leaving a trail of burnt-out and destroyed buildings. Many buildings were marked with insulting and threatening graffiti, a practice that in turn prompted efforts to mark the façade of homes and businesses with quotes from the Qur'an so as to convey that the place was Muslim-owned (Avonius 2004: 71–72).[5]

During the rioting, Balinese men armed with daggers and spears guarded the entrance to their neighborhoods, seeking to prevent the mobs from setting homes and churches on fire. Most neighborhoods in both Cakranegara and Mataram are religiously and ethnically mixed. In fact, the only churches saved were those located in neighborhoods that Balinese residents chose to defend. At least twelve churches were more or less completely destroyed. Months after the situation had calmed down, rumours that Islamic vigilantes were about to "take revenge" on the Balinese because they had protected churches and shielded the homes of their Christian neighbors caused near panic in Balinese circles in Cakranegara and Mataram. This recurring rumor captures the paranoid sensibility generated by the riot, which occurred in a context where militant crime-fighting groups had assumed a growing influence in local affairs, operating in ways suggesting that they somehow were licensed to act with impunity. Effectively, rumors about revengeful attacks to be visited on the Balinese cast the riot as a rehearsal of more shattering events yet to come. These fears were also nurtured by evidence indicating that the violence had been carefully planned.

Despite the seemingly spontaneous nature of the violence, the Lombok riots followed a familiar script which includes the advance circulation of leaflets and video recordings. This included VCR and CD-roms depicting violence allegedly perpetrated against Muslims and mosques in eastern Indonesia. In the week before the rally a so-called "open letter" addressed to local Christians was put up in the Mataram area. Demanding that they issue a statement condemning the atrocities committed by Christians in Maluku, the letter warned that unless Christians issued a written statement within 2 x 24 hours they would face dire consequences. The statement was signed by members of the *tabliq akbar* committee, including the local leader of an Islamic trade union (PPMI) and the founder of Amphibi, a civilian crime-fighting group that has been tied to several cases of vigilante justice (ICG 2003). Provocative pamphlets have become a staple in sectarian conflicts and communal violence in Indonesia (Sidel 2006; Spyer 2006). In an insightful study of the thriving pamphlet politics accompanying the Maluku wars, Bubandt

(2008) has shown how inflammatory pamphlets tapped into a culture of rumor and served to provoke and legitimize acts of violence. Understanding pamphlets as social agents, Bubandt argues that their social efficacy is tied to "their capacity to be 'in the true' in a variety of evocative plots" (ibid.: 792). In order to be effective their narratives must, in other words, be taken as believable accounts.

Even though the "open letter" made no mention of the local Balinese, in the tense post-riot climate it served to confirm Balinese fears of a broader agenda of Islamization. Suspicions that the riot was part of a plot to overturn the nation's secular constitutional ideology (Hefner 1997) were boosted by the fact that the conflict in Maluku had become a national concern, eliciting militant Muslim support in a string of rallies across the country. That the rioting occurred at the turn of the millennium, following on the heels of a series of bomb attacks targeting local churches, added another sinister dimension to these fears.[6] Apocalyptic expectations and the notion that cosmic battles usher in new eras are found in many Indonesian societies (Hobart 2000; Bubandt 2001). The Sasak have messianic traditions (Cederroth 1977) and are deeply familiar with the Islamic notion of the Day of Judgement. Signs that this cataclysmic event is drawing near are assumed to manifest themselves in the form of disasters, upheavals, and warfare in the human realm. These general religious ideas acquired new urgency during the political and economic crisis of the late 1990s, when Sasak friends noted that the year 2000 would likely mark the end of this world and warned me that this cataclysmic event would be presaged by battles between Muslims and "infidels." By the time the riot occurred, many locals, irrespective of their religious identity, were probably familiar with the notion of an imminent battle of cosmic proportions. This scenario may well have inspired some of the rioters, who took to the streets wearing white headbands inscribed with *Allahu Akbar* ("God is great"), lending their actions higher purpose and a sense of inevitability.

Balinese fears that the riot was part of a grand scheme to wipe out or drive all religious minorities away from Lombok spurred a firm resolve to resist. As one man put it to me in 2001, echoing a common sentiment: "We were prepared, if necessary, to fight to the finish (*puputan*), to defend our homes and neighborhoods." By invoking the notion of the *puputan*, my interlocutors framed the contemporary situation in terms of the all-out resistance put up by the small court of Singasari in Cakranegara and their retinue in 1894, when they refused to surrender and marched, white-clad and armed with krisses and lances, into the fire of the Netherlands Indies army. In official Balinese historiography, the term *puputan* has come to signify the heroic fight against colonial oppression, and warrior virtues like courage and readiness to sacrifice (Wiener 1995, 1999). Given the centrality of this trope in nationalistic historiography it is perhaps not surprising that many Balinese invoked the charged notion of the *puputan* to describe their unflinching commitment to defend homes and neighborhoods. What is more remarkable is the fact that this resolve included heroic acts for the sake of their Christian compatriots.

Responding to the violence, the Lombok Balinese did not simply draw on the recollected past as a model for action. At this moment, aspects of the past became an immediate resource. The issue of spiritual intervention is a recurring theme in the narratives and recollections I have gathered about the rioting. I suggest that this moment became a "clearing," a term borrowed from Lambek (2002: 13), when the past and present intermingled and what is normally hidden from view momentarily became visible. At this frightful time, spirits of the past emerged and confronted the present. For instance, a retired teacher recalled how an advancing mob about to torch a Protestant church in a predominantly Balinese neighborhood in Cakranegara turned around and, for no apparent reason, fled in panic. The mob, he explained, had been terrified by the sight of a group of "spirit warriors" (*bale samar*) assuming a wild and ferocious demeanour. The issue of spiritual intervention also came up in an interview with Anak Agung Made Djelantik, Dharma Wisesa's commander-in-chief in 2006.[7] Underlining the seriousness of the information he was about to divulge, the young man leaned forward and lowered his voice: "Just imagine, suppose that the *bale samar* had not intervened during those days, I am confident that Cakranegara would have been utterly destroyed (*hancur total*)." He added that the Dharma Wisesa headquarters now serve as the earthly base (*pusat*) for the spirit army.

The suspicion that the city of Cakranegara would have been leveled were it not for the intervention of spiritual forces inscribes the riot within an almost apocalyptic imaginary in which the actual violence was but a pale taste of violence intended to be far more destructive. Combining conspiracy theory with a firm belief in the agency of non-human beings, this account illustrates that "occult cosmologies" not only are tools for deciphering a complex world but provide persons and groups with a measure of agency in confronting the interplay of the manifest and the invisible world. As Schrauwers observes, writing about a Christian minority group in the highlands of Sulawesi under the New Order, "'occult cosmologies' offer 'occult technologies' by which the larger, unseen powers that be can be manipulated and corruption transcended" (Schrauwers 2003: 129). Conspiratorial fears aside, Made Jelantik's comments articulate cosmological understandings that most Balinese take for granted, namely that what happens in the "visible" (*sekala*) or material realm is shaped by a host of "invisible" (*niskala*) powers. What happens in the realm of spiritual relations exerts a decisive influence on the material and physical word; it is somehow more "real" (Wiener 1995). In other words, the manifest reality of the senses is encompassed by an invisible world of spiritual forces which can be harnessed for positive or harmful ends. Balinese cosmological ideas and the importance of establishing auspicious connections with the forces of the "invisible" realm will be further discussed as I now turn to Dharma Wisesa and the spiritual economy in which the movement is embedded. This will also make sense of the remarkably bold claim that the spirit army's base is the command post of a (hyper)modern security group.

Re-enchanting "Security"

The initiative to establish a Hindu-inspired civilian security force was taken by prominent members of the Balinese community in Cakranegara and Mataram in late December 1999.[8] This initiative arose out of anxiety and disillusionment with the state's willingness and ability to control crime-fighting groups operating under the banner of Islam, which had assumed a growing influence in local affairs since the demise of the New Order regime (Telle 2009, 2010b). The recent death of a Balinese man and the maiming of another at the hands of members of a militant crime-fighting force were fresh in the minds of the four hundred men who gathered in the Meru temple on 25 December to discuss the need to step up security measures.[9] During this meeting it was agreed to establish neighborhood night-watches (*ronda*) around the city, a form of community self-policing common in both urban and rural areas of Indonesia. But the scale of the subsequent January 2000 rioting convinced many Balinese of the need for an island-wide organization comprised of territorially-based units to be coordinated by a central headquarters. By adopting this solution, they also took advantage of the new political climate in which it had become possible to mobilize around security and to do so along ethnic or religious lines.

The transition to the Reformasi era entailed major changes in the meaning and organization of "security" in Indonesia. Long before the all-encompassing role of security in the post-9/11 world, the Suharto regime turned its statist version of security into a fundamental societal discourse (Bubandt 2005). Presenting itself as the guarantor of "safety and order," the armed forces had the dual function of defending the nation against foreign enemies and the mandate to secure regime stability by "guiding" the development of society. The myth propagated by the regime was that the nation had fallen prey to disorder but was rescued by General Suharto, the "father of development," who put the nation on the road towards modernization. What remained unspeakable was the violence committed by the regime itself, especially the 1965/66 massacres of hundreds of thousands of people charged with being communists (Zurbuchen 2005). With the shift from state-secured development to democracy, the military lost its former near-monopoly of the "securitization" of society.

Seeking an alternative to the New Order regime's top-down authoritarian rule, many provincial governments now welcomed greater civilian involvement in security management. On Lombok, popular initiatives to combat lawlessness and fight crime were welcomed as "a new form of 'people's power'" (MacDougall 2007: 287) embodying the spirit of democracy. Following the January 2000 rioting, influential government officials concluded that civilian security groups (*pam-swakarsa*) might prevent further outbreaks of sectarian violence. Consequently, Balinese leaders easily obtained permission to form a security force. In May 2000, several hundred delegates from all over Lombok gathered in the provincial capital to draw up a program. Prominent politicians, police, and military personnel attended the "big assembly" (*maha sabha*), including the governor of the province, who expressed the wish that Dharma Wisesa would help foster peace and stability, and promote inter-religious harmony.

The new security group was set up to safeguard Balinese interests on Lombok by mediating relations, not just among people but also with the forces of the "invisible" realm. For those who devoted themselves to develop Dharma Wisesa and to bring the entire Lombok Balinese community within its protective fold, it was obvious that genuine ontological certainty could not be achieved simply by emulating the modern state's security discourses. Although they adapted many terms and practices from the police and military, like organizing the guards into regiments (*regu*) headed by commanders (*komandan*), performing "patrols" around the city, and using modern communication technologies, this mobilization arose from a deep dissatisfaction with the Indonesian state's ability to deliver security and justice. Consequently, it was felt that this goal could only be achieved by infusing, hence qualitatively transforming, conventional modern security measures with religious as well as spiritual force. Put in other terms, it was necessary to bring such "outer" organizational forms in touch with far more effective "inner" spiritual powers.

To reflect the favorable connections with the spiritual realm, the name Dharma Wisesa, which means "Dharma Power," was chosen for the new movement that

Figure 2.2: The Dharma Wisesa logo: Lord Siwa meditating on a lotus throne surrounded by eternally spinning *cakra* weapons. Photograph by Kari Telle, 2006.

was inaugurated and "blessed" by several prominent Brahmana priests (*pedanda*). The notion of *dharma* is a key concept in Hindu Balinese thought and can be glossed as "truth" or "balanced cosmic order." The antithesis of *adharma*, meaning chaos or disorder, *dharma* carries a sense of moral virtue and the duty to behave according to socio-religious norms (Pedersen 2006). The term *wisesa* connotes power or force, and is semantically linked to the notion of *kesaktian*, connoting magical or mystical power. According to Hildred Geertz, *sakti* is "not only the power of the gods but also a human competence," albeit one that is by nature ephemeral (Geertz 1994: 85). Geertz also observes that Balinese talk about *sakti* tends to be "pervaded with a rhetoric of battle" (ibid.: 85). In her view, this reflects an understanding of the world as comprised of a multitude of beings, human as well as non-human, in endless competition for control of one another. In such a world it is vitally important to align oneself with those who have the capacity to mediate and act in an intercessory capacity with the realm of *niskala* powers.

While it was important to secure support from agents of the modern Indonesian state, Dharma Wisesa was from the outset located within a longer trajectory of Balinese kingship. This is evident from the fact that the man chosen to head this new supra-local civilian defence force was Anak Agung Gedé Biarsah, the grandson of the last Balinese king to rule Lombok. Besides the need for a leader who could act effectively on the political scene, I suggest that this choice was guided by the conviction that descendants of the royal clan possess regalia, heirlooms (*pusaka*), and forms of valuable knowledge associated with the last dynasty. Although the Mataram dynasty is long gone, the regalia and forms of knowledge that once constituted the ruler's claim to power continue to play vital roles to this day. At the time of the Dutch conquest, the supreme ruler was Anak Agung Ngurah Karangasem who had amassed great wealth. While many treasures and important chronicles were taken to the Netherlands or auctioned off in Java, some possessions, including sacred cloths and daggers, were saved. Connecting the past to the present, these durable tokens of former state power are treated with respect and given offerings, as they are conduits of magical power.

Scholars of precolonial kingdoms in much of Southeast Asia have stressed how regalia, ritual practices, and processions served to constitute the power that allowed kings to rule. On Lombok and Bali the foremost heirloom object was the royal keris; various texts indicate that the "keris rather than the king was the divinely 'true' (*wyakti*) source of power" (Schulte Nordholt 1996: 152). Conversely, it is a recurring theme that the loss of the named keris, conceived as a conduit of power, entailed the loss of kingship. Another dimension of the precolonial Balinese state that must be emphasized is "the imminence of death and, hence, the necessity to seek protection" (ibid.: 11). As Schulte Nordholt (ibid.) points out in his history of the Mengwi dynasty, an important task of royal centers was to provide protection from threats, both from the "visible" world as well as the "invisible" one, in order to guarantee the continuation of life.

Informing Lombok Balinese historical consciousness is an understanding of the past such that it is not completed but continuous in the present. By extension, present-day power and well-being derives from a carefully maintained relationship to aspects of the ancestral past. During the rioting of January 2000 and in the tense post-riot atmosphere, much activity was aimed at bringing the magical power of royal ancestors to bear on the present. Hundreds of people flocked to Puri Pamotan, Gedé Biarsah's spacious residence in Cakranegara, seeking assistance. Some asked for charms to boost their courage, others requested protective amulets (*bebadong*) to confer invulnerability. Many men brought daggers and spears to the palace in order to have these weapons re-enlivened (*pasupati*) so as to render them potent and "hot."[10] This spontaneous "return to the palace" involved the recognition of centuries-old historical relationships between members of the royal family and various kinds of subjects. Turning to the palace, people acted on the assumption that the objects and forms of knowledge associated with the former royal dynasty were accessible at this dramatic juncture.

By making himself available and working tirelessly to fashion protective devices, Gedé Biarsah nurtured the idea of an imagined Balinese state (*negara*) that protects its subjects. My host family in Cakranegara was not alone in claiming that the royal heirs had activated their auspicious connections to their ancestors and forces of the "invisible" realm during the rioting. The apparent success of these efforts, as evidenced by the fact that no Balinese were seriously hurt and that the only churches saved were those located in Balinese neighborhoods, indicated that these connections remained strong and vibrant. In Balinese conceptions, the "invisible" and "visible" worlds interpenetrate. Hence, for a person or ruler to be recognized as powerful it is necessary "to realize power in practical terms in the manifest world" (Pedersen 2006: 21). The relatively favorable outcome of the riot thus boosted people's confidence that the royal heir was well suited to imbue the security group with power and charisma.

Spirited Warriors, Emerging Myths

Since early 2000, the Dharma Wisesa headquarters in Cakranegera has been staffed, day and night, by rotating teams of uniformed guards who range in age from their twenties to their mid sixties. Although many guards cultivate a tough image, most of them were quite approachable and I soon found myself hanging around the office, listening in as they called up fellow guards by using police radio, discussed upcoming rituals, or complained about the difficulties facing religious minorities on Lombok. It was during these casual meetings that I first learned that many guards feel protected by a battalion of spirits (*bale samar*). Some guards were adamant that sightings of the spirit army had become more frequent over the past decade. Others, including Dharma Wisesa members, doubt that this is the case. The profound ambivalence surrounding such sightings is worth noting.

While glimpses of these spirits bring reassurance because they reveal that supernatural assistance is forthcoming, their appearance implies that the situation is growing precarious.

Finding that the spirit army was often brought up in connection with the Mataram dynasty, in 2006 I asked Anak Agung Gedé Biarsah to tell me more about these forces:

> As a matter of fact this is sacred (*sakral*). Let me put it this way. What we call *bale samar* are a certain kind of spirits who are still connected to the material world. Christians believe in the devil (*setan*), but there are other kinds of spirits that are good and benevolent. These spirits are good, and they can be controlled by kings (*raja*) who have the ability to see into the invisible realm. These spirits have the ability to manifest themselves in the shape of humans. They manifest at certain times [brief pause]. Only powerful persons, like Balinese kings, command such forces. In the past, the gods (*dewa*) bestowed an invisible spirit army to help the *raja* assume control over Lombok. At that time, the king was not accompanied by many followers but the *bale samar* aided the king. Let me give an example. Think about the irrigation system running all the way from the Lingsar temple to Mayura [Cakranegara]. The channel is deep and set with stones that have the same size. It would not be possible to construct this channel except by advanced modern tools or supernatural strength (*kekuatan ghaib*). The channels are proof (*bukti*) that the *raja* invited the *bale samar*.

At first, Gedé Biarsah seemed somewhat reluctant to discuss this "sacred" subject with me. This reluctance can be attributed to the fact that the legacy of Balinese rule has become a sensitive political issue in Lombok, where memories of colonization run deep.[11] Another reason is that activities involving traffic with "invisible" forces tend to be shrouded in secrecy. As such forces are eminently Janus-faced, having both life-giving and destructive powers, the motives of those who get involved with such forces can be questioned. Considering the emphasis scholars working on Bali and Java have paid to indirectness, dissimulation, and the reluctance to make direct claims to one's personal skills (Keeler 1987; Wilson, this volume), Gedé Biarsah's response was surprisingly direct. There is nothing in this account to suggest that these forces no longer are available. In fact, people who are close to Dharma Wisesa's leader note that he often meditates in a special room (*kamar suci*) to seek advice from his father and grandfather.

The centrality of supernatural power in constituting and exercising kingship is underscored in this account, which ties the spirit battalion to the origin of Balinese control over Lombok. The aspiring ruler's agency is amplified by his command of spiritual forces, described as a divine gift bestowed on powerful persons. To demonstrate that the king was endowed with supernatural powers, Gedé Biarsah points to the channels running from the natural springs in Lingsar, twenty kilometers east of Cakranegara, feeding water to the lowland plains of west Lombok that are ideally suited for rice cultivation. Pointing to the engineering feat that produced these life-giving channels, he claims that the *raja* was so close to the gods that he could put spiritual forces to work. During the reign of the Mataram dynasty, the temple festival at Lingsar assumed the status of state ritual. Celebrated to secure abundant rainfall and fertility, the festival constituted, to quote Harnish, "a political demonstration of spiritually concentrated power, water and fertility, and the rulers became associated with prosperity" (Harnish 2006: 53). Today, the Lingsar temple festival remains a large-scale event in Lombok, drawing as many as 20,000 Balinese and Sasak participants, including some Sasak Muslims, who perform rituals in a separate section of the temple.

Set within a cosmology of divine kingship, the historical narratives in which the spirit army figure centrally serve to legitimize the founding of a new political order. The importance of spiritual assistance is a major theme in the corpus of narratives chronicling how a branch of the rising Karangasem dynasty established itself on the island of Lombok.[12] What follows is a truncated narrative told in 2005 by one consultant who preferred to remain anonymous:

> There was a kingdom ruled by three siblings in Karangasem who lived in Puri Kelodan [the south palace]. Sometime earlier, their sister had born a child who was fathered by Batara Gunung Agung, the powerful deity of Mount Agung [in east Bali]. When the child, named Batara Alit Sakti, was about six months old, he asked his family to carry him towards the mountain where he vanished (*moksha*) and crossed into the "invisible" realm. The family built a temple, Pura Bukit, in his honour. Later, a messenger arrived with a letter from the king of the Pejanggik kingdom in Lombok, requesting help to defeat a rival kingdom. Before leaving for Lombok, the prince, I Gusti Ketut Karangasem paid a visit to the Bukit temple and asked Batara Alit Sakti for blessings. As the boats of the expedition left the shores of Bali, they were accompanied by leaves from the *kepel* trees around Pura Bukit which turned into yellow butterflies. Having safely guided the boats to the shore of Padang Rea, in west Lombok, the butterflies disappeared but later assumed the shape of warriors, a regiment of about 200 men.

The narrative goes on to tell how the prince, who led the first Lombok expedition, climbed to the top of the small mountain, Mount Pengsong, to meditate and seek inspiration. The voice of the mountain deity, Batara Gunung Pengsong, tells him to head northeast and to rest when the men become tired. Moving through the thick forest, the men eat and rest in an area called Punikan, where they suddenly hear the sound of running water, and come upon a spring, later named Lingsar, or "spouting water," which later becomes the site of a major public temple. When the prince prays to Batara Alit Sakti and to the deity of the spring, Batara Gedé Lingsar, there appears a regiment of spirits dressed in yellow sarongs and headpieces. Together the two armies defeat several smaller Sasak kingdoms before striking a deal with the Selaparang kingdom to rule different parts of Lombok. Owing to the prince's intimacy with "invisible" forces and powerful deities dwelling on mountain tops, the expedition becomes more of a divinely blessed mission than an ambitious conquest.[13]

To solely dwell on the legitimizing function of these historical narratives would be to miss the current salience of these spirits, which by no means are locked away in a distant past. As the following narrative—told by Ketut Sudiartha, a retired headmaster, in 2006—demonstrates, these spirits constitute a living presence and turn up in surprising settings:

> Shortly after the riot, Dharma Wisesa members were ordered to attend a flag ceremony and marching exercise (*apel*) at the provincial police headquarters (Kapolda) in Ampenan. At first we felt confused and nervous. We didn't quite understand why we should participate. You see, this order came before our security group had been properly established with different sections and so on. Our men were just regular folks, civil servants and teachers like myself. But we formed a "special unit" called Bayu Mandala. I also took part that day [he starts to grin]. There was just a few of us, no more than forty men or thereabouts. But the word that spread after the ceremony was that the large field in front of the police command was packed with people. What people said, including journalists, was that almost one thousand people were present. Strange, heh! Why was our number so grossly exaggerated? We are simply forced to acknowledge that the *bale samar* took part in the *apel* ceremony. Their form was exactly like that of ordinary people. During the ceremony, we wore the Dharma Wisesa uniform. They were dressed exactly like us. It was just as if humans had been present.

Told with a sense of amazement, this account underscores how spiritual forces blend perfectly into the militarized setting of a flag-raising ceremony (*apel*) in post-New Order Lombok. From the perspective of state agents, the public saluting of the flag and the marching exercise was intended to discipline the new civilian security force and make it answerable to the state. But in Ketut Sudiartha's rendition, this state ritual became an occasion for asserting the power of Balinese mobilization. Having supernatural "backing," the tiny Dharma Wisesa regiment appears as a formidable force of close to one thousand spirited warriors. As men and spirits stand shoulder to shoulder, "everyone"—not least journalists—is said to have been impressed by the turnout. Having privileged access to the mass media, journalists might have transformed the relatively inconsequential talk about the turnout into the authoritative language of print. Though it is doubtful that this talk ever made it into the mass media, this account speaks to pressing concerns about power and representation. There is a defiant tone in this narrative where the Balinese come off as a formidable force despite their numerical weakness.

By the time this flag-raising ceremony took place, the Islamic crime-fighting group Amphibi boasted of having more than 200,000 members who were busy putting up security posts across the island. Under these circumstances, it was clearly in the interest of a fledgling Balinese counter-movement to be seen as endowed with supernatural powers. This desire to come off as powerful also operates in different registers. What can only be described as a deliberate inflation of Dharma Wisesa's organizational and numerical strength is apparent in the documents produced around this time. For instance, one official booklet puts the number of elite "core forces" (*pecalang inti*) at 10,000 men. The total number of members is estimated at 60,000, more than half the entire Balinese population on Lombok.

This narrative also tells us something about the transformative capabilities of spirits, and how Lombok Balinese spirit beliefs become relevant in contemporary circumstances. Dressed in gleaming black Dharma Wisesa uniforms, the spirit army becomes virtually indistinguishable from ordinary men. The presence of these forces imbues the Dharma Wisesa guards with a sense of enhanced agency, exactly what was needed at this moment. One might say that the "real" strength of these imagined forces lies in their ability to take shape of the situation and problematics that they address (Kapferer 2003: 105–7). It almost goes without saying that they would appear differently under other circumstances. In my view, the fluid and ambiguous qualities attributed to spiritual agents contributes to the resilience of Lombok Balinese spirit traditions. This fluidity also allows spirit beliefs to be easily grafted onto and made relevant in new social circumstances. By bringing the mysterious *bale samar* that aided the precolonial Balinese kings to establish sovereign power over Lombok to bear on an uncertain postcolonial present, Ketut Sudiartha's narrative is an example of how contemporary myth-making elaborates on longstanding oral traditions. As long as such narratives and reports of spontaneous sightings continue to be the stuff of everyday talk and historical consciousness, these occult forces are likely to remain a living presence. But perhaps we should not be surprised if they eventually begin to roam about on their own, cut loose from the grip of royal heirs.

The fact that spirits have assumed a more influential role in public life and politics after the fall of the Suharto regime is part of a broader revival-of-tradition trend in Indonesia. Local elites who claim some hereditary title have been active proponents of this neo-traditionalism (Davidson and Henley 2007). When the Balinese minority on Lombok began experimenting with new forms of security, they looked to neighboring Bali. In 2001, the Balinese provincial government passed a new law that greatly increased the power of the village council and authorized the village to run more aspects of its internal affairs. This legislation recognized *pecalang* as a traditional security force (*satgas keamanan tradisional*), especially with regard to custom and religion.[14] They were supposed to represent "traditional authority, in contrast to the corrupt practices of an external and often absent police force" (Schulte Nordholt 2007: 31). Santikarma (2003) offers a critique of this development and the "strong Bali" (*ajek Bali*) discourse. Under the New Order, he argues, Balinese culture was increasingly conceived in material terms, as a commodity that could be bought, sold, or even lost. *Pecalang* groups emerged to safeguard this precious possession, and are likely to breed violence and xenophobic exclusion of non-Balinese "outsiders" and migrants. While these concerns are clearly legitimate, I am not convinced that "tradition" is used in purely instrumental ways or simply serves as a foil for other interests as Santikarma suggests.

There is no denying that elements of Lombok Balinese "tradition" have also been objectified and mobilized for particular, partially politically-motivated, ends. Like their counterparts on Bali, the men who joined Dharma Wisesa call themselves *pecalang*, a term they say means "traditional Balinese police" or "palace guards." This terminology reflects the new value "tradition" and the idea of the "local" have assumed in the post-Suharto period. But we should not forget that the penchant for borrowing authority from older state formations is an integral element of modern Indonesian political culture. As Tsing (1993) and Pemberton (1994) have shown, the high-modernist New Order regime, through a combination of political rhetoric and state rituals, played up its alleged connections with ancient Javanese empires. Moves to legitimate a regime or group's position by drawing on the past are hardly innocent. A significant portion of Dharma Wisesa's income is collected from Sino-Indonesian businesses in Cakranegara, a practice that many local Balinese residents find problematic. Others see no problem with this, claiming that it is a voluntary donation as the Balinese protected this vulnerable group during the rioting in January 2000. Yet others insist that this informal taxation is justified because the city used to be a center of the Balinese state.

Conclusion

Religious ideas and idioms returned with a vengeance in public life and politics in Indonesia following the fall of the New Order regime in 1998. But it is not only organized religions that are thriving in the new political landscape of democratic reform and decentralization. Indonesia's monumental political transformation also appears to have given fresh impetus to conspiratorial thinking, sorcery concerns, and renewed interest in supernatural protection (Bubandt 2006; Siegel 2006; MacDougall 2008). Here I have examined how the conspiratorial sensibility that gripped members of the Lombok Balinese community around the turn of the millennium provided the grounds for a return of spirits to the realm of contemporary politics. Formed in response to an acute sense of insecurity, the establishment of Dharma Wisesa was also enabled by calls for greater civilian involvement in policing and security in the new era of democracy. Fusing spirit beliefs with modern discourses of security, Dharma Wisesa illustrates that Lombok Balinese "alternative modernity" (Taylor 1999) remains enchanted.

Lombok Balinese historical consciousness, I have argued, entails an ongoing creative process of "imagining continuity" (Lambek 2002) which renders aspects of the past available in the present. Central to this historical consciousness is the sense that figures of the past occasionally irrupt in and confront the present, as when a woman is possessed by the ancestors during a temple festival, or a young man tells me how spirit forces descend from a mountain to protect a Hindu temple from an angry mob. When the guards staffing the headquarters of a Balinese security group consult spirits forces who aided their forebears to settle on Lombok, this is because ancestral idioms of power remain deeply meaningful, offering ways to deal with a challenging present. In this and numerous other ways, they draw on the past to endow their routine acts with dignity and power.

This attitude does not, I should stress, imply conservatism or blind acceptance of authority figures who claim special closeness with past rulers and their entourage of spirits. Indeed, when Anak Agung Gedé Biarsah made efforts to consolidate control by appointing his eldest son as Dharma Wisesa's commander-in-chief in 2004, this prompted harsh criticism that this authoritarian streak was appropriate for a ruler in the time of Hindu Balinese dynasties but wholly inappropriate in a modern democracy. Heated discussions about the role of the past in the post-authoritarian present also flared up when the leader announced his intent to change Dharma Wisesa from a *pamswakarsa*, an Indonesian term designating a voluntary civilian defence force, into a Balinese *pecalang* group. For those who preferred the original name, which they associate with a cosmopolitan civic nationalism, the renaming signalled an inward-looking nostalgic return to a time of aristocratic privilege. Rejecting what they took to be an attempt to symbolically reclaim the authority of the former king, a number of high-ranking and commoner men withdrew, going on to form new security groups.

Central to the day-to-day operation of these civilian security groups is the sense that personal as well as collective well-being requires efforts to bring the power of the past to bear on the present. When spirit forces like the *bale samar* burst into the visible world, their presence lingers for a long time. However brief, such glimpses generate ontological certainty and the assurance of spiritual backing brings a sense of enhanced agency. Although such sightings give reassurance that spiritual protection is forthcoming, the fact that these spirits manifest in moments of insecurity is significant. The ambivalence surrounding the sightings of these spirit warriors probably stems from the fact that they are a potent reminder that Balinese inhabit a dynamic world comprised of a multitude of beings in endless completion for control of one another.

Notes

1. Anyone familiar with Balinese religious aesthetics will associate these colours with the gods who make up the Hindu Trinity: red is the colour of the creator Brahma, black is associated with Wisnu, the preserver of life, and white is associated with Siwa, the destroyer of life. While Siwa is known as the destroyer, this is the deity from which everything emanates.
2. This chapter is based on eight months of fieldwork carried out between 2001 and 2010 in Cakranegara. I have previously conducted thirteen months of fieldwork in Sasak villages in Jonggat, Central Lombok.
3. This formulation is inspired by Bubandt's discussion of ontological uncertainty, which refers to "the socially constructed anxiety that shapes pertinent kinds of dangers, fears and concerns for a particular community at a particular time" (Bubandt 2005: 277).
4. For an intriguing analysis of different phases of religious violence in Indonesia, see Sidel (2006).
5. Official records report seven deaths and fifty-four severely injured, but the actual number of casualties is probably higher. Several deaths were caused by Indonesian security forces, who followed instructions to "shoot-on-sight" issued after three days of rioting.
6. During the 1999 Christmas celebrations, bombs went off in two churches in Mataram, one of ten cities targeted in coordinated attacks. Jemaah Islamiyah, the radical Islamist group responsible for the 2002 Bali bombings, claimed responsibility for these acts. On this group, see Sidel (2006).
7. I use real names for people who hold leadership positions in Dharma Wisesa. Other names are pseudonyms.
8. Parts of this section are taken from Telle (2010a).
9. The assault occurred on 18 December 1999 when members of the Amphibi crime-fighting force entered Desa Sengkongo looking for "criminals." My sources, including the two men who reported the incident to the police, claimed that the case was not properly investigated.
10. The day known as Tumpek Landep is sacred to metal objects and weapons. On that day, keris and other weapons are cleaned, rubbed with oil, purified, and provided with offerings to recharge their sharpness and potency.
11. A sense of having endured a long history of domination by "outsiders" has become central to Sasak collective self identity; see Telle (2007: 123–26).
12. Several versions of these narratives are discussed in Harnish's rich ethnographic study of the Lingsar temple festival (Harnish 2006).
13. Important Hindu Balinese deities dwell on mountain tops. When the Balinese established themselves on Lombok, Gunung Rinjani—considered as the "sibling" of Gunung Agung in east Bali—became the focal center of their ritual practice. On mountains and spiritual landscapes in Southeast Asia, see Allerton (2009).
14. For a more detailed discussion of this law (Perda no. 3/2001), see Schulte Nordholt (2007).

References

Allerton, Catherine. 2009. "Introduction: Spiritual Landscapes of Southeast Asia," *Anthropological Forum* 19(3): 235–51.

Avonius, Leena. 2004. "Reforming Wetu Telu: Islam, Adat and the Promises of Regionalism in Post-New Order Lombok," Ph.D. dissertation. Leiden: University of Leiden.

Bubandt, Nils. 2001. "Malukan Apocalypse: Themes in the Dynamics of Violence in Indonesia," in *Violence in Indonesia*, eds I. Wesssel and G. Wimhofer. Hamburg: Abera, pp.228–53.

———. 2005. "Vernacular Security: The Politics of Feeling Safe in Global, National and Local Worlds," *Security Dialogue* 36(3): 275–96.

———. 2006. "Sorcery, Corruption, and the Dangers of Democracy in Indonesia," *Journal of the Royal Anthropological Institute* 12(2): 413–31.

———. 2008. "Rumours, Pamphlets, and the Politics of Paranoia in Indonesia," *Journal of Asian Studies* 67(3): 789–817.

Cederroth, Sven. 1977. "Religiösa Reform rörelser på Lombok [Religious reform movements on Lombok]," *Historisk Tidsskrift* 4: 350–73.

Davidson, Jamie, and David Henley, eds. 2007. *The Revival of Tradition in Indonesian Politics: The Deployment of Adat from Colonialism to Indigenism.* London: Routledge.

Day, Tony. 2002. *Fluid Iron: State Formation in Southeast Asia.* Honolulu: University of Hawaii Press.

Geertz, Hildred. 1994. *Images of Power: Balinese Paintings Made for Gregory Bateson and Margaret Mead.* Honolulu: University of Hawaii Press.

Harnish, David D. 2006. *Bridges to the Ancestors: Music, Myth, and Cultural Politics at an Indonesian Festival.* Honolulu: University of Hawaii Press.

Hefner, Robert W. 1997. "Islamization and Democratization in Indonesia," in *Islam in an Era of Nation-States*, eds R.W. Hefner and P. Horvatich. Honolulu: University of Hawaii Press, pp.75–128.

Hobart, Mark. 2000. "The End of the World News: Television and a Problem of Articulation in Bali," *International Journal of Cultural Studies* 3(1): 79–102.

Hobsbawm, Eric, and Terence Ranger, eds. 1983. *The Invention of Tradition.* Cambridge: Cambridge University Press.

ICG. 2003. "The Perils of Private Security in Indonesia: Guards and Militias on Bali and Lombok," International Crisis Group Asia Country Report, No. 67.

Kapferer, Bruce. 2003. "Sorcery, Modernity and the Constitutive Imaginary: Hybridising Continuities," in *Beyond Rationalism: Rethinking Magic, Witchcraft and Sorcery*, ed. B. Kapferer. Oxford: Berghahn Books, pp.105–28.

Keeler, Ward. 1987. *Javanese Shadow Plays, Javanese Selves.* Princeton, NJ: Princeton University Press.

Kraan, Alfons van der. 1980. *Lombok: Conquest, Colonization and Underdevelopment, 1870–1940.* Singapore: Heinemann Educational Books.

Lambek, Michael. 2002. *The Weight of the Past: Living with History in Mahajanga, Madagascar.* New York: Palgrave Macmillan.

MacDougall, John M. 2005. "Buddhist or Buda Buddhists? Conversion, Religious Modernism and Conflict in the Minority Buda Sasak Communities of New Order and Post-Suharto Lombok," Ph.D. dissertation. Princeton, NJ: Princeton University.

———. 2007. "Criminality and the Political Economy of Security in Lombok," in *Renegotiating Boundaries: Local Politics in Post-Suharto Indonesia*, eds. H. Schulte Nordholt and G. van Klinken. Leiden: KITLV, pp.281–303.

———. 2008. "The Political Dimension of Emasculation: Fantasy, Conspiracy, and Estrangement among Populist Leaders in Post-New Order Lombok, Indonesia," in *Postcolonial Disorders*, eds M. Del Vecchio Good, S.T. Hyde, S. Pinto and B.J. Good. Berkeley: University of California Press, pp.109–31.

Pedersen, Lene. 2006. *Ritual and World Change in a Balinese Princedom.* Durham, NC: Carolina Academic Press.

Pemberton, John. 1994. *On the Subject of "Java."* Ithaca, NY: Cornell University Press.

Reuter, Thomas A. 2003. "Introduction," in *Inequality, Crisis and Social Change in Indonesia: The Muted Worlds of Bali*, ed. T.A. Reuter. London: Routledge Curzon, pp.1–16.

Santikarma, Degung. 2003. "The Model Militia: A New Security Force in Bali is Cloaked in Tradition," *Inside Indonesia*, January–March, p.73.

Schrauwers, Albert. 2003. "Through a Glass Darkly: Charity, Conspiracy, and Power in New Order Indonesia," in *Transparency and Conspiracy: Ethnographies of Suspicion in the New World Order*, eds H. West and T. Sanders. Durham, NC: Duke University Press, pp.125–47.

Schulte Nordholt, Henk. 1996. *The Spell of Power: A History of Balinese Politics, 1650–1940*. Leiden: Leiden University Press.

———. 2007. *Bali: An Open Fortress, 1995–2005. Regional Autonomy, Electoral Democracy and Entrenched Identities*. Singapore: National University of Singapore Press.

Sidel, John. 2006. *Riots, Pogroms, Jihad: Religious Violence in Indonesia*. Ithaca, NY: Cornell University Press.

Siegel, James T. 2006. *Naming the Witch*. Stanford, CA: Stanford University Press.

Spyer, Patricia. 2006. "Some Notes on Disorder in the Indonesian Postcolony," in *Law and Disorder in the Postcolony*, eds J. Comaroff and J.L. Comaroff. Chicago: University of Chicago Press, pp.188–218.

Taylor, Christopher. 1999. "Two Theories of Modernity," *Public Culture* 1(1): 153–74.

Telle, Kari. 2007. "Nurturance and the Spectre of Neglect: Sasak Ways of Dealing with the Dead," in *Kinship and Food in Southeast Asia*, eds M. Janowski and F. Kerlogue. Copenhagen: Nordic Institute of Asian Studies Press, pp.121–48.

———. 2009. "Swearing Innocence: Performing Justice and 'Reconciliation' in Post-New Order Lombok," in *Reconciling Indonesia: Grassroots Agency for Peace*, ed. B. Bräuchler. London: Routledge, pp.57–76.

———. 2010a. "Dharma Power: Searching for Security in Post-New Order Indonesia," in *Contemporary Religiosities: Emergent Socialities and the Post-Nation State*, eds B. Kapferer, K. Telle, and A. Eriksen. Oxford: Berghahn Books, pp.141–56.

———. 2010b. "Seduced by Security: The Politics of (In)Security on Lombok, Indonesia," in *Security and Development*, eds J.A. McNeish and J.H. Sande-Lie. Oxford: Berghahn Books, pp.130–42.

Tsing, Anna. 1993. *In the Realm of the Diamond Queen*. Princeton, NJ: Princeton University Press.

Vanvugt, Ewald. 1995. *De Schatten van Lombok: Honderd jaar Nederlandse oorlogsbuit uit Indonesie*. Amsterdam: Mets.

Wæver, Ole. 1995. "Securitzation and Desecuritization," in *On Security*, ed. R. Lipschutz. New York: Columbia University Press, pp.46–86.

West, Harry, and Todd Sanders. 2003. "Power Revealed and Concealed in the New World Order," in *Transparency and Conspiracy: Ethnographies of Suspicion in the New World Order*, eds H. West and T. Sanders. Durham, NC: Duke University Press, pp.1–37.

Wiener, Margaret J. 1995. *Visible and Invisible Realms: Power, Magic, and Colonial Conquest in Bali*. Chicago: University of Chicago Press.

———. 1999. "Making Local History in New Order Bali: Public Culture and the Politics of the Past," in *Staying Local in the Global Village: Bali in the Twentieth Century*, eds R. Rubinstein and L.H. Connor. Honolulu: University of Hawaii Press, pp.51–90.

Zurbuchen, Mary S., ed. 2005. *Beginning to Remember: The Past in the Indonesian Present*. Singapore: Singapore University Press.

3

FROM THE MYSTICAL TO THE MOLECULAR: MODERNITY, MARTIAL ARTS, AND AGENCY IN JAVA

Lee Wilson

Introduction

Perhaps the only thing that is constant about the notion of modernity is the disagreement and debate prompted by attempts to define the term in social analysis. For some, modernity is a clearly locatable moment in human history, an epochal transformation marked by faith in the ability to bring nature to heal, industrialization, capitalist development, and the dominance of the institutions of the nation-state (e.g., Giddens and Pierson 1998: 94). Others, arguing for the consideration of "multiple modernities," have voiced concerns over engagement with the "cultural programme of modernity," the implicit bias shown in how this has transpired in the "West," and the imposition of a narrative of a modern age wracked by rationalization, reason, and spiritual disenchantment upon the world more generally (e.g., Eisenstadt 2000: 24). Others still have argued that accounts of multiple modernities are similarly biased towards "meta-narratives" of modernity that naturalize a shift in analytical scale. That the contextualization of the particular experience of modernity effects closure and runs the risk of subverting reflexive engagement in ethnographic enquiry (Englund and Leach 2000: 236). While such criticisms themselves run the risk of reifying the notion of modernity (in part a logical necessity of formulating an argument against such a "meta-narrative"), the point is well made. While it is undeniable that "certain forms of modern action" have "achieved tremendous historical modifications of human behavior" (Pels 2003: 30), to assume the constituent elements of an abstract notion of modernity,

---

Endnotes for this chapter begin on page 79

plural or otherwise, or indeed the ways that these elements might bear upon the forms that social relations take, begs the question. Rather, modernity is better thought of as a relational term (Jonsson 2004: 674), and in this respect it is possible to recover some comparative ground for the analysis of the particularities of forms of sociality in a modern age, and to engage critically with conceptions of "modernity" and "tradition" in diverse cultural and political contexts. Such is my aim in this chapter in which I examine transformations in knowledge practices associated with Sundanese and Javanese martial arts in Indonesia.

Associated with the practice of the martial art of pencak silat in Indonesia is the acquisition of "inner knowledge." Such knowledge may facilitate the mediation of relations with the ancestors and denizens of the unseen world, the *alam ghaib*, to afford protection to self and others through the manifestation of supernatural abilities such as invulnerability. Recently, these knowledge practices have been transformed in modern, nationalist martial-art schools. Conceptions of citizenship and fealty to the state are actively promoted in these more modern schools. Unlike the supernatural abilities that are a consequence of the possession of inner knowledge, exponents of modernist pencak silat schools work to cultivate their "inner power" through physically cultivating the self. Bounded conceptions of personhood prevail in these groups, and the development of inner power is explained via recourse to modern, scientific paradigms. I argue that framing these transformations as local appropriations of global discourses of modernity, or as characteristic of instrumental rationality in a modern age, can potentially obscure political modalities not so easily shoehorned into secularist paradigms of sociological explanation.

I develop this argument through a brief consideration of Michel Foucault's account of shifts in the ways in which power relations are constituted through disciplinary practices in modernity. I argue that the utility value of ascetic practices is neglected in favor of a more repressive account of the institutionalization of bodily practices and the rise of regimes of surveillance. To see transformations in the relationship of the body to power only as the reconfiguration of sovereign authority by more recent modes of regimented and secularized power elides cultural dynamics that have important implications for understanding forms of political process and the articulation of modes of governance in Indonesia under the New Order and since (cf. Steinmetz 1999: 23). Relationships engendered with powerful non-physical social entities are commonplace throughout Indonesia (Chambert-Loir and Reid 2002), and are a means through which political authority might be mediated and contested (see Bubandt 2009). Continuities in the ways in which inner knowledge and inner power are embodied and enacted, particularly in the indexical relationship of the body to power, are typical of the ways in which connections to potential sources of authority such as the ancestors might be rendered visible. My aim in this chapter is then to attempt to bracket out the secularism implicit in much social scientific theorizing of modernity in order to elicit presuppositions in models of power that circulate in Indonesia, models that are sensitive to the role that violence plays as both a coercive and compelling force, and which accurately reflect the intrinsic instability of political authority consolidated through personal relations.

The Power of Narrative

In west Java, training in pencak silat usually involves apprenticeship to a *guru*, and incorporates a corpus of ascetic techniques that are a means of tempering the *batin*, the inner self. An oft-cited aphorism, *ngolah rasa, raga dan jiwa*, refers to the development of "feeling, body, and soul" in training. Through practice in pencak silat, exponents are said to simultaneously cultivate both the *lahir*, the physical or manifest aspects of our bodies, and *batin*, the inner or more refined, spiritual aspects of being (cf. Mulder 1998: 81). It is through the practice of *ilmu batin* and temperance of the body that one might become *sakti*, and that the possibility of supernatural abilities, or *kesaktian*, be realized.[1] Indeed, tales of the fantastic abilities possessed by legendary pencak silat players are the common currency of the myths, folklore, and oral histories that surround the art. Si Pitung, the folk hero of Jakarta and a scourge of the Dutch colonial oppressors, was able to thwart his enemies and evade capture with the aid of magical abilities (van Till 1996). Mas Djakaria, a champion of some renown in Banten in the nineteenth century, was widely held to be invulnerable (Kartodirdjo 1984: 4–5). More recently, popular accounts of pencak silat champions and the incredible feats attributed to them are recounted in the literary genre of "silat stories." The heroes of these novels, characters of great martial prowess, make use of their supernatural abilities as they engage each other in combat (Gartenberg 2000). Yet when explaining *kesaktian*, pencak silat exponents rarely claim to be in control of such abilities. Rather, agency is deferred or attributed to a higher, spiritual authority.

Accounts of the manifestation of *kesaktian*, usually autobiographical, are remarkably consistent in the telling. Typical of these narratives, spoken to a room full of attentive students, was that told by Bapak Rifai'i one evening after training at his home in south Jakarta. As was often the case after training sessions with Bapak Rifai'i, a teacher of the Sundanese style of *cimande*, conversation late in the evening had strayed towards consideration of *ilmu batin* and the attributes it might engender. Bapak Rifai'i recalled that upon returning home one day he had witnessed three men beating another unconscious in a small compound ringed by a high chain-link fence. In his account, he remembered crying out to the man's assailants to stop. He was not conscious of actions or the events that followed, knowing only that a few moments later he stood outside the enclosure, the victim's prostrate form cradled in his arms. He explained that he was only aware of what had happened from the accounts of witnesses who later told him what had occurred. After his calls to cease the assault on the man had gone unheeded, onlookers told him of the incredible jump he had made to clear the fence in a single bound, brushing aside the man's attackers, picking up their hapless victim from where he had fallen and carrying him to safety. On leaving the compound he had once more become conscious of his surroundings. Looking down he became aware of the man that he bore in his arms. As he explained to us, all those that had witnessed the event were in agreement that something extraordinary had occurred, but he himself was at a loss to explain what had transpired.

On another occasion in Bandung, west Java, Bapak Harun, a well respected teacher, similarly regaled a group of fellow pencak silat practitioners of similar experience and status with tales of the extraordinary. Whilst walking in the street a man brandishing a rock had rushed at him, threatening to brain him. Bapak Harun had let out a loud shout that, he insisted, was not of his volition. Rather, an involuntary cry had sprung from his lips and stopped the assailant dead in his tracks. Thus disabled with a single shout, Bapak Harun had then made the slightest gesture towards the man with his fingers, which had resulted in the man instantly dropping the stone. How this had happened he did not know, he had not been conscious (*sadar*) of events as they transpired. Yet the manifestation of *kesaktian* beyond his conscious control had enabled him to overcome the attacker.

Common to both these narratives is an emphasis placed on the lack of understanding of how or why the protagonists were able to perform these amazing feats. They went to some lengths to avoid any direct claims to be responsible for what had transpired. In Rifai'i's account he had learnt of what had taken place after the fact from the accounts of onlookers. This deferral of agency is a common motif in these stories. What transpired is attributed to training in pencak silat; there is never any attempt made at explaining how *kesaktian* might manifest. Importantly, the manifestation of *kesaktian* was not in any way volitional. Bapak Rifai'i had not sought to develop such abilities. The events that transpired in Bapak Harun's account were as much a surprise to him as they were to his would be assailant. Thus the narrators of these accounts, through studiously avoiding any direct claims to agency, make an indirect claim to their level of spiritual development, and their possession of supernatural abilities.

Of the many times that I listened to the telling of these tales in a variety of settings with a number of different teachers, I never once heard these narratives called into question. Veracity, it seemed, was not at issue. Yet these narratives of the manifestation of *kesaktian* are not the only way in which one may lay claim to being efficacious. Discourse has its limits, and the undisputed acceptance of the existence of these abilities is due to the very practical ways in which the possession of *ilmu batin* might be demonstrated.

The Practice of Invulnerability

There are many kinds of *ilmu* practices, but perhaps not surprisingly, a form of *ilmu* commonly associated with pencak silat is knowledge of invulnerability, or *ilmu kebal*. Historically, invulnerability practices are commonplace throughout

Southeast Asia.[2] The public performance of invulnerability in west Java has an analogue in the practice of *dabus* in the Sufi order Qadiriyyah. Founded by Shaikh Abdul Qadir Jilani in the twelfth century in present day Iraq, in Indonesia the order developed mainly in Java (Lombard 1996), and *ilmu* Abdul Qadir Jilani was taught in both Banten and Cirebon from at least the seventeenth century (van Bruinessen 1995: 209). In the performance of *dabus*, participants hammer sharp spikes into one another's bodies, climb ladders of blades affixed to poles, or dance energetically on piles of broken glass, all seemingly without any apparent injury to the performer (Vredenbregt 1973: 316; cf. Winstedt 1938: 191). *Dabus* is both a demonstration of the faith of the performer in God, and of the omnipotence and beneficence of God in protecting them from coming to harm. Whilst many pencak silat teachers in west Java differentiate between the practice of *dabus* and *ilmu kebal*, the higher levels of learning in pencak silat are predominantly associated with the order Qadiriyyah, and demonstrations of imperviousness to injury are standard practice amongst many pencak silat groups.

In Jakarta, Bapak Achmad Bunawar, head of the school Tiga Berantai, is typical of many of the teachers found in the teeming sprawl of the capital city. Well respected as a pencak silat *guru*, he teaches a small and relatively informal group training in pencak silat styles common to Jakarta. I had visited Bapak Achmad one afternoon to learn more of the silat particular to the city. He had spent some time demonstrating the intricacies of the particular styles of silat that he practiced with his students, a group of young men in late adolescence. After the training session had finished we sat talking about the art, how he had come to practice it, and his role as a teacher. There was, Bapak Achmad stated with quiet intent, far more to the practice of pencak silat than the physical aspects of the art. After pausing for a moment, he summoned three of his students, asking them to sit in front of him. He prayed briefly for a moment, asking Allah to protect the young men, then proceeded to break a small glass on the table next to him. Picking up three pieces of the shattered vessel, he handed one to each of his students. They held the glass before them, and on Bapak Achmad's instruction, popped the pieces of glass into their mouths and began to chew. Each of them followed their teacher's commands without hesitation, crunching upon the shards. After a minute or so, Bapak Achmad ordered them to rinse their mouths with water, and to spit out the glass. He was quite clear in his instructions, forbidding them to swallow.[3] In answer to my questions about the demonstration, Bapak Achmad explained to me that it was God's strength (*kekuatan*) that had protected his students from harm during the demonstration. Furthermore, the exercise was a testament to the students' faith in the strength of God, and a test of their trust in and devotion (*bakti*) to him as their teacher or *guru*. In training in pencak silat one should follow the instructions of one's *guru* regardless of how potentially injurious the consequences of compliance might seem to be, and his teacher had similarly tested him on a number of occasions.

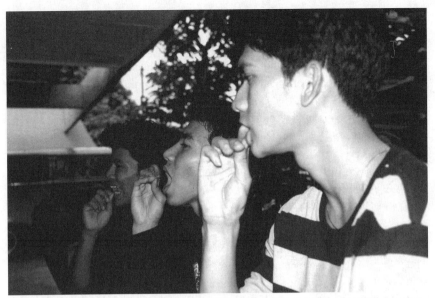

Figure 3.1: Demonstration of glass chewing in Jakarta by Bapak Achmad's students. Photograph by Lee Wilson, 2003.

Bapak Achmad made no claim to understand how protection from injury was afforded his students. It was, he told me, by the will of God (*keinginan Tuhan*) that they came to no harm. The knowledge that he used to safeguard them was part of the training in pencak silat. There is much in this world that we cannot see, and knowledge of the invisible world (*alam ghaib*) might be utilized in this way. Through submission to the will of their *guru*, the students demonstrated their absolute obedience to him and faith in his ability to afford them protection. That they came to no harm was attributable to the *ilmu* that enabled him to act in an intercessory capacity on their behalf as both instrument/agent of God in this world. His students considered him to be spiritually potent or efficacious, able to act in the world in a way that others were not. Their demonstration of invulnerability was therefore far more than an affirmation of individual prowess; it was a means through which the spiritual potency of Bapak Achmad, in his capacity as *guru* and protector, signified itself, and in this respect he was considered to be efficacious, or *sakti*, by his students.

Some years ago in a seminal essay on forms of power in Java, Benedict Anderson argued for a conception of *sakti* as a form of spiritual or cosmic energy (Anderson 1972) that might be concentrated in a person or place. Contrary to European conceptions of power as an abstract aspect of relationships, Anderson posited that power in Java is held to be concrete, finite, and embodied. Individuals held to be "potent" thus become the center of political authority, which is held to be a manifestation of their potency (Keeler 1987: 39). While Anderson himself later took issue with his theory (Anderson 1990), the uncritical use of his model has resulted in the common occlusion in academic accounts of the relational aspects of concepts of power in circulation in Indonesia, and indeed in Southeast Asia.[4] Hildred Geertz, writing on Bali but relevant here, argues that *sakti* is used in reference to an attribute, "not a force or measurable energy"; it is not just "potency in an abstract or physical sense, but rather a competence in a personalistic sense" (Geertz 1995: 10). Conceptualizing *sakti* as substantive energy or an impersonal force elides the interpersonal aspects of transactions between social agents that are *sakti*. Such relations are personable relations between efficacious beings, both visible and non-visible (Geertz 1995: 10; 2004: 43; see also Winzeler 1983: 438; Needham 1976; cf. Keesing 1984). The importance of the maintenance of interpersonal relations is especially clear in the spiritual hierarchy of the style of pencak silat known as *cimande*.

Personhood and Place in *Cimande*

The village of Cimande sits in the highlands to the south of Jakarta, on the outskirts of the town of Bogor. It is the birthplace of the style of pencak silat that takes its name from the area. Of the many different schools and styles of pencak silat in Indonesia, *cimande* is perhaps the most well known of all, and elements of the styles are found in the repertoires of systems and schools of pencak silat throughout the island of Java and beyond. The village of Cimande, with a population of around five thousand people, is divided into three "hamlets" or *kampung*. The original settlement was the *kampung* Tari Kolot, and it is here that previous generations of practitioners of *cimande* are laid to rest. Etymological speculation is a popular pastime in Indonesia, and among the several accounts of the origins of the name Tari Kolot in circulation is the claim that the settlement was originally called Tarekat Kokolot, the spiritual path or way of the elders. Indeed, it was often stressed to me by teachers of *cimande* that I knew and trained under that while ostensibly a system of self-defense, of more importance are the teachings of the order Qadiriyyah , and the practice of *cimande* was in fact a means through which one might draw closer to God. Yet *cimande* is nonetheless a highly developed and practical combative system.

Those who come to Cimande in search of instruction in pencak silat, or *penca* as it is known in Sundanese, do so by apprenticing themselves to a teacher, usually one of the elders in the village. Arsan, a young man of sixteen from Badui, had lived in Cimande for five months. He was undergoing instruction in *penca cimande* at the behest of his father. Knowledge of the art is highly valued, and this was the reason his father had dispatched him to Tari Kolot to apprentice to a teacher. Dani, a young man from Banten just turned twenty, had been living in Cimande for two years, having been similarly ordered by his father to learn *penca*. His father's intention was that he would then teach the art in an Islamic boarding school (*pesantren*) run by a relative in Banten. In exchange for food, board and instruction in *penca*, Arsan, Dani, and others like them, would work in the day for their teacher as a servant or helper, or planting and harvesting rice, exchanging their labor for knowledge.[5] In the evening they would train in *penca*, sitting opposite one another exchanging blows in the series of choreographed exchanges that constitute the training repertoire in *penca cimande*, a process which both trains the body to move in accordance with the principles of the art and serves to harden players' limbs through a painful conditioning process as they repetitively clash arms with their training partners. After training is finished, medicinal oil (*balur penca*) is massaged into the bruises, haematomas, and contusions of the players. The oil is much sought after for its healing properties, and is manufactured by the elders (*sesupuh*) of Cimande during *mulud*, the auspicious month of the prophet's birthday. The ingredients of the oil are a closely kept secret, passed down through a select group of families from one generation to the next. The arms of adepts of *cimande* are thus conditioned to the degree that they become a formidable weapon, capable even of cracking an opponent's bones.

It is common consensus in Cimande that it is not the ingredients of the medicinal oil that are of primary importance in its manufacture. Rather, its healing properties are attributed to the blessings (*berkah*) and prayers said by the elders during the production process. It is by right of descent from the founder of the village, Embah Buyut, and the founder of pencak silat *cimande*, Embah Kahir, that the elders are capable of bestowing such blessings. The genealogical seniority of the elders is figured vertically through patrilineal descent from these two ancestors. The elders are considered to be intermediaries in the *wasila*, an unbroken chain of "spiritual mediation" (van Bruinessen 1994: 125, cf. Woodward 1985: 1010) that is detailed in the genealogy, the *silsilah*, which stretches from them, via the ancestors, to Sunan Gunung Jati, one of the nine apostles of Islam in Java, on to the prophet and hence to God.

Prior to the practice of *penca* in Cimande, the names of the ancestors are remembered in the *amalan tawasul* (*amalan* implies a charitable or good deed; *tawasul* refers to a means of approaching God via intermediaries). The genealogy is recited in the *amalan tawasul* before the beginning of the session in order to receive the blessings of the ancestors (Heryana 1995: 31–32). Knowledge of the *amalan tawasul* remains guarded and is passed down from *guru* to student. Those privy to its secrets are themselves part of this tradition, and it is the very act of its recitation that defines them as recipients of guarded knowledge and incorporates them into this lineage. The elders remain extremely reticent on the matter of the *silsilah*, a state of affairs that grants this information value as political currency. Since the *silsilah* is the source of the recognition of one's authority, why such information should not be openly shared is a hint as to the presuppositions that inform its recital. It is far more than an evocation of the expert knowledge of the enunciator. It is a communicative act, an affirmation of the personal relationship with the ancestors, the *karuhun*, prayer being made more efficient through their participation. Knowing the names of the ancestors is an important part of the "interpersonal technology" (Harrison 1998: 1) through which relations with the ancestors and denizens of the unseen world (*alam ghaib*) are mediated. Thus the limbs of *cimande* practitioners are forged into potent weapons through harsh conditioning and, importantly, the technical proficiency of the elders in their capacity as instruments of God in this world.

From the Mystical to the Molecular

The practice of *penca cimande* is a far cry from the modern sporting practice of pencak silat promoted by the Indonesian Pencak Silat Federation (IPSI). Under President Suharto's New Order, pencak silat was widely promoted as a means of cultivating the Unitarian values and ideals of the regime. Sponsored by leading members of the political and military elite, under the auspices of the IPSI, the art was aligned with nationalist imaginaries of a common cultural heritage and linear historical development (L. Wilson 2009). New Order ideology was firmly anchored in conceptions of Javanese culture, drawing on cosmological notions of divinely ordained kingship to frame the authoritarian leadership of Suharto (Barker 2008: 532). A commonly expressed ideal in the rhetoric employed by Suharto and other proponents of the state, informed by Javanese conceptions of personhood, was the necessity for the state to attend to both the external, physical (*lahir*) and inner, spiritual (*batin*) well-being of its citizenry. It was through the cultivation of the cultural inheritance of the nation that its spiritual needs might be addressed (Pemberton 1994: 154), a shared ancestry to be venerated and revered.[6] In his address at the opening of national headquarters of IPSI in Jakarta in 1997, President Suharto expressed his view that the cultural heritage (*warisan budaya*) of pencak silat, "laden with noble values, needs to be preserved as well as possible to become the pride of continuing generations of the nation," in order that it become "an active component in the development (*pembangunan*)[7] of nation (*bangsa*) and state (*negara*)" (IPSI n.d.: 14). Spiritual well-being is thus associated with the stability of a homogeneous antiquity, a common heritage that acts as a counterbalance to the materialism of the modern world. Through the practice of pencak silat as a means for the promotion and propagation of these ideals, continuity with a particular conception of the past is thus cultivated.

Within IPSI the practice of pencak silat is sub-divided into four aspects, mental/spiritual, self-defense (*bela diri*), sport (*olah raga*), and "artistic" (*kesenian*), each of which has its own administrative section within the organization. Through the ministrations of IPSI the art has come to be practiced throughout the archipelago and internationally, promoted as an aspect of Nusantara cultural heritage by the International Pencak Silat Federation (see PERSILAT 2000: 3).[8] Yet it is only within IPSI that the different facets of Pencak Silat are differentiated to this degree. Matters relating to the acquisition of *ilmu*, the use of modes of ascetic practice through which one may become *kebal* (invulnerable) are eschewed. While falling within the remit of the "mental/spiritual," the emphasis within IPSI has been on sporting competition, with which esoteric aspects of the art are held to be incommensurate. Loyalty to any agency other than the state is thus reoriented to suit an institutional agenda and the particular brand of spiritual hegemony articulated through the rhetoric of the New Order. Through the regulation of pencak silat, and of the cultivation of athletes in IPSI, the potentially transformative capacity of the pencak silat *guru* is incorporated in a "corporeal pedagogy" (Turner 2003: 106) informed by New Order meta-narratives of national unity, progress, and development. An organization that is favored by IPSI and that embodies these values is the pencak silat school Merpati Putih.

Founded by Saring Hadi Poernomo in Yogyakarta, central Java, in 1963, Merpati Putih claims to have over one hundred thousand members in seventy-six branches throughout Indonesia, with representation in the USA, Japan, and Holland. The organization has a formal constitution and governing board, and every three years stages a conference and general meeting for all branch members. The school traces its origin to a system of self-defense and spiritual development taught in the royal palace of Amangkurat II, the sultan of Mataram, in the seventeenth century, and the cultural heritage of Javanese mysticism and cosmology, or *kejawèn*. Practices such as *kanuragan*, ritual initiation, through which *aji*, supernatural powers invoked through the recital of mantra, are imparted to the initiate, are part of the cultural repertoire of *kejawèn*. Yet whilst rooted in *kejawèn*, the emphasis in Merpati Putih is upon modernization and serving national interests. The organization has striven to rid itself of the mysticism associated with these practices, attempting to validate them scientifically (de Grave 2001: 229). Members of the school wear a red and white uniform in imitation of the Indonesian flag, and even the five rows of stitching on the collar have significance, representing the five principles of *Pancasila*, the Indonesian state doctrine or national philosophy.[9] Exponents of the school are well known for their ability to develop inner power, or *tenaga dalam*. It was the spectacular demonstration of inner power that first attracted Bambang Rus Effendi, a former Chairman of the school, to training in Merpati Putih. He first witnessed the shattering of large blocks of ice by exponents of the art, a performance that led him to give up his practice in other martial arts and to begin to train in Merpati Putih. After training for some time in the art, he explained that he began to develop inner power to the extent that he could emulate the feats that had first impressed and attracted him to study Merpati Putih.

In a typical Merpati Putih training session the instructor leading the group opens the practice with an oath stating belief in one God, the students first pledging subservience (*mengabdi*) and devotion (*berbakti*) to the nation and the state of the Republic of Indonesia, and to be faithful and obedient to the school (see ibid.: 242). The instructor then leads the class through a series of dynamic breathing exercises. The focus of training is upon the cultivation of inner power, which is achieved through a series of coordinated breathing exercises performed in conjunction with specific bodily postures. Practitioners perform these exercises in unison, and claim that through their constant and disciplined practice inner power may be channeled to any part of their body. Exponents demonstrate their ability to manifest inner power through smashing stacks of iron pump handles or concrete blocks with their hands, feet and heads. These performances are a means of testing one's ability and of progression in the school's grading system, and are the main feature in spectacular public demonstrations. At the school's complex in Jakarta, the head of the organization, Bapak Poerwoto Hado Poernomo, or Mas Poeng as he is known less formally, explained to me that it is not *ilmu*, but *ilmiah*, or science, through which Merpati Putih players are able to develop inner power. All living things require energy to exist, and respiration (*pernafasan*) releases energy in a chemical reaction in the cells in our bodies through oxidation. Through dynamic breathing techniques, inhalation is controlled, the breath being held before exhaling, thus causing a decline in oxygen levels immediately available to the body and the body to go anaerobic. Anaerobic respiration is responsible for an increased rate of production of the molecule adenosine triphosphate, or ATP. ATP is the molecule responsible for the storage and transfer of energy within the body. It is this chemical reaction that is claimed to be the source of inner power. The instructor (*pelatih*) in Merpati Putih is no longer viewed as a spiritual preceptor or repository of recondite knowledge, but as a facilitator of self-development for all who participate in group instruction and the sequence of breathing exercises taught as part of the school's curriculum. Their authority is thus depersonalized and subordinated to the school's organizational hierarchy. The development of inner power, permeated with the values of the New Order, the self proclaimed developmental order (Heryanto 1988), both articulates and affirms the rational, technocratic superiority of science over supernaturalism. While homage is paid to the founders of the school, and its lineage is traced back to the royal court in Mataram in a manner characteristic of New Order historiography, care is taken to distinguish the past from the present and the modern school of Merpati Putih. Conceptions of the New Order citizen, loyal to the nation and state, take precedence over genealogical relations that bear upon personhood and place. Intersubjective relationships and intermediary practices are thus reconfigured through an overdetermination of paradigmatic relations centered upon the bounded individual (cf. Headley 2006: 518).

In contrast to invulnerability practices in which one trusts to the will of God and to one's *guru* to prevent oneself from coming to harm, in Merpati Putih one activates one's own inner potential through dedicated practice and self development. Exponents do not withstand attacks upon their person, but instead demonstrate their invincibility by smashing apparently unbreakable objects, aggressively imposing their authority upon the world. In contrast to the figure of the *guru*, the teacher in Merpati Putih is no longer viewed as a spiritual preceptor or repository of recondite knowledge but as a facilitator of self-development for all who participate in group instruction and the sequence of breathing exercises taught as part of the school's curriculum. In contrast, the overt demonstration of *ilmu kebal* (invulnerability) by the students of Bapak Achmad is a compelling presentation of his efficacy and ability to act on the world. The elders in Cimande, as a consequence of their being the locus of relational identities articulated in the genealogy, the *silsilah*, similarly act in an intercessory capacity. It is via their instrumentality that God's agency might become manifest in this world. It is not so much that "power" is in any way homogeneous and concentrated in the elders, but rather that they possess both the "technical means" (*elmu pangaweruh*) and, by virtue of descent, the capacity to mediate relations with the denizens of the unseen world (*alam ghaib*). The agency of the ancestors—Embah Buyut, Embah Kahir, and the *karahun*—in narrative accounts of their actions and in the social life of Cimande continues beyond their deaths, acting through people and things, and can be seen to be located in a field of spatio-temporal relations in which agency is not confined to the body (Gell 1998: 96–154). Thus, as individual persons they might be seen in Gell's sense to be "multiple"—that is, "the precipitate of a multitude of genealogical relationships, each of which is instantiated in his/her person; and conversely, an aggregate of persons, such as a lineage or tribe, is 'one person' in consequence of being one genealogy: the original ancestor is now instantiated, not as one body but as the many bodies into which the one body has transformed itself" (ibid.: 140).

In Merpati Putih inner power is substantive and focused in the individual, cultivated through disciplined practice. Instruction is standardized, and taught openly in large schools in which allegiance to the state and the organization takes precedence over loyalty to one's teacher. Tradition is relegated to a relatively powerless past, a point from which progress might be measured. *Tenaga dalam*, a large scale, institutionalized practice defined by rational scientific explanation, is a consequence of individual agency. The acquisition of *ilmu batin* may involve secretive study with a *guru*, or may even be transmitted directly from the *guru* to the student. It incorporates the cultivation of spiritual potency, often through the use of extra-mundane agency or by right of descent. Within Merpati Putih, conceptions of the New Order citizen, loyal to the nation and state, take precedence over genealogical relations that bear upon personhood and place. In modernist schools such as Merpati Putih, a new kind of instrumental rationality might be seen to operate in the collective cultivation and institutionalized dissemination of *tenaga dalam*. However, these rationalities take very specific forms, and should not be seen simply as a consequence of state appropriation of extant discourses and practices as a means of subjugation.

Personal Sovereignty and the Practicalities of Power

With regard to *ilmu batin* and those potential practices such as *ilmu kebal* to un-
derpin informal authority, efficacy, agency, and the possession of knowledge are
equally important, if not defining aspects of being *sakti*. In becoming *sakti* one
becomes agentive, able to act upon the world in a new way for oneself and in the
interests of others, a process that involves the negotiation of intermediary relationships, and may be understood not only as a concentration of power in a person
or place, but also as collective agency. In this respect action is not necessarily re-
ducible to individual, or for that matter human, agents (see Taylor 1985: 90). This
stands in contrast to modernist pencak silat schools in which more substantive
conceptions of power and potent individuals hold sway. Ward Keeler, writing on
what he terms "personal sovereignty" in Java (Keeler 1985: 138), argues that it is
a Javanese "concern to demonstrate and assure one's status by remaining impervious to external influence of any sort, including political influence" (ibid.: 107). It
is "dissimulation of a superior's control [that] mitigates the impression of a loss of
personal control or autonomy. The dissimulated self also gains a particular authority: a diffuse but idealized and highly respected position as agent both operating
within and surpassing the world" (ibid.: 268). However, in knowledge practices
such as *ilmu kebal* it is not just that one is capable of remaining impervious to outside interference, defining relations of interiority through circumscribed boundaries. Rather, a more subtle account of power is predicated upon the recognition of
the importance of relations of exteriority to the instantiation of authority.

The importance of entering into and maintaining relations with persons, both
visible and invisible, is paramount to the task of consolidating power (cf. Strathern 1995: 22). In this respect, signs of the visibility of power are important to its
consolidation, and "an audience [is] necessary in these systems as both witness
and substance of power" (Errington 1989: 110). Knowledge of invulnerability is
thus an important aspect of power relations. In demonstrating this knowledge the
guru is dependent upon their students to substantiate their role, which is corrobo-
rated by the protection they are able to afford their students. Direct claims to their
own agency in preventing their students coming from harm are overtly deferred
(cf. Hobart 1990: 118), an indirect assertion of one's capacity to act as spiritual
intermediary.

In the standardized regimen of breathing exercises through which *tenaga
dalam* is cultivated in modernist pencak silat schools, New Order imperatives are
clearly discernable. The body is transformed in conjunction with the wider transformation of the social body in the developmental discourse that was the mark
of governance in Suharto's Indonesia. Yet it is not just power/knowledge that
cross-cuts the body (Lash 1991: 270) in the practices of "inner power." Rather, the
self-disciplined and disciplining body is the site of potentialities, not just of sub-
jectification and constraint. To think of it in this way is to see power only as envel-

oping, constrictive, with subjectivities being shaped purely in response to external forces. Moreover, while strategic deployments like the New Order cultural project served to define and maintain a distinction between "traditional" and "modern" practices in relation to the state as an agent of change, they did so through extant technologies of power. The formally organized pencak silat school thus serves not to efface relationships based upon devotion to one's teacher but to reorient them towards the state as the progenitor of knowledge and material gain. Individuality is formalized in a way that denies connectivity except with the anteriority of a nationalist past. The invulnerable body, the product of alignments in assemblages that transcend the authority of the state, to the ancestors and ultimately God, is not so much pacified or colonized as exiled to this traditionalist past.

Joshua Barker argues that the "*kebal* body" is resistant to the surveillant technologies of the state, and is in a sense territorial, describing an "interiority" that is impenetrable, impervious to outside interference (Barker 1999: 109). While Barker's account is insightful, it is limited by the emphasis placed on logics of surveillance and the Foucauldian framework that frames his thinking on forms of power in Indonesia. While Foucault's ethical and political oeuvre is a convenient point of departure for the exploration of the effects of technologies of power, it is limited in its scope. Framed historically against the backdrop of the Rousseauist state (Siegel 2006: 19), a pervasive secularism shapes the forms that theory takes in Foucault's canon.

Michel Foucault famously distinguishes between old economies of power, which proceeded by deduction, on the principle of "levying-violence," and the development of disciplines, which "make it possible to adjust the multiplicity of men and the multiplication of the apparatuses of production" (Foucault 1995: 219). It was the accumulation of capital in the West that:

> made possible a political take-off in relation to the traditional, ritual, costly, violent forms of power, which soon fell into disuse and were superseded by a subtle, calculated technology of subjection ... a specific modality of disciplinary power, whose general formulas, techniques of submitting force and bodies, in short, "political anatomy," could be operated in the most diverse political régimes, apparatuses or institutions. (ibid.: 220–21)

Foucault insisted that disciplinary mechanisms "were different from asceticism and from 'disciplines' of a monastic type, whose function was to obtain renunciations rather than increases of utility and which, although they involved obedience to others, had as their principle aim an increase of the mastery of each individual over his own body" (ibid.: 137). Yet arguably the *kebal* body, to continue with Barker's turn of phrase, has a capacity for transformation with a utility value in excess of that posited by Foucault with regard to ascetic practices. As I have endeavored to show, such impenetrability is as much a consequence of aligning oneself and maintaining relations with a higher authority—an alignment that Suharto himself was careful to maintain publicly.

It is possible to discern similar strategies underpinning the spiritual authority of the pencak silat teachers in west Java, the representatives and mediators of relations with the ancestors, and Suharto, the figure and instrument of the state. The New Order was renowned for its construction of buildings and monuments, of the use of urban space in the establishment of its cultural order (Nas 1993; Korff and Evers 2001). Development thus served as sign of the material well-being of the nation and the agency of the Suharto administration as the self-proclaimed developmental order. Curiously though, there was very little celebration of Bapak Suharto, the father of the nation, in public space in Indonesia. There were no buildings, bridges, or streets named after him in the fashion of the celebration of the revolutionary heroes of the state. He ensured that no "cult of personality" sprang up around him (Ratih 1997). Yet it is this absence of personalization that provides the discursive potential for a surfeit of signification. Suharto, the father of development, was thus portrayed as immanent in all things, in bureaucratic agencies, in the material benefits of ordered development, and in the retribution meted out upon those that threatened the social order. His perceived detachment from the affairs of state could be adduced as evidence of this. Through deferral of agency he was thus constituted as the instrument of state. Careful to perpetuate the image of a legitimate, even divinely ordained, ruler, Suharto never superseded the authority of the state. State legislation, although it may have been rewritten to suit the interests of Suharto and other members of the political and military elite, was never overtly transgressed. Suharto was thus conceptualized as mediating relations on behalf of a divinely protected citizenry, a theocratic conception of kingship that was justified through the maintenance of order.

In a convincing argument as to the differences in the role that violence plays in processes of state formation and governance in Southeast Asia and the West, Tony Day stresses the strategic significance of the threat of chaos and disruption to the social order. "It is impossible to imagine the Orde Baru, the 'New Order'," he writes, "without contiguous mayhem to give that order its raison d'être" (Day 2002: 278). Disorder, in Day's reckoning, is a defining characteristic of both the Dutch colonial state and successive incarnations of the Indonesian state. Exploring alternative readings of the "mysterious killings" (*penembakan misterius*, or *petrus*), the extra-judicial murder of thousands of petty criminals in 1983/84, Day argues that spectacular violence serves to define the boundary between state and society and establish the state as the source of both death and invulnerability. The corpses of the victims were left in their local territories after being abducted at night. They were often riddled with bullet wounds or stabbed many times. As Siegel argues, the danger presented by those abducted "made it necessary to kill each criminal several times … [Thus] the force of the government was made equivalent to the power attributed to these corpses precisely when the victims were murdered multiple times" (Siegel 1998: 115). Spectacular and brutal violence thus served to both constitute and eradicate threat to the social order.

Giorgio Agamben, taking issue with Foucault's thinking on sovereignty, argues that in the final analysis, all power can be seen to rest on the ability to take or preserve life. Exploring the notion of *homo sacer* in Roman law, a person who is banned and who may not be sacrificed ritually but can be killed by anyone, Agamben asserts that the sovereign state's dominion over the subject rests ultimately on the reduction of *bios*, "the form or way of living proper to an individual or group" (1998:1), or political life, to *zoe*, to "bare life," or natural, biological life. *Homo sacer* thus "presents the orginary figure of life taken into the sovereign ban and preserves the memory of the originary exclusion through which the political dimension was first constituted" (ibid: 83). Sovereignty retains its sacrality, as evidenced by the continuing presence of *homo sacer* in the sovereign state's capacity to inaugurate a state of exception, to suspend law in the interests of national security that, with the advent of biopolitics, contributes to the franchisement of the decision over life or death and the monstrous transformation of the biopolitical into the thanatopolitical (ibid.: 122). Thus, for Agamben, sovereignty is not a mode of power belonging to an earlier age, superseded by biopolitical power that is characteristic of modernity. Rather, "the production of a bio-political body is the original activity of sovereign power" (ibid.: 6).

Agamben's account of sovereign power resonates with the exclusionary practices of the Indonesian state and its terratoid presence in the lives of its citizenry. However, there is an important difference to account for in the conception of power that is operationalized in transformational technologies such as *ilmu kebal*, in which *all* persons are potentially sovereign. The possession of knowledge of invulnerability, however it is gained, via self-transformation through ascetic practice or the possession of talismans, is, as Tony Day notes, not the sole dominion of the state or any one party, and cannot therefore be considered simply as an instrument of class domination. Rather, it is a form of knowledge "directly concerned with relations of power … [I]ts function is to assist the knowledgeable to exercise power, make it protective, or elude it. Such powerful knowledge also attracts adherents who form communities of the 'protected'. *It is a state-forming kind of knowledge*" (Day 2002: 160, emphasis added).

Conclusion

In sketching the transformation of knowledge practices in pencak silat, my purpose here has been to muddy the theoretical waters a little with regard to what might and might not be seen as indicative of "modernity" or "modernities." Viewing these transformations as a mode of cultural nationalism, a coping mechanism "constituted by an ambivalence vis-à-vis modernity" (Hansen 1996: 140), or the cultivation of a disciplined citizenry as a hegemonic articulation of the authority of the state that works to displace and reorient existing modes of authority and technologies of power, might be theoretically productive. However, if care is not taken, such modes of explanation may also work to subvert the elucidation of cultural logics that are not just attempts to recuperate power as an appropriation of or reaction to the global in a modern age.

Informal sites of authority such as the *kebal* body are fundamental to the constitution of relations of power rooted historically in ascetic practices. *Ilmu kebal* is a technology through which personal sovereignty might be constituted and maintained. In the promotion of bounded individualism and the realignment of relationships in modern pencak silat schools with the state there is an acknowledgement of the right to life embodied in the practice of invulnerability. Whether framed in the pronouncements of scientism, or explained via recourse to the mystical, common to both fields of practice are processes through which one may become efficacious. The corpus of knowledge practices through which one may become invulnerable can be seen not just as resistance in response to power but also as indicative of "resistance that is found in the social ontology from the start" (Hoy 2004: 82), in which it is possible to discern an eminently practical conception of power as mutable, personable, and in constant need of reaffirmation.

Governance under the New Order was itself shaped by the inherent instability of political power in a field of social relations in which the possession of *ilmu kebal* lent itself to the consolidation of political authority (cf. Schulte Nordholt 1991: 76). In ideal conceptions of power and its ritualistic representation under the New Order there was recognition of the volatility and mutability of authority, of the necessity for sovereignty to be violently performed if it was to endure. More than a decade after Suharto's New Order was proved to be vulnerable, invulnerability practices are increasingly prominent throughout Indonesia. For members of Banser, the paramilitary wing of Indonesia's largest Islamic organization, Nahdatul Ulama, the practice of *ilmu kebal* is a prerequisite of membership (D&R 1999: 19; see also I. Wilson 2008). Throughout Java, Kalimantan, and Sulawesi, members of militia groups solicit supernatural agency and lay claim to invulnerability to establish their authority (Schiller and Garang 2002; Peluso 2003; Dove 2007; Wilson et al. 2010); and in Lombok, Balinese security groups maintain relations with and are protected by an invisible spirit army (Telle, this volume). Such practices demand a closer examination of spiritualized authority in forms of political process in Indonesia. The consideration of political efficacy and affect with the spirits in mind is an issue that draws into question the theoretical crutch provided by materialist models in social scientific discourse.

The importance of maintaining relations with a higher form of authority, of demonstrating efficacy and rendering visible non-manifest agencies in practices such as invulnerability, is suggestive of a notion of power in which authority is recognized as relative, mutual, and constituted through display. The reconfiguration of knowledge practices and relational agencies in modernist pencak silat schools is a continuation of political modalities in which the body gains significance as a means through which efficacy might be established. Foucault, in his enquiries into sovereignty, posed the question how it was that "people begin to perceive a war just beneath the surface of peace" (Foucault 2003: 267). Ironically, looking beyond Eurocentric models of material agency and power propagated by following too closely in Foucault's theoretical footprints may well grant novel insights into this question and the ways in which social order is predicated on the basis of perceived threat.

Notes

1. *Kesaktian* is formed from the root *sakti*, and is often equated with supernatural "power" concentrated in an individual or object. The notion of *sakti* is also used in reference to male sexual potency, and an implicit phallocentrism frames the use of the term and the spiritual strength of males (Hatley 1990: 180–82; Brenner 1998: 147–49).
2. In the *Suma Oriental*, an account of Malacca in the sixteenth century, Tomo Pires mentions the *cabaées,* a Portuguese derivation of *kebal* used in reference to noblemen from the regions of Linga, Brunei, and Pahang who were given to believe they could not die by the sword (Pires 1967: 266). In the Philippines, amulets, or *anting anting*, protect the wearer from blade and bullet (Kayme 1901; Ileto 1979; Kowalewski 1991: 246), and similarly the knowledge of invulnerability in Thailand is widespread (Turton 1991; see also Ffennell 1897). Tanabe and Turton (1984) note the significance of invulnerability practices within peasant rebellions throughout Southeast Asia, and in Java, revolt against the Dutch colonial administration was often led by local *jago*, figures held to be invulnerable, their followers making use of spiritually charged amulets or *jimat* to similarly ensure their imperviousness to injury (Kartodirdjo 1984: 18–19; Onghokham 1984: 328).
3. Bapak Achmad also explained that although there was a method for ingesting the glass, the means of providing protection for his students was considered to be "black magic" or *ilmu hitam*, and therefore forbidden for them to practice. Training in *ilmu kebal* is seen by some to be *syirk*, at odds with Islamic prescriptions, and more conservative pencak silat teachers in west Java may eschew such practices (cf. I. Wilson 2008: 202 n.21). Pencak silat schools such as Tapak Suci, associated with the modernist Islamic organization Muhammadiyah, generally avoid such practices. For members of Pagar Nusa, the pencak silat school associated with Banser, the paramilitary wing of Indonesia's largest Islamic organization, the traditionalist Nahdatul Ulama (NU), *ilmu kebal* is an important part of training. Religious orientation within Islam is thus reflected in attitudes towards the practice of *ilmu kebal.*
4. Anderson's account, as he later explained, was an attempt to address problems he perceived with Weber's notion of charismatic authority and the ways in which it was at times implied to be an attribute of certain persons, rather than such authority being attributed to them by their followers. As such, he sought to explain why culturally specific perceptions of charismatic authority were particularly compelling by focusing on assumptions about power, which, he asserts, "in any culture is fundamentally a metaphor for causality—why things happen the way they do. From the Javanese data it seemed plausible to argue that all human societies at one time or another had had a *substantive* view of power as an emanation of the cosmic or divine" (Anderson 1990: 78–79). Thus Weber had been wrong to contrast charismatic modes of authority with traditional or rational-legal modes of domination. From a historicist perspective there were in fact "only *two* general forms of domination, one linked to substantive and the other to instrumental/relational concepts

of power" (ibid.: 79, original emphasis). Taking himself to task, Anderson observes that he had been too keen to read Weber sociologically, and so mistook what were actually "'tropes' for 'types'" of authority (ibid.: 79).

5. In 2003 there were fifteen such apprentices working in Tari Kolot and the surrounding *kampung*.

6. The conception of culture, or *kebudayaan*, as it was promoted under the New Order, encompassed the notion of culture as a "civilising agent of human behaviour" and a source of common identity (Lindsay 1995: 659). "Regional culture" (*Kebudayaan daerah*) referred to the specific cultural attributes of the ethnolinguistic groups of Indonesia and the "provincial differentiation" of culture through its association regionally with the administrative provinces of the state (Picard 1996: 176–79). National Culture, on the other hand, embodied the linear, unidirectional trajectories of modernity (Hough 1999: 234; see also Brenner 1998: 1). Through this association of culture and place, local knowledge and existence patterns became contained and disempowered, subsumed within the broader narrative of *Indonesia Raya*, or "Greater Indonesia" (Rodgers 1993). While elements of Indonesia's "traditional" past were to be treasured, it was through "national culture" (*kebudayaan bangsa*) that progress (*kemajuan*) was deemed possible.

7. The notion of development, or *pembangunan*, employed by Suharto is typical of the New Order narrative of nation-building (Hooker and Dick 1993: 3). *Pembangunan*, from the root *bangun*, which may be glossed as "rise, awake, construction" (Langenberg 1986: 19), is suggestive of a process which does not recognize itself automatically but needs outside action or encouragement (Quarles van Ufford 1985: 57).

8. The term *nusantara* is used in reference to the Indonesia archipelago, or more generally, to the archipelagic region comprising the states of Indonesia, Malaysia, Singapore, and Brunei.

9. The Indonesian state doctrine or national philosophy consists of five principles; belief in one God; just and civilized humanity; national unity; democracy arising from the wisdom of the unanimity of the deliberations of representatives; social justice for the whole of the Indonesian people (see Bourchier and Legge 1994: x). Suharto, soon after assuming the Presidency from Soekarno in 1967, stated that the goal of the New Order "is to secure and purify the implementation of *Pancasila* and the 1945 Constitution. Every Indonesian, every organization, every form of business which calls itself New Order must accept the twin foundation of *Pancasila* and the 1945 Constitution" (Bouchier and Hadiz 2003: 37). This culminated with a pronouncement in August 1982 that all "socio-political forces," including all political parties and religious groups, should adopt *Pancasila* as their sole principle or foundation (*azas tunggal*, Prawiranegara 1984: 74), a law being passed to this effect in 1986.

References

Agamben, Giorgio. 1998. *Homo Sacer: Sovereign Power and Bare Life.* Stanford, CA: Stanford University Press.

Anderson, B. 1972. "The Idea of Power in Javanese Culture," in *Culture and Politics in Indonesia*, eds. B. Anderson, C. Holt, and J. Siegel. Ithaca, NY: Cornell University Press, pp.1–70.

———. 1990. "Further Adventures of Charisma," in *Language and Power: Exploring Political Cultures in Indonesia*. Ithaca, NY: Cornell University Press, pp.78–93.

Barker, Joshua. 1999. "Surveillance and Territoriality in Bandung," in *Figures of Criminality in Indonesia, the Philippines, and Colonial Vietnam*, ed. V.L. Rafael. Ithaca, NY: Cornell University Southeast Asia Program Publications, pp.95–127.

———. 2008. "Beyond Bandung: Developmental Nationalism and (Multi)cultural Nationalism in Indonesia," *Third World Quarterly* 29: 521–40.

Bourchier, David, and Vedi R. Hadiz, eds. 2003. *Indonesian Politics and Society: A Reader*. London: Routledge Curzon.

Bourchier, David, and John Legge, eds. 1994. *Democracy in Indonesia: 1950s and 1990s*. Victoria: Monash University.

Brenner, Suzanne A. 1998. *The Domestication of Desire: Women, Wealth and Modernity in Java*. Princeton, NJ: Princeton University Press.

Bruinessen, Martin van. 1994. "Pesantren and Kitab Kuning: Maintenance and Continuation of a Tradition of Religious Learning," in *Texts from the Islands: Oral and Written Traditions of Indonesia and the Malay World*, ed. W. Marschall. Berne: University of Berne.

———. 1995. *Kitab Kuning, Pesantren, dan Tarekat: Tradisi - Tradisi Islam di Indonesia*. Bandung: Mizan.

Bubandt, Nils. 2009. "Interview with an Ancestor: Spirits as Informants and the Politics of Possession in North Maluku," *Ethnography* 10: 291–316.

Chambert-Loir, Henri, and Anthony Reid, eds. 2002. *The Potent Dead: Ancestors, Saints and Heroes in Contemporary Indonesia*. Honolulu: University of Hawaii Press.

D&R. 1999. Kebal itu Perlu, Katanya. April, 19–24.

Day, Tony. 2002. *Fluid Iron: State Formation in Southeast Asia*. Honolulu: University of Hawaii Press.

De Grave, Jean-Marc. 2001. *Initiation Rituelle et Arts Martiaux: Trois Écoles de Kanuragan Javanais*. Paris: Association Archipel.

Dove, Michael. 2007. "'New Barbarism' or Old Agency among the Dayak? Reflections on Post-Suharto Ethnic Violence in Kalimantan," in *Identifying with Freedom: Indonesia After Suharto*, ed. T. Day. Oxford: Berghahn Books, pp.70–86.

Eisenstadt, Shmuel N. 2000. "Multiple Modernities," *Daedalus* 129: 1–29.

Englund, Harri, and James Leach. 2000. "Ethnography and the Meta-narratives of Modernity," *Current Anthropology* 41: 225–31.

Errington, Shelly. 1989. *Meaning and Power in a Southeast Asian Realm*. Princeton, NJ: Princeton University Press.

Ffennell, M.C. 1897. "Charms from Siam," *Folklore* 8(1): 88–91.

Foucault, Michel. 1995. *Discipline and Punish: The Birth of the Prison*, trans. A. Sheridan. New York: Vintage Books.

———. 2003. *Society Must Be Defended: Lectures at the Collège de France 1975–76*, trans. D. Macey. Harmondsworth: Penguin.

Gartenberg, Gary. 2000. "Silat Tales: Narrative Representations of Martial Culture in the Malay/Indonesian Archipelago," Ph.D. dissertation. Berkeley: University of California at Berkeley.

Geertz, Hildred. 1995. "Sorcery and Social Change in Bali: The *Sakti* Conjecture," unpublished paper presented at the conference "Bali in the Late Twentieth Century," Sydney.

———. 2004. *The Life of a Balinese Temple: Artistry, Imagination and History in a Peasant Village*. Honolulu: University of Hawaii Press.

Gell, Alfred. 1998. *Art and Agency: An Anthropological Theory*. Oxford: Clarendon Press.

Giddens, Anthony, and Christopher Pierson. 1998. *Conversations with Anthony Giddens: Making Sense of Modernity*. Stanford, CA: Stanford University Press.

Hansen, Thomas Blom. 1996. "Recuperating Masculinity: Hindu Nationalism, Violence and the Exorcism of the Muslim 'Other'," *Critique of Anthropology* 16(2): 137–72.

Harrison, Simon. 1998. "The Extended Agency of Alfred Gell," *Anthropology Today* 14(4): 1–2.

Hatley, B. 1990. "Theatrical Imagery and Gender Ideology in Java," in *Power and Difference: Gender in Island Southeast Asia*, eds. J. Atkinson and S. Errington. Stanford, CA: Stanford University Press, pp.177–207.

Headley, Stephen C. 2006. *Durga's Mosque: Cosmology, Conversion and Community in Central Javanese Islam*. Singapore: Institute of Southeast Asian Studies.

Heryana, A. 1995. *Laporan Penelitian Pencak Silat Aliran Cimande di Jawa Barat*. Bandung: Departemen Pendidikan dan Kebudayaan, Direkorat Jenderal Kebudayaan Balia Kajian Sejarah dan Nilai Tradisional Jawa Barat.

Heryanto, A. 1988. "The 'Development' of Development," *Indonesia* 46: 1–24.

Hobart, Mark, 1990. "The Patience of Plants: A Note on Agency in Bali," *Review of Indonesian and Malaysian Affairs* 24: 90–135.

Hooker, Virginia M., and Howard Dick. 1993. "Introduction," in *Culture and Society in New Order Indonesia*, ed. V.M. Hooker. Kuala Lumpur: Oxford University Press, pp.1–23.

Hough, Brett. 1999. "Education for the Performing Arts: Contesting and Mediating Identity in Contemporary Bali," in *Staying Local in the Global Village: Bali in the Twentieth Century*, eds. L. Connor and R. Rubinstein. Honolulu: University of Hawaii Press, pp.231–64

Hoy, David C. 2004. *Critical Resistance: From Poststructuralism to Post-critique*. Cambridge, MA: MIT Press.

Ileto, Reynaldo. 1979. *Pasyon and Revolution: Popular Movements in the Philippines 1840–1910*. Quezon City: Ateneo de Manila University Press.

IPSI. n.d. *Padepokan pencak silat Indonesia*.

Jonsson, Hjorleifur. 2004. "Mien Alter-Natives in Thai Modernity," *Anthropological Quarterly* 77: 673–704.

Kartodirdjo, S. 1984. *Modern Indonesia: Tradition and Transformation, A Socio-historical Perspective*. Yogyakarta: Gadjah Mada University Press.

Kayme, Sargent. 1901. *Anting Anting Stories, and Other Strange Tales of the Filipinos*. Boston: Small, Maynard and Co.

Keeler, Ward. 1985. "Villagers and the Exemplary Centre in Java," *Indonesia* 39: 111–40.

———. 1987. *Javanese Shadow Plays, Javanese Selves*. Princeton, NJ: Princeton University Press.

Keesing, Roger M. 1984. "Rethinking 'Mana'," *Journal of Anthropological Research* 40: 137–56.

Korff, Rüdiger, and Hans-Dieter Evers. 2001. *Southeast Asian Urbanism: The Meaning and Power of Social Space*. Singapore: Institute of Southeast Asian Studies.

Kowalewski, David. 1991. "Cultism, Insurgency, and Vigilantism in the Philippines," *Sociological Analysis* 52: 241–53.

Langenberg, Michael van. 1986. "Analysing Indonesia's New Order State: A Keywords Approach," *Review of Indonesian and Malaysian Affairs* 20: 1–47.

Lash, Scott. 1991. "Genealogy of the Body: Foucault/Deleuze/Nietzsche," in *The Body: Social Process and Cultural Theory*, eds. M. Feathertone, M. Hepworth and B.S. Turner. London: Sage, pp.256–80.

Lindsay, Jennifer. 1995. "Cultural Policy and the Performing Arts in Southeast Asia," *Bijdragen tot de Taal-, Land- en Volkenkunde* 151: 656–71.

Lombard, Denys. 1996. "Les Tarékat en Insulinde," in *Les Ordres Mystiques dans l'Islam*, eds. A. Popovic and G. Veinstein. Paris: Ecole des Hautes Etudes en Sciences Sociales, pp.139–66.

Mulder, Nils. 1998. *Mysticism in Java: Ideology in Indonesia*. Amsterdam: Pepin Press.

Nas, Peter J.M. 1993. "Jakarta City Full of Symbols," in *Urban Symbolism*, ed. P.J.M. Nas. Leiden: Brill, pp.13–37.

Needham, Rodney. 1976. "Skulls and Causality," *Man* 11: 71–88.

Onghokham. 1984. "The Jago in Colonial Java, Ambivalent Champion of the People," in *History and Peasant Consciousness in Southeast Asia*, eds. A. Turton and S. Tanabe. Osaka: National Museum of Ethnology, pp.327–43.

Pels, Peter. 2003. "Introduction: Magic and Modernity," in *Magic and Modernity: Interfaces of Revelation and Concealment*, eds. B. Meyer and P. Pels. Stanford, CA: Stanford University Press, pp.1–38.

Peluso, Nancy Lee. 2003. "Weapons of the Wild: Strategic Uses of Violence and Wildness in the Rainforests of Indonesian Borneo," in *In Search of the Rain Forest*, ed. C. Slater. Durham, NC: Duke University Press, pp.204–45.

Pemberton, John. 1994. *On the Subject of Java*. Ithaca, NY: Cornell University Press.

PERSILAT. 2000. *Pencak Silat Constitution.*

Picard, Michel. 1996. *Bali: Cultural Tourism and Touristic Culture*. Singapore: Archipelago Press.

Pires, Tomo. 1967. *The Suma Oriental of Tome Pires*, trans. A. Cortesao. Nendeln, Lichtenstein: Kraus Reprint Limited.

Prawiranegara, Sjafruddin. 1984. "Pancasila as the Sole Foundation," *Indonesia* 38: 74–83.

Quarles van Ufford, P. 1985. "Rationalities and Development in Java," in *Development and its Rationalities*, eds. C.A. van Peursen and M.C. Doeser. Amsterdam: Free University Press, pp.51–75.

Ratih, I Gusti Agung Ayu. 1997. "Soeharto's New Order State: Imposed Illusions and Invented Legitimations." M.A. dissertation. Madison: University of Wisconsin.

Rodgers, Susan. 1993. "Batak Heritage and the Indonesian State: Print Literacy and the Construction of Ethnic Cultures in Indonesia," in *Politcal and Legal Anthropology, Vol 9: Ethnicity and the State*, ed. J.D.Toland. New Brunswick, NJ: Transaction, pp.147–76.

Schiller, Anne, and Bambang Garang. 2002. "Religion and Inter-ethnic Violence in Indonesia," *Journal of Contemporary Asia* 32(2): 244–54.

Schulte Nordholt, Henk. 1991. "The Jago in the Shadow: Crime and 'Order' in the Colonial State in Java," *Review of Indonesian and Malay Affairs* 25(1): 74–91.

Siegel, James. T. 1998. *A New Criminal Type in Jakarta: Counter Revolution Today*. Durham, NC: Duke University Press

———. 2006. *Naming the Witch*. Stanford, CA: Stanford University Press

Steinmetz, George. 1999. "Introduction: Culture and the State," in *State/Culture: State-Formation After the Cultural Turn*. Ithaca, NY: Cornell University Press, pp.1–49.

Strathern, Marilyn. 1995. *The Relation: Issues in Complexity and Scale*. Cambridge: Prickly Pear Press.

Tanabe, Shigeharu, and Andrew Turton, eds. 1984. *History and Peasant Consciousness in South East Asia*. Osaka: National Museum of Ethnology.

Taylor, Charles. 1985. *Human Agency and Language*. Cambridge: Cambridge University Press.

Till, Margreet van. 1996. "In Search of Si Pitung: The History of an Indonesian Legend," *Bijdragen tot de Taal-, Land- en Volkenkunde* 152(3): 461–82.

Turner, Bryan. 2003. "Warrior Charisma and the Spiritualization of Violence," *Body and Society* 9: 93–108.

Turton, Andrew. 1991. "Invulnerability and Local Knowledge," in *Thai Constructions of Knowledge*, eds. M. Chitkasem and A. Turton. London: School of Oriental and African Studies, pp.155–82.

Vredenbregt, Jacob. 1973. "Dabus in West Java," *Bijdragen tot de Taal-, Land – en Volkenkunde* 129(2/3): 302–20.

Wilson, Ian D. 2008. "As Long as It's Halal: Islamic Preman in Jakarta," in *Expressing Islam: Religious Life and Politics in Indonesia*, eds. G. Fealy and S. White. Singapore: ISEAS, pp.192–210.

Wilson, Lee. 2006. "Unity or Diversity? The Constitution of a National Martial Art in Indonesia," Ph.D. dissertation. Cambridge: Cambridge University.

———. 2009. "Jurus, Jazz Riffs and the Constitution of a National Martial Art in Indonesia," *Body and Society* 15(3): 93–119.

Wilson, Lee, Gabriel Facal, Jean Marc de Grave, and Tom Green. 2010. "Political Conflict and Martial Arts," in *Martial Arts of the World: An Encyclopedia*, eds. T.A. Green and J.R. Svinth. Santa Barbara, CA: ABC Clio, pp. 619–25.

Winstedt, R.O. 1938. "The Malay Annals, or Sejarah Melayu: The Earliest Recension from MS. No.18 of the Raffles Collections in the Libraries of the Royal Asiatic Society, London," *Journal of the Malay Branch of the Royal Asiatic Society* 16: 1–222.

Winzeler, Robert L. 1983. "The Study of Malay Magic," *Bijdragen tot de Taal-, Land- en Volkenkunde* 139: 435–58.

Woodward, Mark R. 1985. "Healing and Morality: A Javanese Example," *Social Science and Medicine* 21: 1007–21.

4

CHANGING SPIRIT IDENTITIES: RETHINKING THE FOUR PALACES' SPIRIT REPRESENTATIONS IN NORTHERN VIETNAM

Claire Chauvet

In the temple of the Five Mandarins in Hanoi, Mrs Bình is sitting in front of an altar covered with offerings—flowers, incense sticks, cookies, and instant noodles—dedicated to a large pantheon of spirits, called the Four Palaces spirits (*thánh Tứ Phủ*).[1] She wears a Vietnamese medium's ceremonial dress: a long white tunic, white trousers, and a red turban on her head. She is now possessed by the Third Mandarin of the Water Palace (*Quan Tam Phủ*), a popular spirit of the pantheon.[2] Dressed according to common representations of this figure, she performs some dance steps specific to the Mandarin, swinging her arms and the two swords she holds. This incarnation of a male spirit is only one of the incarnations that generally constitute a spirit possession ritual, called *hầu bóng* ("serving the shadows") or *lên đồng* ("mounting the medium").

The performance will last about four hours, during which about fifteen spirits successively possess the medium. Each spirit incarnation (*giá*) starts and finishes with the medium sitting crossed-legged in front of the altar with a red veil on her head, under which each spirit takes possession of her body. For each spirit incarnation, Mrs Bình repeats identical sequences in front of the altars: she first performs solemn salutes, offers incense and rice wine, then performs the dances specific to each spirit and finishes with the redistribution of offerings. Two male musicians and singers (setting up a band, *cung văn*) accompany the medium's (*bà đồng*) performance with lute and percussion. They invoke the spirits to descend (*giáng*) into the temple and to take possession of the medium's body, and then sing the legend of the spirit (*chầu văn*).

Endnotes for this chapter begin on page 99

Mrs Bình, forty-five years old and a medium for seven years at the time of my research, had decided to perform this possession ritual for two main reasons: to solve some health problems she faced and to improve the situation of her declining business. She had invited about thirty people. After the sequence of dances,

Figure 4.1: A medium possessed by a prince. Photograph by Claire Chauvet, 2002.

some members of the audience enter the ritual space one by one, carrying a tray of offerings and whispering some words of invocation to the possessed medium. Mrs Bình listens to each of them, takes their offerings and reciprocates them with some "blessed gifts" (*lộc*) and banknotes. At the end of the seance, the worshipers take these home as lucky charms: they will play the lottery with the banknotes and eat the food for good health. Most of the people attending the performance are women and spirit mediums themselves, or at least regular disciples (*đệ tử*) of the spirits.[3] They know each other and meet regularly in this temple.

The scene described above took place at the end of the 1990s, yet it duplicates accounts and images of Vietnamese mediums' performances drawn in the French colonial literature (Giran 1912; Coulet 1929; Durand 1959). A comparison between contemporary fieldwork observations and literature from the beginning of the twentieth century raises the issue of changes in the ritual and spirit representations. Basic elements of spirit possession rituals (*hầu bóng*)—such as the order in which the spirits possess the medium, the emblematic color of the ceremonial clothes referring to the color of the palaces, and the ritual sequences themselves— seem not to have changed noticeably in the time span of almost a century. But the general context of worship, the meanings of the rituals and the representations of the spirits have markedly changed, as too have anthropological interpretations of spirit possession in northern Vietnam.[4]

The anthropological literature often analyzes spirit possession and shamanism in a dual manner: as permanent and long lasting relics from the past, but also as very dynamic phenomena able to adapt to social change (Hamayon 2000). Even if these two interpretations may be partly contradictory, they clearly show that these phenomena are inscribed in the problematic of the relationship to the past, social change, and the contested concept of "modernity." Specifically regarding Southeast Asia, anthropologists have already examined some aspects of this topic. Aihwa Ong (1987), for example, focuses on the occurrence of spirit possession in Malaysian multinational factories, and looks at transformations in possession compared to its original rural forms. She analyzes this as a kind of protest against capitalism and the modern world. More recently, Rosalind Morris (2000) has studied the practices of mediums in Chiang Mai, Thailand. Her interpretation presents mutual connections between spirit possession and modernity, in the form of a back-and-forth movement between the origins, the past, and the present. These two examples, along with many others, challenge arguments about modernity and the disenchantment of the world which have long dominated the social sciences.

The tension between modernity and religion in Vietnam has a long history (Taylor 2007; Endres and Lauser, this volume) and has already been questioned by scholars. This chapter focuses on the post-reform period and aims at presenting some specific elements of change in the Four Palaces cult in relation to the social and economic changes which have marked Vietnamese society since the "renovation" policy (*đổi mới*, lit. "change for the new") launched by the government in the late 1980s. The transition to a market economy introduced by this reform has had a major impact on ritual life by providing the economic surplus necessary to perform ceremonies and has led to a questioning of the governmental agenda of socialist ideological transformation (Hy Văn Lương 1993, 2003; Malarney 1996). As a result, the beginnings of sustained economic growth and the modernization of the country emerged in tandem with important religious developments.

Over the last twenty years, the Four Palaces cult has experienced unprecedented growth, as have other religious practices. The number of worshipers and spirit mediums making their way toward the temples dedicated to the Four Palaces spirits for specific requests (health, prosperity, family happiness, and so forth) has noticeably increased. Spirit possession rituals and pilgrimages to the main temples of the Four Palaces spirits located in the northern part of the country—which are the two major events of the cult—are, first and foremost, growing in visibility and popularity in the capital Hanoi.

If this process differs in some ways from other Southeast Asian cases, it is similar insofar as spirit possession is not disappearing with economic development and modernization, but developing into new forms. A comparison of data from the contemporary and colonial periods leads us to examine changes in representations of the spirits of the Four Palaces that have occurred in the light of Vietnam's recent social and political transformations. Significantly, this process toward the elaboration of new spirit representations takes place thanks to the mediation of the past and falls in the scope of long-lasting Vietnamese traditions. Two main trends are noteworthy. First, the Four Palaces' spirits are now compared with contemporary heroes who sacrificed themselves in order to "save the country," a notion that is deeply anchored in the tradition of the cult of national heroes. Second, the spirits are thought to be benevolent toward the market economy and trade, which is due, among other elements, to the long-lasting influence of merchants on this cult (Dror 2007).

As well as drawing on published accounts, this chapter is based on ethnographic data collected in Hanoi since 1999.[5] The data was mainly collected at the temple of the Five Mandarins, located close to Hanoi's old city. The temple—led by Mr Hải, a male medium, born in the late 1960s—is one of numerous places of worship in the capital.[6] The worshipers who regularly take part in the temple's ritual activities form a group (*đoàn*) of worship and regularly meet on the first and fifteenth days of the lunar month for spirit possession performances and pilgrimages.

The Four Palaces Cult and Anthropological Literature

Religion in general, and spirit possession and the Four Palaces cult in particular, have long been major issues in the anthropological literature on Vietnam. This curiosity reached a peak during the French colonial period, not only through detailed anthropological and folkloric investigations but also through descriptions and reports by military and clerical staff. French scholars, as well as French-trained Vietnamese scholars, were the first to pay in-depth attention to this form of worship, and their writings remain of major interest to understand this cult (see, e.g., Dumoutier 1899; Diguet 1906; Giran 1912; Nguyễn Văn Huyên 1944; Durand 1959). Many early studies considered the Four Palaces cult as a relic of the past, despite its increasing popularity. For instance, Maurice Durand, the major scholar of the cult, depicted the mediums as "a toned-down survival of a widespread primitive shamanism" (Durand 1959: 11). Some years later, Nghiêm Thẩm, a Vietnamese scholar, considered spirit possession to be a "bastardization of Taoism that gives birth to scenes of witchcraft" (Nghiêm Thẩm 1965: 19).

Since the 1970s, interpretations of spirit possession have significantly changed. Southeast Asian spirit possession was depicted by Georges Condominas as "the heart of the local religious system" (Condominas 1976: 216). In his attempt to compare Southeast Asian spirit possession, he argued that the Four Palaces cult was an expression of a specific local historical context and that *hầu bóng* rituals were an evocation of the vanished class of the mandarins (Condominas 1973). After decolonization, the study of the Four Palaces cult faded in Vietnam, though worshipers carried on their ritual activities in secret. For several decades, due to war and the political situation, Vietnamese and foreign scholars could not carry out fieldwork in Vietnam, especially to study forbidden religious practices. The cult was therefore mainly studied abroad, such as in France (Simon and Simon-Barouh 1973), the United States (Fjelstad 1995), and Canada (Dorais and Nguyễn Huy 1998).

Following "renovation," the development of all components of the Vietnamese religious landscape—including ancestor worship (*thờ cúng tổ tiên*), Buddhism (*thờ Phật*), tutelary spirit worship (*thờ thánh hoàng*), and divination—have been well studied by anthropologists (e.g., Hy Văn Lương 1993; Endres 2001; Malarney 2002, 2007), and transformations of the Four Palaces cult have also been analyzed by many scholars (see Fjelstad and Nguyễn Thị Hiền 2006). Barley Norton (2000, 2003, 2009), for example, has studied the impact of the prohibition on mediumship on invocatory songs, while Phạm Quỳnh Phương (2006, 2009) has analyzed connections between the Four Palaces and Trần Hưng Đạo cults, the latter being in the past mainly practiced by men. Other aspects of the revitalization of spirit possession, such as the motivations and experiences of spirit mediums (Chauvet 2005; Endres 2006; Nguyễn Thị Hiền 2007) and their ritual performances (Nguyễn Thị Hiền 2006; Endres 2007), have also been analyzed.

Spirit Possession and the Four Palaces Cult: A Troubled History

The studies of the colonial period are neither complete nor unbiased, but they may help us analyze contemporary transformations of the cult and, more precisely, changes in the ways the spirits are thought of and represented by their disciples. In this chapter I will focus on spirit representations as modes of identification and classification of spiritual entities. As Gilles Tarabout has demonstrated concerning Hindu divinities (Tarabout 1992), representations may be observed in different forms—such as visual forms, narratives, rituals, and so on—that may overlap, contradict, and transform each other. In the Four Palaces cult, spirit representations are mainly expressed in legends and invocatory songs, in ritual practice, in the statues located in temples, private shrines and pagodas, and in the discourse of spirit mediums and worshipers.

Two main upheavals that occurred after the end of French colonial rule deserve mention: the establishment of the communist government in the 1950s in northern Vietnam, and the economic liberalization that commenced at the end of the 1980s, known as "renovation." These phenomena have undoubtedly deeply influenced spirit worship. However, despite these changes, the Four Palaces cult appears to be a reasonably stable and permanent element of the Vietnamese religious landscape.

In its present form, with Princess Liễu Hạnh as the main figure, the Four Palaces cult has existed for about 150 years, though it has a much longer history. As Olga Dror (2007) has shown, the history of worship of Liễu Hạnh and the practice of spirit possession has been a troubled one, even if only a broad outline of this history is known. The origins of the Four Palaces cult are not well known, only that the activities of mediums (though we do not know which kind) were already forbidden in the fifteenth century (Nguyễn Thế Anh 1991). Possession by female spirits (*Thánh Mẫu*) was described in the eighteenth century (Lãn Ong 1972). In the nineteenth century, under the last dynasty of the Nguyễn, spirit possession was alternately forbidden and rehabilitated, depending on the ruling emperor. Gia Long (1802–1820), the first emperor of the dynasty, published a decree prohibiting and punishing spirit mediums, while Đồng Khánh (1885–1889) was a follower of the cult and funded the restoration of Hòn Chén temple, the main shrine of the cult in Huế, the capital of the dynasty in central Vietnam (Bertrand 1996). From this time on, a major trend of worship became apparent: a shift swinging between times of prohibition by those in power and periods of acceptance or rehabilitation.

This ambivalent relationship with the holders of political power is not specific to Vietnamese spirit possession. In other Southeast Asian countries, spirit possession and political power are also closely linked. For instance, in Burma, the thirty-seven *nats* who regularly possess spirit mediums are thought to be tutelary spirits who have suffered from an unfair death caused by the monarchy. The king decided to gather these spirits together in an official cult (Brac de la Perrière 1989). In Laos, conflictual relationships between political power and spirit mediumship are also reported, since before the establishment of communism the spirits were linked to Buddhism and royalty (Sélim 2000). After years of restriction, spirit possession in Laos now benefits from religious liberalization, thus allowing a kind of reconciliation between spirits and political power.

At the beginning of the twentieth century, the French colonial government in Vietnam adopted a similar ambivalent political stance, oscillating between tolerance and local bans. Indeed, as with other religious practices, the cult was forbidden in the 1950s by the newly established communist government in the north of the country, and after 1975 it was banned across the whole of Vietnam and considered a "superstition" (*mê tín dị đoan*). As different authors have shown (Kleinen 1999: 162; Malarney 2002: 227), the category of "superstition" gathers together different aspects: the wasteful dimensions generated by feasts, the incompatibility of religious practices with the political project of the creation of a new order, and the retrograde nature of religious practices. Nowadays, the Four Palaces cult is tolerated by the government, but its situation is still uncertain.[7] Even as the Four Palaces cult attracts more and more worshipers and spirit mediums, it is still considered by some to be a superstition, an old-fashioned and marginal practice. Nevertheless, far from being marginal and in decline, since the period of economic development of the country began in the late 1980s, spirit mediums and worshipers have been gaining in visibility and in legitimacy, finding their place and contributing to the recent economic and social transformations of the country.

The recent history of the temple of the Five Mandarins reveals this link. With the prohibition of the cult, difficult times began for spirit mediums and worshipers. Surveillance of rituals and arrests of spirit mediums and disciples by the police were common. Spirit mediums and disciples had to worship and carry out their rituals secretly (*hầu trốn*). The temple of the Five Mandarins was used for other purposes and became a community hall for local organizations. This echoes what happened in many temples in northern Vietnam—for example, the shrine in Bắc Lệ (Lạng Sơn province), dedicated to the "Mountains and Forests" Palace spirits, was closed and used as headquarters of the people's committee and as a school (Vũ Ngọc Khánh 2000: 267). The festivals where Hanoi mediums and worshipers used to gather in large numbers were officially banned by local authorities. The festival held annually in Phủ Giầy (Nam Định province), the main shrine dedicated to Liễu Hạnh, was officially banned until 1995. Nevertheless, some ritual activities continued secretly and the Four Palaces cult did not disappear. Under conditions of state surveillance and intervention, worshipers therefore redirected their worship to domestic shrines in order to perpetuate the cult outside the public sphere.

Over the past twenty years, the Four Palaces cult has benefited from the liberalization of religious practices. The temple of the Five Mandarins in Hanoi, for example, reopened at the end of the 1980s. Nowadays, spirit possession rituals are carried out on a nearly daily basis during the most active periods of the ritual calendar linked to the celebrations (*tiệc*) of popular spirits of the pantheon. Small groups of about ten or twelve worshipers are regularly led by Mr Hải on pilgrimages during the annual festivals organized in the main temples of northern Vietnam dedicated to important figures.

Mr Hải has seen an increasing number of spirit mediums and disciples coming to the temple of the Five Mandarins over the past two decades. These new mediums and worshipers have influenced ritual practices and created new ritual rules and styles since each medium tries to develop their own creativity and style in order to be recognized by their peers. This sometimes leads to discussions and even conflicts between older and younger generations of mediums about the rituals' rules, the legends of the spirits, and so on.

Even if the ritual activities performed in the temples of the Five Mandarins are common knowledge in the area, strategies of secrecy remain employed. During rituals the temple gate may be closed and a bamboo screen opened up in order to prevent neighbors' curiosity. At the city scale, even if worship became more visible in the public sphere, discretion remains the rule in some circumstances. In some places of worship which are generally open to the public, the doors may be closed and visitors may be checked when rituals are performed. Those who want to attend a ritual must be known by the medium, or at least recommended by him. Musicians are sometimes asked to arrive in the temple discretely and to hide their instruments.

Significantly, official discourse concerning the Four Palaces has changed over the past ten years or so. The cult is now no longer considered to be a "superstition" but is rather seen as a national tradition which deserves to be preserved. Its reconceptualization as "Mother Religion" is indicative of the cult's new image in official discourse. Although some still point to some of its "negative sides," scholarly articles and books generally present the Four Palaces cult as a national tradition that must be preserved as part of the nation's heritage (e.g., Ngô Đức Thịnh 2004). In the following section, I turn to the question of what impacts these historical trends and changes have had on the spirits' representation.

Princes, Princesses, and Revolutionary Heroes

Even if our knowledge of the Four Palaces cult's history is incomplete, it is possible to look at changes in spirit representations over the past few decades using the available literature and worshipers' remarks. Considering these elements, the transformations that have occurred over the past half century in the ways the spirits are thought of and represented by their disciples become apparent.

Significantly, the disciples intrinsically link the general identity of these spirits to the imperial past. As Rosalind Morris (2000) shows with regard to the mediums established in northern Thailand and their performances involving representations of origins, modernity is definitely inscribed in representations of the past. If we consider Vietnamese worshipers' points of view, it appears that the past — more specifically, Vietnam's precolonial imperial past — lies at the heart of their representations. The legends related by worshipers show that many spirits owe their elevation to supernatural status to their merits in important battles or other major events that took place in the past. Generally, legends about spirits refer to glorious historical events, mainly from the time of the struggle against Chinese invaders, even if not all the legends mention a precise historical period. The reference to the past is extended to Vietnamese mythical references, as some of the male figures of the Water Palace are linked to the mythical foundation of the country and they are considered to be descendants of the Dragon King of Động Đình, father of the mythic founder of the country, Lạc Long Quân.

Images from this past are enacted during spirit possession rituals, such as Mrs Bình's, by dressing in the appropriate ritual costumes and in the songs of the *chầu văn* musicians. The long and colorful ceremonial tunics Mrs Bình wore are in this way inspired by the design of imperial robes and are viewed as the outfits of mandarins, princes, or princesses. Her place in front of the altars may also be seen as a reference to the past: surrounded by four assistants (*hầu dâng*), this is supposed to refer to the practice when emperors received audiences. Furthermore, the architecture of temples is closely related to palace architecture (Lê Văn Hảo 1963; Trần Văn Toàn 1969).

The course of Mrs Bình's performance at the Five Mandarins temple strengthens these references to the past. She is possessed by different spirits according to their hierarchical rank in the general structure of the pantheon, inspired by the imperial regime. Even if there are variations in the spirits' legends and identities from one region to another, and from one worshiper to another and from one period to another, the structure of the pantheon seems to have been quite stable over the past few decades. Its six hierarchical ranks (*hàng*) persist: the Mothers at the top, while in hierarchically descending order are the Five Mandarins (*Quan Lớn*), the Twelve Ladies (*Chầu*), the Ten Imperial Princes (*Ông Hoàng*), the Twelve

Figure 4.2: An altar in Hanoi. Photograph by Claire Chauvet, 2007.

Princesses (*Cô*) and the Small Princes (*Cậu*). In this pantheon, some figures emerge thanks to specific identities that are embedded in different elements, such that their legends are known through invocatory songs, iconography (such as the symbolic color of the Palace and their ceremonial clothes), and through the main temple where they are worshiped and the date of their celebrations.

Worshipers solicit the spirits for different reasons, since they consider that the Four Palaces have numerous and miscellaneous abilities (*phép*), from a general power to improve people's lives to specific powers of answering requests. Invocatory songs recall that the spirits have also saved the people (*cứu dân*) from epidemics and, more generally speaking, they are seen as benevolent and able to solve any problems. Worshipers ask the spirits to maintain the means of existence (health, work, studies, and marriage in general). Nevertheless, the spirits are also potentially malevolent since they send illness and misfortune to potential mediums—people who have a *căn* or *đồng*[8]—in order to force them to recognize that they have to worship and serve them.

Besides being figures from the imperial era, spirits are now also considered to be heroes (*anh hùng*) who saved the country from Chinese invaders.[9] Interestingly, the vocabulary used by cult followers is the same as the state's revolutionary one: the spirits are said to have sacrificed (*hy sinh*) themselves during their life on earth to protect the country and the people. Worshipers reinforce this idea by drawing comparisons between the spirits of the Four Palaces and Hồ Chí Minh and other revolutionary and contemporary heroes. Although worshipers' comparisons are taken from the contemporary period, the worship of heroes has a long history in Vietnam (Huê-Tâm Hô Tâi 2001; Tréglodé 2001; Malarney 2002, 2007). Mythical and historical characters, who worked and battled for the preservation and glory of the state, as Confucian ethics required, have been honored as national heroes since precolonial times.

Despite Vietnam's long history of hero worship, the literature available in the first part of the twentieth century never listed the spirits of the Four Palaces in the ritual category of heroes. Before the communist revolution, the literature clearly distinguished two forms of worship: the cult dedicated to the "Saint Mothers" and, more generally, to the spirits of the Four Palaces; and the cult dedicated to "heroes," such as General Trần Hưng Đạo (a national hero who defeated the Chinese in the thirteenth century) or other military men and women who distinguished themselves during armed struggles against Chinese invaders (Lê Văn Hảo 1963). This distinction was based on gender differences between ritual specialists (male for the cult of heroes and female for the Mothers), differences in ritual performance (such as elements of self-mortification in the male cult), and also in spirit representations.

These scholars may have underestimated existing links between male and female rituals. Nowadays, as Phạm Quỳnh Phương (2009) has noted, a strict distinction between the Mothers' cult and the cult of Trần Hưng Đạo is no longer upheld, and the cult of Trần Hưng Đạo has largely merged with the Four Palaces cult. It is as yet difficult to conclude that transformations of ritual practices are effects of recent social and historical trends within the country. Nevertheless, this trend may be connected to contemporary political issues. Unlike the Four Palaces cult, the Trần Hưng Đạo cult has had a high status for centuries, and is thus able to confer greater legitimacy on female spirit possession. This is reinforced by the fact that from the 1950s onwards the government, while banning some religious practices, also established a cult dedicated to the veneration of soldiers and revolutionary heroes who sacrificed themselves in the defense of national freedom and independence. Today, worshipers conceive of the spirits of the "feudal era" as warriors who sacrificed themselves for the nation, thus inscribing their worship in a more politically correct way. As such, they provide a legitimization of their contemporary practices.

Prosperity Spirits

Even if Mrs Bình's ritual was performed in the third lunar month, to honor the Third Mandarin, disciples linger in order to offer numerous gifts to other popular spirits. They address the spirits regarding their abilities. The Third Princess (*Cô Bơ*), dressed in white, and the Ninth Princess (*Cô Chín*), in pink, are believed, for example, to have healing abilities. One of the reasons for this is to be found in the fact that the starting point of a medium's career is often illness, and the belief that possession rituals may cure this illness. Earlier approaches predominantly focused on the healing abilities of the spirits (Durand 1959; Condominas 1976; Heinze 1988), while neglecting their other abilities. But the scope of the spirits' abilities is in fact much larger. Among the abilities of spirits most commonly solicited by worshipers is their ability to ensure success in business and gambling.

My own observations and recent literature (Norton 2009) show that two popular spirits are dedicated to protecting businesses, the Tenth Prince (*Ông Hoàng Mười*) for retailers and the Little Princess (*Cô Bé*) for wholesalers,[10] while the Seventh Prince (*Ông Hoàng Bảy*) is popular for his ability to confer good luck in gambling. While the colonial literature mentioned their popularity, neither the authors nor invocatory songs report these abilities. The invocatory songs emphasize only the classical aspects of the spirits' identities. The Tenth Prince is shown as a strategic talent, raising his sword and fighting against the enemy. The Little Lady's song mentions the beauty and the elegance of this spirit, who wears a blue scarf on her head, a green shirt, and walks on the clouds and moves with the wind. We must turn toward the remarks of mediums and worshipers and discuss some sequences of the possession ritual to understand how the spirits of the Four Palaces are closely associated with prosperity and business.

One of the longest and most important ritual sequences of Mrs Bình's ritual, as for many other mediums, is the redistribution of offerings, called *phát lộc*. Presented on altars or to the spirits through the possessed medium, offerings are converted into blessed gifts (*lộc*). So, one of the principal aims of these rituals is to implore generosity (*xin lộc*), which means to exchange goods for advice and to show the generosity of the spirits. Even if not all of the spirits distribute goods, their liberality contributes toward their popularity, and the spirits associated with business and prosperity are known to be generous and to redistribute large amounts of offerings. Disciples address pressing requests to the spirits, as the vocabulary shows. They beg (*xin*) and they pray (*cầu*) to the spirits while they present offerings to the mediums, telling them their names and how many people bought the goods. Most of the time the requests are uttered in a stereotyped form, asking for blessed gifts (*xin lộc*), for talent (*xin tài*), for health. If the request is fulfilled, the worshipers' obligations are increased. They have to perform a thanksgiving ritual (*lễ tạ*), which is a luxurious presentation of offerings.

The redistribution of offerings follows a precise order. Mrs Bình begins with her assistants and the musicians, continues with important people in the social network of the medium who bring a lot of offerings, and finishes with the other guests. Nobody wants to be excluded from the spirits' generosity. So some of the disciples check the amount of the goods, and others, in a friendly atmosphere, gently quarrel during the redistributions since possession rituals are a kind of transaction between worshipers and spirits. Sometimes worshipers try to negotiate with the spirits according to their own generosity. The more they offer to the spirits, the more generous the latter are expected to be in return. When worshipers present offerings directly to the spirits—embodied in the mediums—the spirits estimate the quality and quantity of the goods placed on a tray. Depending on the attitude of the worshipers, the spirits will be more or less generous.

The sequence of the redistribution of offerings was noted by Maurice Durand (1959: 14) at the beginning of the twentieth century. But it appears that nowadays the offerings are increasing in number, thus emphasizing the ostentatious nature of *hầu bóng* rituals. The efficacy of these rituals and the spirits partly lies in these exchanges. After *hầu bóng* rituals, people go back home with a plastic bag full of blessed gifts (*túi lộc*) which are supposed to protect people and be good omens.

A second element which establishes specific connections between the spirits of the Four Palaces and prosperity and business is that many storekeepers engage in the Four Palaces cult with the intention of controlling the risky elements of their activity. One of the most salient facts concerning followers of the Four Palaces is that, nowadays as in the past (Dror 2007), most of them are traders: door to door vendors, shopkeepers, manufacturers, and so forth. Even if it is well known that traders generally invest a lot in religious activities (Malarney 2002: 243), their influence on this cult may be without parallel in other Vietnamese religious practices. This trend is reinforced in the case of the temple of the Five Mandarins by the fact that most regular worshipers are traders.

The Four Palaces cult and business have several elements in common, such as the fundamental importance of the exchange of goods and promises, and of negotiations in long-lasting relationships between partners. These elements are one reason for the over-representation of traders among the worshipers. The fact that certain spirits are considered particularly benevolent toward business may be regarded as a reaction to commercial liberalization and the tolerance, and even encouragement, shown toward personal enrichment, which after decades of hardship is no longer banned (ibid.).

In the Four Palaces cult, as in other Southeast Asian spirit possession cults, particularly those in Thailand (see Kitiarsa 2005, 2008), mediums and spirits are in a close relationship with prosperity and the market economy. Nevertheless, on this point, spirit possession in Vietnam differs from contemporary spirit possession in Malaysian factories. According to Aihwa Ong's analysis, spirit possession in Malaysia may be seen as being in clear opposition to the capitalist industrialization process (Ong 1987). In northern Vietnam, however, spirit possession in the Four Palaces cult does not challenge the process of change, but rather adapts to new local social and economic conditions. Changes in spirit representations help in giving a new sense to this worship rooted in the past but adapted to the preoccupations of each historical period.

Urban Mediums and the Expression of Modernity

Mr Hải and his disciples regularly leave Hanoi to go on pilgrimage to the main temples of the spirits (*đền thờ chính*), located in different parts of northern and central Vietnam. Early in the morning, a dozen worshipers meet in the temple and leave on a trip of one or two days, sometimes longer. Traveling by minibus, private car, or even by train, they make their way toward popular shrines during festivals which are organized annually in order to celebrate the spirits in their home temple—that is, in the historical location of their legend. Worshipers go to display offerings (food, flowers, and money) in front of the altars, and sometimes also to perform spirit possession rituals. Each year, Mr Hải and some of his disciples regularly go to the main temples dedicated to the spirits of the Four Palaces, following the festival calendar.

During these trips they join the crowd of pilgrims from all over the northern part of the country, as well as from farther afield. The festivals are a rare occasion for different kinds of worshipers, specifically urban and rural worshipers, to meet. However, even though they gather at the same shrines, honoring the same spirits, performing the same kinds of rituals, they do not really communicate.

The pilgrimages undertaken by Mr Hải and his fellow worshipers reveal that as a group they want to arrange practical details of their trips themselves, and to be on their own to perform rituals. They prefer not to rely on the services provided by the temples they visit during their trips but to purchase and prepare offerings and food in Hanoi and bring them along with them. When the rules of a temple allow it, the mediums hire the regular musicians of the temple of the Five Mandarins to come along with them as well. As a result they are sometimes in competition with other groups of worshipers, trying to reach the altars to present their offerings, trying to occupy ritual space in order to start their own performance, or trying to find places to eat or sleep near the shrines.

Festivals are events where oppositions between different categories of worshipers are expressed and sometimes strengthened. The main distinction drawn is that between urban and rural worshipers. For Mr Hải's disciples, as for many urban worshipers, rural rituals appear to be poor, with cheap-looking ceremonial clothes and meager offerings, shrines—except important ones—sometimes poorly furnished, food which may taste good but is not regarded as clean, and facilities (such as bathrooms and kitchens) that are basic and dirty. Indeed, rural practices are considered to be "backwards" by urban worshipers.

In spite of these oppositions, urban spirit possession is often considered to be the leading practice, the standard to achieve. The fact that urban spirit mediums, such as Mrs Bình, use modernity's attributes—high-tech cellphones, motorbikes, and very fashionable and expensive dresses—in their rituals is taken into consideration by the worshipers. "Modernity" also means wealth, which is revealed notably through modern means of transport and communication: railways, roads, cars, and cellphones. These means of transportation and communication enable urban disciples to make shorter pilgrimages, thus increasing the number of pilgrimages they are able to accomplish every month.

In the same way, the mediums' performances are regularly recorded on audio and video tape, and nowadays on DVD. As some mediums say they cannot remember their performance since the spirits took control of their body, these recordings are for them a kind of proof and a recollection of their performance. Even if mediums prefer distributing recordings to friends and relatives, many of these recordings are sold during festivals. These recordings are then another means of diffusing and promoting urban standards of spirit possession throughout the country. Urban mediums thus express their modernity through the circulation of persons, goods, and ideas, echoing Appadurai's definition of modernity: "This mobile and unforeseeable relationship between mass-mediated events and migratory audiences defines the core of the link between globalization and the modern" (Appadurai 1996: 4).

Conclusion

Based on a comparison of depictions of spirit possession rituals in older literature and my own observation of these events, this chapter aimed at showing some of the transformations of representations of spirits of the Four Palaces that have occurred over the last few decades. Within a relatively stable and structured pantheon and ritual framework stretching back over a century, representations of Four Palaces' spirits have experienced different and deep transformations. From an identity rooted in the past of the imperial regime, they are now also seen as national heroes and spirits of prosperity.

This illustrates the creativity of spirit possession and the malleability of spirit representations that has been observed elsewhere in Asia (Tarabout 1992; Kendall

1996). Far from disappearing with modernization and social change, Vietnamese spirit mediums give sense to contemporary upheavals of social and historical change. These transformations in ritual practice and spirit representations are likely to bring up to date this long tradition and attract new worshipers.

Notes

1. This name refers to a large pantheon of about sixty spirits that belong to four domains or "palaces": Heaven (represented as red), Mountains and Forests (green), Water (white) and Earth (yellow). The Four Palaces cult is also known as *Đạo Mẫu* or the "Mother Goddess religion."
2. This spirit is a scholar mandarin. His main shrine is located in Lảnh Giang (Hà Nam province) and his annual festival is on the twenty-sixth of the sixth lunar month.
3. The full expression is *con hương đệ tử* or *con nhang đệ tử*, which broadly means "incense child." This term refers to anyone who actively worships the spirits: spirit mediums, other rituals specialists, musicians, and worshipers.
4. In this chapter I use the term "spirit possession" according to the definitions provided by Luc de Heusch (1971) and Gilbert Rouget (1980), and in opposition to shamanism. The distinction between the two phenomena lies in the difference between the upward movement of immaterial components of the shaman into the spirits' world and the downward movement of spirits into the body of the medium. From the medium's point of view, the spirits enter (*nhập*) their body and act or talk by this means. According to this ritual logic, many mediums—though not all of them—say they cannot remember what happened during the time they embody the spirits.
5. Fieldwork in Hanoi was conducted between 1999 and 2002, and again in June 2007 and November 2009.
6. The Four Palaces spirits may be worshiped in different places: local temples, private shrines, and even sometimes Buddhist temples.
7. For instance, a recent decree of the Ministry of Culture (75/2010/NĐ-CP, issued 7 July 2010) bans mediumship (such as *lên đồng* performances) along with divination from cultural events or festivals.
8. This expression is generally translated as "spirit root" and is the mediums' special potential of being possessed by the spirits, which is usually discovered through divination and other signs such as illness. People have this potential from birth, but they need to understand the spirits' call and then go through the requisite initiation rituals.
9. Chinese domination lasted about a millennium, from 111 BC to AD 939, and was briefly restored in later periods.
10. The Prince, belonging to the Earth Palace, is a military mandarin, born in Nghệ An, where the main temples dedicated to him are based. He is famous for his therapeutic power, but also for his abilities to promote business. The Princess is an ethnic spirit, a native of Bắc Lệ (Lạng Sơn province). She belongs to the Mountains and Forests Palace.

References

Appadurai, Arjun. 1996. *Modernity at Large.* Minneapolis: University of Minnesota Press.

Bertrand, Didier. 1996. "Renaissance du lên đồng à Hue (Việt Nam): Premiers éléments d'une recherche." *Bulletin de l'Ecole Française d'Extrême Orient* 83: 271–85.

Brac de la Perrière, Bénédicte. 1989. *Les rituels de possession en Birmanie: du culte d'Etat aux cérémonies privées.* Paris: Éditions Recherches sur les Civilisations.

Chauvet, Claire. 2005. "Une femme médium d'esprits de Hà Noi: un destin pas comme les autres," in *Vietnam au Féminin*, eds G. Bousquet and N. Taylor. Paris: Les Indes Savantes, pp.253–65.

———. Forthcoming (2011). *Sous le voile rouge: rituels de possession et réseaux cultuels à Hà Nội (Việt Nam)*. Paris: Les Indes Savantes.

Condominas, Georges, ed. 1973. "Chamanisme et possession en Asie du Sud-Est et dans le Monde Insulindien," *Bulletin du Centre de documentation et de recherche sur l'Asie du Sud-Est et le Monde Insulindien* 4(1).

———. 1976. "Quelques aspects du chamanisme et des cultes de possession en Asie du Sud-Est et dans le Monde Insulindien," in *L'autre et l'ailleurs: hommage à Roger Bastide*, eds J. Poirier and F. Raveau. Paris: Berger-Levrault, pp.215–32.

Coulet, Georges. 1929. *Cultes et religions de l'Indochine annamite*. Saigon: Imprimerie Commerciale.

Diguet, Émile. 1906. *Les Annamites: société, coutumes, religions*. Paris: Augustins Challamel Editeur.

Dorais, Jean-Louis, and Nguyễn Huy. 1998. "Le thờ Mẫu, un chamanisme vietnamien?" *Anthropologie et Sociétés* 22(2): 183–209.

Dror, Olga. 2007. *Cult, Culture and Authority: Princess Lieu Hanh in Vietnamese History*. Honolulu: University of Hawaii Press.

Dumoutier, Gustave. 1899. *Études d'ethnographie religieuse annamite: sorcellerie et divination*. Paris: Imprimerie Nationale.

Durand, Maurice. 1959. *Techniques et panthéon des médiums vietnamiens (đông)*. Paris: École Française d'Etrême Orient.

Endres, Kirsten. 2001. "Local Dynamics of Renegotiating Ritual Space in Northern Vietnam: The Case of the Dinh," *Sojourn* 16(1): 70–101.

———. 2006. "Spirit Performance and the Ritual Construction of Personal Identity in Modern Vietnam," in *Possessed by the Spirits: Mediumship in Contemporary Vietnamese Communities*, eds K. Fjelstad and T.H. Nguyễn. Ithaca, NY: Cornell University Southeast Asia Program, pp.77–94.

———. 2007. "Spirited Modernities: Mediumship and Ritual Performativity in Late Socialist Vietnam," in *Modernity and Re-enchantment: Religion in Post-revolutionary Vietnam*, ed. P. Taylor. Singapore: Institute of Southeast Asian Studies, pp.194–220.

Fjelstad, Karen. 1995. "Tứ Phủ Công đồng: Vietnamese Women and Spirit Possession in the San Fransisco Bay Area," Ph.D. dissertation. Honolulu: University of Hawaii.

Fjelstad, Karen, and Nguyễn Thị Hiền, ed. 2006. *Possessed by the Spirits: Mediumship in Contemporary Vietnamese Communities*. Ithaca, NY: Cornell University Southeast Asia Program.

Giran, Paul. 1912. *Magie et religion annamite*. Paris: Augustin Challamel.

Hamayon, Roberte. 2000. "Avant-propos," in *La politique des esprits: chamanisme et religions universalistes*, eds D. Aigle and B. Brac de la Perrière. Nanterre: Société d'ethnologie.

Heinze, Ruth-Inge. 1988. *Trance and Healing in Southeast Asia Today*. Bangkok: White Lotus.

Heusch, Luc de. 1971. *Pourquoi l'épouser? Et autres essais*. Paris: Gallimard.

Huệ-Tâm Hồ Tài, ed. 2001. *The Country of Memory: Remaking the Past in Late Socialist Vietnam*. Berkeley: University of California Press.

Hy Văn Lương. 1993. "Economic Reforms and the Intensification of Rituals in Two North Vietnamese Villages, 1980–90," in *The Challenge of Reform in Indochina*, ed. B. Ljunggren. Cambridge: Harvard University Press, pp.259–91.

———. ed. 2003. *Postwar Vietnam: Dynamics of a Transforming Society*. Singapore: ISEAS.

Kendall, Laurel. 1996. "Korean Shamans and the Spirits of Capitalism," *American Anthropologist* 98(3): 512–27.

Kitiarsa, Pattana. 2005. "Magic Monks and Spirit Mediums in the Politics of Thai Popular Religion," *Inter-Asia Cultural Studies* 6(2): 209–26.

———. ed. 2008. *Religious Commodifications in Asia: Marketing Gods*. London and New York: Routledge.

Kleinen, John. 1999. *Facing the Future, Reviving the Past*. Singapore: Institute of Southeast Asian Studies.

Lãn Ông. 1972. *Thuong kinh ky-su (Relation d'un voyage à la capitale)*. Paris: École Française d'Etrême Orient.

Lê Văn Hảo. 1963. "Introduction à l"ethnologie du den et du chùa," *Revue du Sud-Est Asiatique* 2: 79–114.

Malarney, Shaun K. 1996. "The Limits of 'State Functionalism' and the Reconstruction of Funerary Ritual in Contemporary Northern Vietnam," *American Ethnologist* 23(3): 540–60.

———. 2002. *Culture, Ritual and Revolution in Vietnam*. Honolulu: University of Hawaii Press.

———. 2007. "Festivals and the Dynamics of the Exceptional Dead in Northern Vietnam," *Journal of Southeast Asian Studies* 38(3): 515–40.

Morris, Rosalind. 2000. *In the Place of Origins: Modernity and its Mediums in Northern Thailand*. Durham, NC: Duke University Press.

Nghiêm Thẩm. 1965. *Esquisse d'une théorie sur les interdits chez les Viêtnamiens*. Saigon: Ministère de la culture et de l'éducation.

Ngô Đức Thịnh, ed. 2004. *Đạo mẫu và các hình thức shaman trong các tộc người ở Việt Nam và Châu Á*. Hanoi: Nhà xuât bản khoa học xã hội.

Nguyễn Thế Anh. 1991. "Thien-Y-A-Na, ou la récupération de la déesse Cam Pô Nagar par la monarchie confucéenne vietnamienne," in *Cultes populaires et sociétés asiatiques: appareils culturels et appareils de pouvoir*, ed. A. For est. Paris: L'Harmattan, pp.73–86.

Nguyễn Thị Hiền. 2006. "'A Bit of a Spirit is Equal to a Load of Mundane Gifts': Votive Paper Offerings of *Len Dong* Rituals in Post-renovation Vietnam," in *Possessed by the Spirits: Mediumship in Contemporary Vietnamese Communities*, eds K. Fjelstad and T.H. Nguyễn. Ithaca, NY: Cornell University Southeast Asia Program, pp.127–43.

———. 2007. "'Seats for Spirits to Sit Upon': Becoming a Spirit Medium in Contemporary Vietnam," *Journal of Southeast Asian Studies* 38(3): 541–58.

Nguyễn Văn Huyên. 1944. *Le culte des immortels au Viêt Nam*. Hanoi: Imprimerie d'Extrême Orient.

Norton, Barley. 2000. "Vietnamese Mediumship Rituals: The Musical Construction of the Spirits," *World of Music* 42(2): 75–97.

———. 2003. "'The Moon Remembers Uncle Ho': The Politics of Music and Mediumship in Northern Vietnam," *British Journal of Ethnomusicology* 11(1): 71–100.

———. 2009. *Songs for the Spirits: Music and Mediums in Modern Vietnam*. Chicago: University of Chicago Press.

Ong, Aihwa. 1987. *Spirits of Resistance and Capitalist Discipline: Factory Women in Malaysia*. Albany: State University of New York Press.

Phạm Quỳnh Phương. 2006. "Tran Hung Dao and the Mother Goddess Religion," in *Possessed by the Spirits: Mediumship in Contemporary Vietnamese Communities*, eds K. Fjelstad and T.H. Nguyễn. Ithaca, NY: Cornell University Southeast Asia Program, pp.32–76.

———. 2009. *Hero and Deity: Tran Hung Dao and the Resurgence of Popular Religion in Vietnam*. Chiang Mai: Mekong Press.

Rouget, Gilbert. 1980. *La musique et la transe: esquisse d'une théorie générale des relations de la musique et de la possession*. Paris: Gallimard.

Sélim, Monique. 2000. "Génies, communisme et marché dans le Laos contemporain," in *La politique des esprits: chamanisme et religions universalistes*, eds D. Aigle and B. Brac de la Perrière. Nanterre: Société d'ethnologie, pp.105–24.

Simon, Pierre-Jean, and Ida Simon-Barouh. 1973. *Hàu bóng: une culte de possession transplanté en France.* Paris: Mouton.

Tarabout, Gilles. 1992. "Quand les dieux s'emmêlent: point de vue sur les classifications divines au Kerala," *Purusartha* 15: 43–74.

Taylor, Philip, ed. 2007. *Modernity and Re-enchantment: Religion in Post-revolutionary Vietnam.* Singapore: Institute of Southeast Asian Studies.

Trần Văn Toàn. 1969. "Le temple Hue-Nam à Hué (étude précédée d'une note sur la sainte religion de l'immortelle céleste dans la région de Hué)," *Bulletin de la Société des Etudes Indochinoises* 3/4: 243–81.

Tréglodé, Benoit de. 2001. *Héros et révolution au Viêt Nam (1948–1964).* Paris: L'Harmattan.

Vũ Ngọc Khánh. 2000. *Đền Miếu Việt Nam.* Hanoi: Nhà Xuât Bản Thanh Niên.

5

GODS, GIFTS, MARKETS, AND SUPERSTITION: SPIRITED CONSUMPTION FROM KOREA TO VIETNAM

Laurel Kendall

The trajectory for this paper might begin in a Korean shaman's shrine in 1991 when a greedy god, enticed by my offering of Chivas Regal, threatened to become intoxicated on the whiskey and derail the entire ritual. He also ordered me to provide his shaman with a bottle of Chivas whenever I visit Korea, an obligation that I have since honored such that the Chivas bottle in the shrine has become a personal symbol of my longstanding relationship with this particular shaman and her patron deity (Kendall 2008, 2009: 162–66). Or it might begin even earlier, in the summer of 1977, when this same shaman told me how she had learned in a dream that Grandmother Buddhist Sage and the Mountain God would favor me if I dedicated a water vessel and an incense pot to her shrine. Taking this request as a sign of my deepening relationship with a key informant—as well as her gods—I accompanied her to a shaman supply shop in Seoul where we purchased these items and had them inscribed with my Korean name and the phrase, "please grant the wish of." They still sit in her shrine, a little retro looking since the stainless steel that was ubiquitous in the 1970s has otherwise been replaced with porcelain and more self-consciously retro brass (Kendall 1985).

Fast forward to spring 2010 in Hanoi.[1] I had joined a team of researchers from the Women's Museum of Vietnam to prepare an exhibit on the Mother Goddess religion, a subject that has engaged my interest over the last ten years. *Lên đồng*, the central ritual, involves performances by mediums that manifest representatives of the pantheon—mandarins, dames, princes, princesses, and pages[2]—by donning a sequence of spectacular costumes, much as shamans do in Korea. *Lên đồng* are artful and highly photogenic rituals involving music and dance against a

---

Endnotes for this chapter begin on page 117

temple backdrop that has been enhanced by exquisitely arranged stacks of offerings and bunches of flowers. Even simple offerings of cash and areca nuts, ceremonially presented on trays, are arranged with care and artistry. Devotees pray to receive the favor or *lộc* of the Mother Goddess which comes back to them in the tangible form of offerings accepted and dispersed by the deity or as fistfuls of cash, in small denominations, that a smiling medium flings into their midst. All of this largess, carried home from the *lên đồng* in a plastic bag, has been transformed by ritual contact into vehicles of disbursed auspiciousness and is consequently also called *lộc*.

Before the team and I make our first visit to a temple together, I have a question for one of my hosts. Madame T. is an unabashed devotee of the goddess, although not herself a medium. I tell her that I ought to "give something to the Third Princess (*Cô Bơ*)," a goddess from the realm of water, and wondering what would be appropriate. I explain how, on a visit to California the previous year, my friend Karen Fjelstad[3] had given me a bottle of water when I left for the airport. "It's the Third Princess's water," she said, something she had received as *lộc* from the Princess at a recent Silicon Valley *lên đồng*. At the Monterey Airport, my backpack was already making its way through the X-ray machine when I remembered that I had forgotten to remove the water bottle—but happily and most mysteriously, the Princess's water never registered on the inspection screen. "She's a traveler herself, she helps travelers," Karen said when I told her.

At this point in my retelling, Madame T.'s eyes are wide with wonder. "It gets even better," I say. Just before Christmas I was returning home from Edinburgh when I missed a connection in London and found myself amid multitudes of stranded travelers, all of us in various stages of meltdown, in the purgatory of Heathrow Airport. "Third Princess," I said, "if you really do help travelers, get me back to New York in time for Christmas and I will give you a present when I go to Vietnam." I received the last stand-by ticket on the first flight out the next morning, and once aboard the aircraft was asked if I wouldn't mind changing seats with a fellow passenger who wanted to sit next to her husband. I agreed and happily ascended to business class, thanking the Third Princess as I stretched out my legs in these relatively commodious accommodations. "Give the Third Princess some Perrier water," Karen had suggested when I told her this story, "She likes luxury."

Madame T. agrees that of course I ought to give something to the Third Princess, but it has to be the right thing. Taking the charge seriously she places a call on her cellphone to a friend who is a meticulous and elegant spirit medium. I learn that a fan would be appropriate but a nice big vase with artificial flowers in it would be even better, white flowers, the color of the water realm. I am dispatched in the museum's car with a member of the research team whose mother, aunt, and mother-in-law are all spirit mediums and who knows what I should buy. We go to a street with several ceramic venders and artificial flower shops where my designated advisor helps me select a pair of vases, the sort that are set on ancestral altars. He makes the tactful suggestion that a pair of the large ones would be "better" and carefully inspects each possible vase, rejecting candidates that have paint smudges, incipient cracks, or rough edges. In the shop next door, I purchase two enormous bouquets of white silk lotus flowers which the vender skillfully installs in the vases, then covers everything with cellophane for the trip to the temple the next day. It all costs a great deal more than the suggested Perrier water, about US$60, probably on the assumption that for an American who can afford an impressive purchase, it would be shabby to spend less.

I have told this tale at some length because it suggests the ease with which at least some of my Korean understandings translate into a Vietnamese popular religious logic. The gods' favor is acknowledged in the form of tangible gifts, which become signs of tangible relationships—of different intensity and duration—between human and spirit. The flip side of this equation was also true, in Vietnam no less than in Korea or China: this same religious materiality is the most abundantly criticized aspect of popular religion. In modern thinking, there should be no causal relationship between immaterial forces and material acts; offerings are at best "symbolic" and to see them as productive of positive or negative outcomes is "superstition." I had thought that I knew the intellectual history of the term "superstition" and how it was being deployed in modern East Asian contexts. "Superstition" comes to us from early Christianity as an indication of false or heterodox religious practice; in the Enlightenment, it took on its modern gloss as bad science, a mistaken understanding of the material world (O'Neil 1987; Pietz 1987; Tambiah 1990; Latour 1993). Its Chinese (*mixin*), Japanese (*meishin*), Korean (*mishin*), and Vietnamese (*mê tín*) translation preserves this implication with paired ideographs signifying "bewitched" or "deluded" (*mê)* "beliefs" (*tín*) and anti-superstition campaigns have been carried out in all of these places by modernizing regimes from across the political spectrum. But time spent in Vietnam has also challenged what I thought I knew about the word "superstition" while simultaneously deepening my awareness of the braided economic and religious significance of sacred goods in Asian material markets.

This chapter explores the burgeoning market in the production and consumption of sacred goods—particularly those used by devotees of the Mother Goddess religion—in the Red River Delta of Vietnam. It also explores how those who produce, buy, sell, and ritually deploy sacred goods negotiate the concept of "superstition" as part of the lexicon of modernity and socialism that they have been living with and speaking for a long time (Marr 1981; Malarney 2002: 80–84, 105–7; Pelley 2002: 228–29). I will argue that while "superstition" is part of the common language of Vietnamese modernity, spirit mediums and devotees deploy it in a manner compatible with their own moral understandings and devotional practices that are inextricable from religious materiality. I begin by addressing the initiating question of this project: What does it mean to believe in spirits in a modern Asian setting? I am particularly concerned with how the construction of spirits is at play within and against modernity and the material world, how in fact the popularity of spirits and the materiality of devotional practices have forced the redefinition of "superstition" among devotees in contemporary Vietnam.

Material Religion

Taken together, my three anecdotes illustrate some fundamental premises about the spirit world as Korean, Vietnamese (and Chinese) devotees might see it. Spirits ("gods" and "ancestors" in an East Asian context)[4] are local rather than transcendent, more like Catholic saints to whom one can appeal in the face of intimate, familial, or communal afflictions, than the Christian God who would encourage us to bear our misfortunes as part of a grand plan.[5] The gods of East Asian popular religion are amenable to relationships with human beings; indeed they expect it, and humans establish, cultivate, and maintain these ties as a means of averting affliction and acquiring blessing. By honoring prior promises and obligations, devotees also try to circumvent divine anger and retribution, which can be experienced as illness, domestic problems, business set-backs, trouble with the authorities, and other difficulties whose sources may be as immediate as a child's credit card debt or as distant as the decrees of the IMF.

A relationship with a deity is necessarily unequal; the devotee seeks a beneficent deployment of the god's power and, as in relationships with influential human beings, curries favor with gifts and other tribute. Sometimes the gift may be an expression of gratitude (my gift of silk flowers in vases) or a response to a command (the incense bowl and water vessel and most of the other accoutrements in a Korean shaman's shrine). Devotees also make offerings as generalized reciprocity, enjoying the god's favor and providing seasonal or periodic offerings (the Chivas Regal I bring each time I visit Korea, the temple offerings that Vietnamese make early in the year with a request and at the end of the year in gratitude, the visits of Korean women to shamans' shrines on the seventh day of the seventh lunar month and early in the new year). Both the *kut* that Korean shamans perform and the *lên đồng* that Vietnamese spirit mediums perform can be construed as meta-offerings including food, drink, music, and entertainment enjoyed by gods who appear in colorful antique-cut garments that have been dedicated to their use.

In these instances, popular religion becomes material religion. Indeed it would be difficult to imagine popular religion in the absence of decorated temples and the prospect of gifting vases of silk flowers to the Third Princess. Popular religion intersects with the market not only because the market breeds the aspirations and anxieties that prompt prayers and offerings (Kendall 1996, 2008, 2009: 129–53) but as the source of religious accoutrements that are used to effect invocations and petitions to the divine. In this part of the world, the market has provided this service for a very long time. Gernet's monumental study of the economic consequences of Chinese Buddhist practice from the fifth to the tenth century (Gernet 1995[1956]) includes mention of temple markets for offering food and other votive goods and the significant employment of artisans who produced objects used in worship or as temple decoration. Art historical evidence suggests that by the sixth century, stone carvers in China were turning out ready-made Buddha images in standardized forms (Swergold et al. 2008). The oldest known votive paper coins were found in a seventh-century Tang Dynasty tomb (Cave 1998), and the still vigorous tradition of making votive paper replicas of houses, goods, and servants can be traced to the Northern Song (AD 906–1125) when they replaced more expensive ceramic versions (Laing and Liu 2004). According to legend, votive papermaking reached Vietnam in the thirteenth century (Nguyễn Thị Hiền 2006).

Contemporary markets in religious paraphernalia are booming in East and Southeast Asia and are sometimes global in their reach. Karen Fjelstad (2010: 61f.) describes Vietnamese spirit mediums in Silicon Valley, California, who upgrade their temples with materials produced in Vietnam. Vineeta Sinha's work on the market in Hindu sacred goods in Singapore (Sinha 2008) and Janet Lee Scott's study of votive paper in Hong Kong (Scott 2007) also suggest that distribution networks for sacred goods can be complex, even global in scope. A visit to any shaman supply shop (*manmulsang*) in South Korea will reveal how completely this market has been saturated with Chinese-made goods (Petersen 2008). Producers of votive paper in the Red River Delta of Vietnam described how some of their wares were being shipped to China.

The recognition that omnipresent spirits—sometimes manifest in shamans and spirit mediums—have appetites and desires carries the likelihood that, like their devotees, they respond to changing horizons of material consumption, fashion, and taste. The Chivas Regal desired by a Spirit Warrior in a South Korean shaman's shrine is a case in point, and I have described how the changing tastes and expectations of Korean gods and ancestors highlight new possibilities for material consumption in contemporary South Korean life (Kendall 2008, 2009: 154–76). But this phenomenon is by no means restricted to Korea. For more than a decade I have collected for the American Museum of Natural History a selection of paper goods intended to be burned and thereby transmitted to the ancestors. These objects – purchased in Vietnam, Malaysia, and New York's Chinatown – witness how ancestors have gained access to cellphones, electric rice cookers, VISA cards, and private automobiles.

In Vietnam, the "renovation" (*đổi mới*) of 1986 heralded a new era of market economics. Relative tolerance of many previously prohibited practices enabled the revival, elaboration, and continuous improvisation of popular religion. The refurbishment of temples, shrines, and sacred sites, and the return to visibility of all manner of ritual life, could be discerned in the 1990s and has become a marked feature of Vietnamese life in the new millennium (Malarney 2002, 2003; Taylor 2004, 2007a; Fjelstad and Nguyễn Thị Hiền 2006a; DiGregorio and Salemink

2007; Lê Hồng Lý 2007). Along with these developments, there appeared a fluid and generally expansive market in sacred goods and related services financed by new wealth (Nguyễn Thị Hiền 2006; Lê Hồng Lý 2007; Nguyên Văn Huy and Phạm Lan Hương 2008; Salemink 2008; Endres 2010). The production of goods for specifically ritual purposes—from altar tables to statues to spirit medium costumes to elaborate votive paper offerings—testifies to an enthusiastic linkage between things material and spiritual in contemporary Vietnamese popular religious life. Most artisans who produce goods used in the Mother Goddess religion are devotees themselves, and many have become spirit mediums in acknowledgement that their enterprise flourishes under the Mother's favor. I have met statue carvers, votive paper-makers, and costume-makers who all double as spirit mediums with their own personal temples. With other new mediums, they feed the market by commissioning statues for their private temples, and costumes and votive paper sculptures for their rituals (Nguyễn Thị Hiền 2006; Kendall et al. 2008, 2010).

At the same time, much of the writing on contemporary religious life in Victnam describes a continuing tension between popular devotion and an official ideology that explicitly denies the existence of gods and ghosts, much less the possibility of their speaking through spirit mediums, receiving offerings of burnt votive paper, or inhabiting statues (Malarney 2002: 103, 106, 219; 2003; Fjelstad and Nguyễn Thị Hiền 2006a: 15; DiGregorio and Salemink 2007: 433ff.; Taylor 2007a: 6–9). In the remainder of this chapter, I will focus on the production of

Figure 5.1: Votive paper attendants at a *lên đồng* ritual. Photograph by Laurel Kendall, 2010.

three genres of sacred goods specific to the world of Vietnamese spirit mediums and the *lên đồng* ritual, and then consider how contemporary Vietnamese, who have grown up amid discourses of anti-superstition, navigate material religion.

The Spirited Production of Temple Statues, Votive Paper, and Costumes

In the densely populated Red River Delta of northern Vietnam, where cottage industries—including the production of temple statues and votive paper—have a long history, the efflorescence of the Mother Goddess religion in the "renovation" era draws households and sometimes entire villages into the production of sacred goods, even in communities where there was no such production tradition in the past. Sơn Đồng village, now a part of greater Hanoi, has long been known for the carving of statues and other temple fittings, activities that have resumed and expanded after a hiatus under high socialism. With the demand for statues in new and refurbished temples, other villages have also begun to produce them. In the recent past, many mediums could not afford wooden statues for their personal temples and used crude woodblock prints of the deities. Some temples also lost their statues in anti-superstition campaigns and replaced them with paper substitutes. Relative prosperity has meant that more mediums are able to install wooden statues either in new temples or as replacements for the older paper images. Because wooden or metal statues are ritually animated with the god's presence once they are installed in the temple, they are more efficacious than paintings or tablets inscribed with the god's name.[6] The market in statue production has diversified with some carvers adhering to old artisanal workshop taboos and punctuating the carving process with appropriate petitions to the spirits and offerings, while others have rationalized the process, quickly turning out less expensive ready-made statues for the Hanoi market. Mediums themselves express a range of opinions about these different options. Some hold that anything less than a statue produced in a traditionalist workshop compromises efficacy and may even cause misfortune. Others maintain that since the animation ritual in the temple transforms the statue into a god they are less concerned with the production process (Kendall et al. 2008, 2010).

Similarly discouraged under high socialism but carried out in secret, votive paper production now flourishes (although it remains technically illegal). Mediums interviewed in the spring of 2010 mentioned several different villages near Hanoi that produced beautiful votive paper in the shape of horses, elephants, dragon boats, servants, and the goddesses themselves. One master medium, eager to help us secure beautiful votive paper for our exhibit, was reluctant to provide a direct introduction to the producers since she brokers votive paper for other mediums who perform *lên đồng* in her temple and seemed to consider this information a kind of trade secret. Several large temple complexes have their own resident votive paper-makers, such that mediums weigh the beauty of an outside artisan's work against the difficulty of transporting these large and fragile sculptures to the temple.

It is impossible to estimate how many people in greater Hanoi and the sur-rounding Red River Delta engage in votive paper production for the Mother God-dess religion, but the role of this industry in generating low-paid employment is not insignificant. In a pioneering study, Nguyễn Thị Hiền (2006) describes the spread of votive paper workshops in the 1990s, some of them producing exclu-sively for *lên đồng*. She also witnesses a tension between families of artisans who have been producing votive paper for several generations, and the newcomers, including the families of spirit mediums, who, while they may claim special favor from the spirits to do this work, do not meet the standards of the older producers.

In April, 2010 I visited Đông Hồ village with the research team from the Women's Museum. Đông Hồ, in the Red River Delta, was once famous for the multi-colored woodblock prints that were auspiciously pasted on the walls of Vietnamese homes to welcome the new year but long ago supplanted by color-printed calendars. The woodblock prints survive as a niche handicraft recognized as intangible cultural heritage, but most Đông Hồ households produce votive pa-per. We visited households where the entire family was engaged in production and one where the family had hired teenage workers from another village as happens in some other Red River Delta handicraft villages. We observed a highly special-ized local industry with some households given over to such tasks as painting recycled paper or fashioning and painting the basic structure of a god's hat which would be lavishly decorated in other workshops with trimmings that had been produced in still other workshops. One family proudly exhibited a machine that could be adjusted to cut custom designs of a variety of paper pieces from the recycled cardboard collar bands of paper clothing to convincing-looking stacks of euros intended for ancestral consumption. Bamboo frames for horses, dragons, elephants, and servants were produced in other family workshops. In this center of votive paper production, one of the producers made an effort to distinguish herself from her product, claiming that the use of votive paper in Đông Hồ village itself was minimal, and that they produced for other people in other places.[7]

Votive paper production is a market-cognizant enterprise. Nguyễn Thị Hiền describes the master paper maker, Mr Thao, as constantly improving his handi-craft techniques "in order to meet the demands of the 'mediums' artful tastes'" (Nguyễn Thị Hiền 2006: 138–39). She also describes the conspicuous consump-tion of spirit mediums who vie with each other to exhibit the most spectacular constructions at their own rituals (ibid.). The spirits have a hand in this as well, as when a medium claimed that a more exquisite work of votive paper is more likely to cause the goddess to want to be present, sentiments that also surround the carv-ing and installation of temple statues.

Conversations with spirit mediums about their costumes reveal similar logics of devotional practice. Mediums describe the provision of costumes as a devotion-al act and beautiful costumes as pleasing to the deities who descend to incarnate themselves in the medium. In addition to her obligation to perform appropriate rituals during the year, she must wear beautiful costumes to "dress up" the spirits in order to receive more favor and compassion. Each spirit in an extensive pantheon has a specific costume, but some mediums will purchase costumes for only the most frequently incarnated spirits until they can afford to purchase the others. One medium explained that if a spirit arrives and does not find the appropriate costume because the medium has not yet purchased it, the attendant must petition the spirit on the medium's behalf, asking the spirit to bless the medium with good

Figure 5.2: The back room of a tailor's shop specializing in costumes for spirit mediums. Photograph by Laurel Kendall, 2010.

fortune so that she will be able to purchase the costume in the future (Kendall and Nguyễn Thị Hiền 2010).[8]

In the *lên đồng*, once the veiled medium has identified with a gesture of her hand the spirit who is about to descend, her assistants find the appropriate costume (usually already waiting in a pre-determined pile), dress the medium, construct a sometimes ornate headdress, and help her put on the appropriate jewelry. At a *lên đồng* performed by master medium Tinh which I observed in 2001, one of the damsels expressed urgent rage when the attendants failed to produce the appropriate costume and would not dance until an inappropriate pink robe was replaced with the desired one. This behavior is not unusual and testifies to the uncanny presence and will of spirits (ibid.).[9]

Mediums replace costumes when they are worn or when they can afford to upgrade the spirits' wardrobe with more beautiful replacements. Our conversations with some affluent Hanoi mediums revealed that their desire for a stylish presentation was not insignificant. Active master mediums may have several sets of costumes and are concerned with the dramatic effect they make. One medium had her costumes styled by one of the best-known fashion designers in Vietnam. Another went to a designer in Ho Chi Minh City so that her costumes would have a unique look among those worn by Hanoi spirit mediums. And yet the costume is also a sacred object, in the first instance an offering which, once it is dedicated, is closely identified with the spirit who wears it, and must be treated with respect as an extension of the spirit's presence. It must be stored carefully and kept apart from ordinary clothing.

The Women's Museum team and I soon learned that costume production is a multi-sited economic enterprise. The cost of costumes varies with the material (blends versus high-quality silk) and process (machine stitches and appliqué versus hand embroidery, workshop ready-mades versus skilled tailoring). Shops along Hanoi's Hàng Quạt Street are at the hub of costume production, with rooms in the back for fittings and a supply of costumes and costume parts from village workshops. One tailor, met on the introduction of a young and popular male medium, described how, within a common understanding of the spirits and the characteristic garments that each spirit wears, she makes adjustments in cut and decoration appropriate to the personalities and tastes of her clients. When I suggested that she was like a high fashion couturier, she beamed her agreement.

The link between Hàng Quạt Street, village cottage industry, and an extensive network for costume production became clear to us when, a few days after our meeting with this tailor, we were interviewing a spirit medium in a village in former Hà Tây province.[10] For her day job, the medium deals in Chinese fabric from the border trade and sells it to workshops producing spirit mediums' costumes, an occupation compatible with her family life and for which she thanks the spirits. She agreed to introduce us to one of her clients in a neighboring village. The cab driver who drove us to this costume workshop was familiar with the tailor we had interviewed on Hàng Quạt Street, having delivered many orders to her address. The proprietor of the workshop also knew her—and everyone else on Hàng Quạt Street, he implied. He was helpful and gracious but extremely busy processing orders for delivery, taking a stream of new orders by telephone, and dealing with drop-in customers. His is one of four workshops in the village, two of which supply Hàng Quạt Street while two others supply provincial shops. His standing workshop employs two men who help with packing and deliveries and some twenty regular workers whom we saw busy at sewing and embroidery machines, packing, cutting, skillfully applying glue and glitter to mandarin robes, pressing metal studs into red velvet bibs of antique-style military dress, or appliquéing imitations of ethnic textiles for the garments of those spirits who are identified with ethnic minorities. But this was just the tip of the iceberg. The workshop distributes and draws in piecework from another hundred village households. The owner is also a spirit medium.

This brief glimpse at the production of three different genres of sacred goods suggests a large and growing market in material religion and a close interface between domains of production, distribution, and religious practice. This is despite the fact that little more than twenty years ago the ban against popular religion was strictly enforced, practices were carried out simply and in secret, and mediums might use only a single costume, carried to a temple in an ordinary bundle (Larsson and Endres 2006). Longtime shopkeepers on Hàng Quạt Street could describe how, to avoid detection, they would pitch bundles of completed costumes out the window to customers waiting in the back alley. Recalling the 1980s, when communities were beginning to quietly repair damaged and decaying temples, a statue carver related that he had sometimes been forced to outrun the local authorities.

Votive paper was produced discreetly and in small quantities during high socialism, and the large, complicated constructions for *lên đồng* were assembled behind the closed doors of a temple where the ritual itself was held in secret (ibid.). As late as 1991, on my first visit to Vietnam, there had been recent raids on the votive paper dealers along Hàng Mã Street whose wares had been confiscated and publicly destroyed. On a quiet Sunday afternoon, I had been ushered into the back room of a votive paper shop and allowed to watch a craftswoman assemble a paper horse and servants, but only when I had given my sincere promise that I would never show the photographs to anyone in Vietnam, a promise I have kept.

The rise of popular religion, and these related industries along with it, recalls what Adam Yuet Chau (2005) has described for China: popular religion tenaciously persists in subterranean ways over long periods of stringent prohibition and bursts out with great flamboyance when the strictures are relaxed. But the botanical metaphor only takes us so far. How are we to account for the world-view of those who have lived through these dramatic changes, who were complicit in both the subterranean tenacity and subsequent flamboyance or were more recently won over from skepticism to full participation? All but the youngest followers of the

Mother Goddess religion lived part of their lives under high socialism, and some are active or recently retired civil servants. It would be naive to assume that devotees—both in the past and in the present—give only lip service to official expressions of public morality, even as it is naive to assume that the state ever effectively suppressed popular religion. What, then, does superstition mean to them?

Pure Hearts versus Superstition

When the researchers from the Women's Museum and I talked with spirit mediums and other followers we found that "superstition" was something they were quick to condemn, even among their own ranks. In a manner that initially surprised me, they identified "superstitions" as violations of their own moral sense of the Mother Goddess religion. Our conversation partners described *tâm*, or pure heart/ mindedness, as fundamental to their practice. In their discourse, *tâm* includes a moral approach to both life and worship: "If we are honest, the gods will support us but the prayers of drug traffickers are unheeded"; "The Mother Goddess does not answer the prayers of those who ask her favor for illegal things." *Tâm* was often invoked to describe how, at least ideally, the spirit medium engages the *lên đồng* with utmost sincerity and a mind focused on worship. Her preparation for the ritual, again ideally, is no less an expression of sincere and whole-hearted devotion to the Mother Goddess, the medium's *tâm*.[11] Spirit mediums spoke of how, as a mark of their gratitude to the Mother, their offerings should be the best that they can afford, selected with thoughtfulness and care, "the best fruit in the market and the most beautiful flowers" (recall how carefully the vases for my offering were selected). Many mediums spoke of the effort they made both to assemble the financial resources for the ritual and the attention they gave to planning and preparing offerings that, once having been accepted by the spirits, are distributed to the participants as *lộc*.

These assertions of high moral purpose may have been colored by our own project. The Women's Museum is, after all, an organ of the Women's Union of Vietnam, a government organization. We described to our interlocutors how we were planning an exhibit and they, understandably, wanted us to present their religion to the public in a favorable light. Some wanted to counter common perceptions of the Mother Goddess religion, such as that people pray to the Mother because they want to be rich, and that one can ask the Mother for help in anything, including morally dubious projects such as gambling.[12] But there is no denying the pervasiveness of *tâm* talk among mediums and the regularity and seeming spontaneity with which they articulated these sentiments.

Devotees were also sensitive to critiques of extravagance and ostentation. Some invoked the very old East Asian notion that simple offerings made with a pure and sincere heart would be more pleasing to the gods than empty show: "The deity accepts when we are sincere." The idea that out of gratitude and as a measure of devotion one should give the best that one is able to provide also raises the specter of conspicuous consumption invoked by critics and by mediums themselves (Larsson and Endres 2006: 157f.). The notion of *tâm* bridges, or at least tries to bridge, an uncomfortable contradiction between the repeated assertion that sincerity and purity of purpose is more pleasing to the Mother than lavish display, and the understanding that beautiful costumes, artistically arranged stacks of offerings and flower arrangements, and well-fitted temples please the Mother and foster her favorable regard.

Those producers of sacred goods who are themselves mediums or devotees take pains to explain their work as motivated by something other than pure profit, even when—almost inevitably—they attribute their business success to the Mother's favor. Master mediums and temple keepers who arrange rituals and commission costumes and offerings on behalf of apprentices or clients claimed that they did not do this in order to make money; that they take "nothing" for themselves and often advance money to destined mediums who cannot finance the necessary initiation on their own. When we were able to interview clients or followers of these same interlocutors, they also commented favorably on the master medium's or shopkeeper's good heart. Our conversation partners also described anonymous greedy master mediums and temple keepers who were just the opposite of this ideal (see also Larsson and Endres 2006; Endres 2010). Some suggested that master mediums who misled clients, temple keepers who overcharged them, and craftsmen or tailors who did not give their clients the quality they had paid for, or encouraged them to buy beyond their means, would subsequently be punished by the gods.[13] Likewise, we were told that mediums with the capacity to function as diviners lose their ability when they become greedy.

Matters of *tâm* are very much a part of a conversation about material religion. In transactions over sacred goods, at least two circumlocutions blunt the normal give and take of the market. Clients of the most traditionalist carvers of temple statues set their payment on the carver's altar in the idiom of an offering, sometimes with fruit, areca nuts, or other offering fare. Several conversation partners claimed that the buyer does not bargain over votive paper or costumes, or at most asks gently whether this is the dealer's "best price." A medium described the buying of votive paper as a matter of *tâm*, both for the buyer who selects goods following their heart-felt devotion to the Mother Goddess, and for the vender who should not exploit a transaction where haggling is muted. The tailor spoke of how the client must necessarily trust the tailor's *tâm*, something that it is easier to do when the tradesperson is a devotee herself and accountable to the moral logics of Mother Goddess religion.

"Superstition" emerged in these interviews not as the practice of material religion per se but as exploitative or excessive material religion. According to our interlocutors, superstition means holding too many rituals, ignoring one's other responsibilities out of religious enthusiasm, or offering things beyond one's means, going into debt in order to hold a fancy ritual. Mediums who make os-tentatious rituals in competition with other mediums, the much criticized *đồng đua*, are likewise "superstitious," as are the master mediums who lead devotees into sponsoring initiations even when the devotee lacks a strong calling (*căn*, lit "root") from the spirits.

Superstition tars the master mediums who pocket some of the money devotees provide for offerings and costumes or who otherwise abuse their authority. Medi-ums, like other Vietnamese, criticized such abuses of religion to one's own finan-cial advantage as *buôn thần bán thánh*, "trafficking in gods and selling the saints" (see also Salemink 2008; Endres 2010).[14] In these discussions, the problem was expressed as either a matter of exploitation (on the part of master mediums) or ir-rational excess (on the part of overly enthusiastic mediums and devotees).

Excess, of course, is relative. One spirit medium, a very successful real-estate speculator, described her son's miraculous cure from a mysterious illness once mother and child both agreed to be initiated as spirit mediums. She spoke with great enthusiasm of how, in her gratitude to the Mother, she provides the spirits with golden bowls, silver swords, and real jewelry, noting that she can well afford to do these things. In other words, ostentation within one's means is still appropri-ate practice and not superstition.[15] But this is a matter of perspective. This me-dium and her similarly affluent friends may well be regarded as competitive and thoroughly inappropriate *đồng đua* by other devotees. A devotee from a less af-fluent group, a former school teacher, happened to observe a *lên đồng* performed by a member of the wealthy medium's circle and wondered if the money spent on gold cups and silver swords would not have been better spent on good works.

Conclusion

This chapter began with a discussion of some of the ways relationships between humans and spirits in contemporary East Asia are realized in and through material forms that could be described as "gifting," "tribute," or "generalized reciproc-ity," an agentive deployment of things to win the benevolent agency of gods and goddesses (Gell 1998). I described the production and procurement of specific goods—votive paper, temple statues, and costumes—in contemporary Vietnam, noting historical depth, a responsiveness to contemporary tastes and markets, and close links between the realms of production, distribution, and religious practice. I suggested that while these activities are a robust component of contemporary popular religion in Vietnam, they are the aspect that is least easily accommodated to common-sense notions of how "modern" people ought to behave. I have de-scribed how followers of the Mother Goddess religion reconcile material religion to a modern moral landscape that has long regarded these things as superstition. Conversations with spirit mediums, devotees, and producers and purveyors of ritual goods suggest that they are very much aware of "superstition" but as the flaws and excesses of others and distinct from their own notions of good religious practice, which includes an appropriate deployment of material goods as a measure of sincerity and devotion.

Are the followers of the Mother Goddess religion sincere when they describe their own behavior in favorable contrast with the superstitious excesses of others? Most of our interlocutors probably believe in their own morality, although sincerity of intention in no sense tells us how these mediums, tailors, carvers, and crafters of votive paper actually behave. Some of our conversation partners described a particular temple keeper, master medium, or tailor as having the attributes of a good *tâm* while the superstitious offenders were inevitably an anonymous negative presence. By no means did I have the opportunity to observe members of this community in depth over time in the way that I have a small group of Korean shamans. The truth or falsehood of these moral assertions, claims of personal sincerity, and rumored counter examples is not what concerns me here but rather how followers of the Mother Goddess deployed these statements to explain what constitutes good religious practice versus superstition. Our conversation partners have solidly incorporated a negative notion of "superstition" into their world-view as modern, moral, and religious people, but they have also recalibrated it such that apart from the now loosely enforced laws against such things as mediumship and selling votive paper as "superstitious" acts, the term has become vaporous and situation contingent.[16] For these conversation partners, conspicuous consumption remains a moral issue, even as the modern Vietnamese (or Korean, or Chinese, or Japanese) state has periodically defined it as a dangerous corollary of religious consumption. These are ideas that followers of the Mother Goddess religion would have been exposed to all their lives. What matters here, and contributes to our discussion of what it means to believe in spirits in a modern Asian setting, is that followers of the Mother Goddess religion have made the term "superstition" tractable to their own discourses about human interactions with the spirit world. They have transformed what was once (and is officially) an overarching critique of popular religion into a relativist understanding of those who do not properly honor the Mother (and will be punished by her in the end). In this instance, the followers of popular religion seem not so much to have resisted modernity as digested it into their own moral understandings of what they do and ought not to do as children of the Mother Goddess. This maneuver allows for the persistence of practices that make manifest some interactions between human and spirit in the transfer of material goods between material and non-material worlds and the entertainment of spirits in the bodies of richly costumed mediums.

Notes

1. Most of the information contained in this paper that has not been previously published comes from interviews conducted in the spring of 2010 during my work with a research team from the Women's Museum of Vietnam led by Mrs Nguyễn Hải Vân and funded with a grant from the (former) Ford Foundation Vietnam. I am grateful to the Women's

Museum of Vietnam for inviting me to work with them and to everyone who gave generously of their time to talk with us. Additional information on statue carving comes from joint research carried out in 2004 with researchers from the Vietnam Museum of Ethnology and funded by the Wenner-Gren Foundation for Anthropological Research. Additional information on costumes comes from fieldwork with Dr Hiền Thị Nguyễn in the summer of 2003 for which my participation was supported by the Jane Tannenbaum Fund of the American Museum of Natural History and hers by the Ford Foundation. I am grateful to participants in the workshop on "Spirits in Modern Asia: Challenges for Societies and Scientists" held at Lichtenberg-Kolleg, Georg-August-Universität, Göttingen, September 18 and 19, 2010, for comments on this chapter and to Kirsten Endres for a Vietnam-sensitive reading. Names are given in Vietnamese order. Kristen Olson at the American Museum of Natural History helped prepare this manuscript for publication. I alone am responsible for the opinions expressed and the shortcomings of this effort.

2. They are also described as "children," "boy attendants," or "young children."

3. Karen Fjelstad has spent many years researching a community of Vietnamese spirit mediums in Silicon Valley. Her scholarship is cited elsewhere in this chapter.

4. In discussions of popular religion, Vietnam's location in Southeast Asia seems almost accidental. It shares in common with China, Korea, and Japan, notions of cosmology, divination, and statecraft, Mahayana Buddhism, and a local appropriation of Confucian rites and ethics.

5. In his study of American Catholic women's devotion to St Jude, Robert Orsi offers a useful discussion of these contrasting world-views and the tension between them in late twentieth-century American Catholicism (Orsi 1996).

6. These may be activated by a ritual master, but as a site of transmission for prayers and petitions rather than as an immediate presence. The animated statue is analogous to the incarnated medium.

7. Interview by Nguyễn Hải Vân (personal communication, 27 April 2010).

8. A similar transaction takes place in Korean *kut* when an initiate or client cannot meet a god's unanticipated demand for clothing or accessories.

9. Before her initiation into the service of the spirits, the medium must purchase suitable costumes, especially those of his or her patron spirits, those whose root the medium carries. Some Mother Goddess temples maintain extra costumes that poor mediums can use. A medium of the Mother Goddess religion is supposed to possess all of the costumes for all of the spirits that she will potentially incarnate when she performs *lên đồng*. A *bà đồng* told Nguyễn Thị Hiền and me that she felt badly when she could not incarnate a spirit in the appropriate costume because she did not yet possess it. When a *bà đồng*'s circumstances improve, she acknowledges the spirits' favor by buying them more spectacular and expensive costumes, carefully preserving the old ones and possibly allowing the mediums she has initiated to use them (Kendall and Nguyễn Thị Hiền 2010).

10. This is now a part of greater Hanoi.

11. Spirit mediums in Vietnam are both male and female and we interviewed both, but since the majority are generally assumed to be women and since most of our conversation partners were women, I use the female pronoun.

12. With respect to gambling, we did meet one woman who claimed that although she had never played the lottery in the past, she made a bargain with the Mother Goddess that if she won the money for her costumes she would accept her calling and be initiated. She drew a winning ticket that abundantly covered her needs. For a description of more unabashed appeals for gambler's luck, see Salemink (2008).

13. See also Kendall et al. (2008) for statues.

14. Salemink offers a more positive gloss on competition between mediums, suggesting that this dynamic is responsible for the artistic realization that garnered the attention of sympathetic scholars in the first instance (Salemink 2008).

15. Although I have not seen her *lên đồng*, I have no reason to think that she was exaggerating, having witnessed similar accoutrements at the *lên đồng* of another spirit medium in her circle.
16. A strict ban on a range of popular religious practices, including many described here, was enacted in 2010 but to date it has had no visible effect on actual practice (Kirsten Endres, personal communication, 13 October 2010).

References

Cave, Roderick. 1998. *Chinese Paper Offerings*. Oxford: Oxford University Press.

Chau, Adam Yuet. 2005. *Miraculous Response: Doing Popular Religion in Contemporary China*. Stanford, CA: Stanford University Press.

DiGregorio, Michael, and Oscar Salemink. 2007. "Living with the Dead: The Politics of Ritual and Remembrance in Contemporary Vietnam," *Journal of Southeast Asian Studies* 38(3): 433–40.

Endres, Kirsten W. 2010. "'Trading in Spirits'? Transnational Flows, Entrepreneurship, and Commodifications in Vietnamese Spirit Mediumship," in *Traveling Spirits: Migrants, Markets and Mobilities*, eds G. Huwelmeier and K. Krause. New York: Routledge, pp.118–32.

Fjelstad, Karen. 2010. "Spirited Migrations: The Travels of *Len Dong* Spirits and Their Mediums," in *Traveling Spirits: Migrants, Markets and Mobilities*, eds G. Hüwelmeier and K. Krause. New York: Routledge, pp.52–66.

Fjelstad, Karen, and Nguyễn Thị Hiền. 2006a. "Introduction," in *Possessed by the Spirits: Mediumship in Contemporary Vietnamese Communities*, eds K. Fjelstad and T.H. Nguyễn. Ithaca, NY: Southeast Asia Program Publications, Cornell University, pp.7–18.

———. eds. 2006b. *Possessed by the Spirits: Mediumship in Contemporary Vietnamese Communities*. Ithaca, NY: Southeast Asia Program Publications, Cornell University.

Gell, Alfred. 1998. *Art and Agency: An Anthropological Theory*. Oxford: Clarendon Press.

Gernet, Jacques. 1995[1956]. *Buddhism in Chinese Society: An Economic History from the Fifth to the Tenth Centuries*, trans. F. Verellen. New York: Columbia University Press.

Kendall, Laurel. 1985. *Shamans, Housewives, and Other Restless Spirits: Women in Korean Ritual Life*. Honolulu: University of Hawaii Press.

———. 1996. "Korean Shamans and the Spirits of Capitalism," *American Anthropologist* 98(3): 512–27.

———. 2008. "Of Hungry Ghosts and Other Matters of Consumption," *American Ethnologist* 35(1): 154–70.

———. 2009. *Shamans, Nostalgias, and the IMF: South Korean Popular Religion in Motion*. Honolulu: University of Hawaii Press.

Kendall, Laurel, and Nguyễn Thị Hiền. 2010. "Dressing Up the Spirits: Costumes, Cross-dressing, and Incarnation," in *Women and Indigenous Religions*, ed. S. Marcos. Santa Barbara, CA: ABC-CLIO, pp.93–114.

Kendall, Laurel, Vũ Thị Thanh Tâm, and Nguyễn Thị Thu Hương. 2008. "Three Goddesses in and out of their Shrine," *Asian Ethnology* 67(2): 219–36.

———. 2010. "Beautiful and Efficacious Statues: Magic and Material in Vietnamese Popular Religion," *Material Religion* 6(1): 60–85.

Laing, Ellen Johnston, and Helen Hui-Ling Liu. 2004. *Up in Flames: The Ephemeral Art of Pasted-Paper Sculpture in Taiwan*. Stanford, CA: Stanford University Press.

Larsson, Viveca, and Kirsten W. Endres. 2006. "'Children of the Spirits, Followers of a Master': Spirit Mediums in Post-Renovation Vietnam," in *Possessed by the Spirits: Mediumship in Contemporary Vietnamese Communities*, eds K. Fjelstad and T.H. Nguyễn. Ithaca, NY: Southeast Asia Program Publications, Cornell University, pp.143–60.

Latour, Bruno. 1993. *We Have Never Been Modern*. Cambridge, MA: Harvard University Press.

Lê Hồng Lý. 2007. "Praying for Profit: The Cult of the Lady of the Treasury (*Bà Chúa Kho*)," *Journal of Southeast Asian Studies* 38(3): 493–513.

Malarney, Shaun Kingsley. 2002. *Culture, Ritual, and Revolution in Vietnam*. New York: Routledge Curzon.

———. 2003. "Return to the Past? The Dynamics of Contemporary Religious and Ritual Transformation," in *Postwar Vietnam: Dynamics of a Transforming Society*, ed. H.V. Luong. Singapore: Institute of Southeast Asian Studies, pp.225–56.

Marr, David G. 1981. *Vietnamese Tradition on Trial: 1920–1945*. Berkeley: University of California Press.

Nguyễn Thị Hiền. 2006. "'A Bit of Spirit Favor is Equal to a Load of Mundane Gifts': Votive Paper Offerings of *Len Dong* Rituals in Post-Renovation Vietnam," in *Possessed by the Spirits: Mediumship in Contemporary Vietnamese Communities*, eds K. Fjelstad and T.H. Nguyễn. Ithaca, NY: Southeast Asia Program Publications, Cornell University, pp.127–42.

Nguyên Văn Huy, and Phạm Lan Hương. 2008. "The One-eyed God at the Vietnam Museum of Ethnology: The Story of a Village Conflict," *Asian Ethnology* 67(2): 201–18.

O'Neil, Mary R. 1987. "Superstition," in *The Encyclopedia of Religion*, Vol. 4., ed. M. Eliade. New York: Macmillan Publishing Company, pp.222–28.

Orsi, Robert A. 1996. *Thank You, St Jude: Women's Devotion to the Patron Saint of Hopeless Causes*. New Haven, CT: Yale University Press.

Pelley, Patricia M. 2002. *Postcolonial Vietnam: New Histories of the National Past*. Durham, NC: Duke University Press.

Petersen, Martin. 2008. "Collecting Korean Shamanism: Biographies and Collecting Devices," Ph.D. dissertation. Copenhagen: University of Copenhagen.

Pietz, William. 1987. "The Problem of the Fetish, II: The Origin of the Fetish," *Res* 13: 23–45.

Salemink, Oscar. 2008. "Spirits of Consumption and the Capitalist Ethic in Vietnam," in *Religious Commodifications in Asia: Marketing Gods*, ed. P. Kitiarsa. London: Routledge, pp.147–68.

Scott, Janet Lee. 2007. *For Gods, Ghosts and Ancestors: The Chinese Tradition of Paper Offering*. Seattle: University of Washington Press.

Sinha, Vineeta. 2008. "'Merchandizing' Hinduism: Commodities, Markets and Possibilities for Enchantment," in *Religious Commodifications in Asia: Marketing Gods*, ed. P. Kitiarsa. London: Routledge, pp.169–85.

Swergold, Leopol, et al. 2008. *Treasures Rediscovered: Chinese Stone Sculpture from the Sackler Collections at Columbia University*. New York: Miriam and Ira D. Wallach Art Gallery, Columbia University.

Tambiah, Stanley Jeyaraja. 1990. *Magic, Science, Religion, and the Scope of Rationality*. Cambridge: Cambridge University Press.

Taylor, Philip. 2004. *Goddess on the Rise: Pilgrimage and Popular Religion in Vietnam*. Honolulu: University of Hawaii Press.

———. 2007a. "Modernity and Re-enchantment in Post-revolutionary Vietnam," in *Modernity and Re-enchantment: Religion in Post-revolutionary Vietnam*, ed. P. Taylor. Singapore: Institute of Southeast Asian Studies, pp.1–56.

———. ed. 2007b. *Modernity and Re-enchantment: Religion in Post-revolutionary Vietnam*. Singapore: Institute of Southeast Asian Studies.

6

CONTESTS OF COMMEMORATION: VIRGIN WAR MARTYRS, STATE MEMORIALS, AND THE INVOCATION OF THE SPIRIT WORLD IN CONTEMPORARY VIETNAM

Kirsten W. Endres and Andrea Lauser

In these days of early Autumn, here is your Altar of Redemption
We sprinkle holy water with willow branches
And pray that merciful Buddha will save you from your suffering
And take your souls to the Promised Land
—Nguyen Du, "Calling the Wandering Souls" (in Pelzer 1993)

It is five o'clock in the morning of a mid November day. It is still dark and a gentle breeze rustles the trees in the woods behind the ten graves. They hold the remains of ten young women who were tragically killed in one single bombing at Đồng Lộc Junction, one of the most violent battlefields on the Ho Chi Minh trail during what the Vietnamese call the American War.[1] Hushed voices fill the eerie space of the memorial. The graves are guarded by a three-dimensional monument reminiscent of a Vietnamese temple gate. Smoke billows from the huge bronze incense burner in front of the structure. Shadowy figures with huge plastic bags and carton boxes scurry to and fro. As the awakening day sheds more light on the scene, the roaming ghosts of countless war dead retreat to their realm and the atmosphere begins to feel lighter. Mrs Thiền,[2] a sturdy spirit medium in her early fifties, starts unpacking the bags and boxes one by one; votive paper houses, paper shirts with matching ties, paper uniforms and paper caps are all carefully arranged on the platform in front of the wall panel. Mrs Hồng, a wealthy Hanoi businesswoman involved in the booming real-estate and construction industry, piles colorful boxes

---

Endnotes for this chapter begin on page 140

Figure 6.1: A memorial turned into a Buddhist-Daoist altar. Photograph by Andrea Lauser, 2006.

of biscuits and crackers on the ledge of the monument and flanks them with cans of soft drinks and beer. Master Hiền, the spirit priest, and his apprentices set out to decorate the memorial with Buddhist-Daoist artefacts and ritual items: paper panels with calligraphy written in parallel sentences, Buddha images printed on waxed paper, wooden plates depicting the Daoist Kings of Hell (*vua ngục*), and so on. On each side of the memorial, fifty meters of red and yellow satin cloth are draped to demarcate the ritual space. Within less than two hours, the socialist war memorial had been turned into a colorful Buddhist-Daoist altar.

The above scene took place in 2006 at the memorial of Đồng Lộc Junction in the central province of Hà Tĩnh. During the American War in Vietnam (1965–1975), the T-junction was a strategically and logistically important part of the legendary road and transport system known as the Ho Chi Minh trail, as virtually every supply truck carrying soldiers, provisions and munitions for the troops had to pass this intersection. Seeing the strategic importance of Đồng Lộc Junction, American aircraft heavily bombarded the area in repeated efforts to destroy the logistical network. However, their aim "to turn this intersection into a dead landscape" failed in view of the immense mobilization of thousands of people and organizations on the North Vietnamese side.[3] In addition to regular military forces, guerrilla warfare led to the mobilization of whole villages, and volunteer groups were formed to survey the supply roads and ensure the transportation process. Among these groups was a squad of ten young volunteer girls between seventeen and twenty-four years of age. Stationed on top of a hill, they had to count the bombs, record the impact locations, and relay the information back to army engineer units. On 24 July 1968 a big bomb hit their trench and killed them in the prime of their youth.

During the "anti-American resistance war for national salvation" (*kháng chiến chống Mỹ cứu nước*), countless people lost their lives under the most in-humane, traumatic, and brutal circumstances.[4] It therefore comes as no surprise that "ghosts of war" still haunt the country in both a metaphorical and literal sense (see Kwon 2006, 2008). Following the example of Europe in the aftermath of the First World War, the commemoration of the enormous sacrifices of those who had fought "on the right side" was a major concern for the Vietnamese state. Central to the official cult of remembrance was the construction of war monuments, me-morials, and cemeteries that serve, to use Bradley's words, "both as shrines of national worship and as physical symbols of the superior claims made by the state on the memories of those who died in battle" (Bradley 2001: 199). In Vietnam, as elsewhere, the official commemoration of wars and fallen soldiers is a prime arena for the construction of national narratives that integrate individual loss and grief into "collectively shared assumptions about the indebtedness of the living to their heroic compatriots and ancestors" (Nelson 2003: 443). Moreover, rituals and practices of commemoration must be seen as a constitutive part of the political project to construct and cultivate a specific interpretation of the past in the present (see Ashplant, Dawson, and Roper 2000; Malarney 2001; Roudometof 2003). As such, memorials dedicated to the commemoration of war dead who fell fighting the French or fighting for national liberation during the American War are a key element in the Vietnamese state's effort to legitimate the war effort and to glorify selfless struggle and personal sacrifice for the revolutionary cause.

This celebration of the "reunification of a victorious country," however, is not designed to heal the wounds of war (Tatum 1996: 642). Neither does it resolve the most pressing concern for the bereaved; that is, the issue of the fate of the war martyrs' souls (see Malarney 2001). In this chapter, we look at the intersection of different discourses—national-patriotic, spiritual-religious, and moral-eco-nomic—at Đồng Lộc Junction and discuss different narratives that have emerged from the commemoration of the ten young women who met their premature death together (hereafter called "the Ten Girls"). While the official narrative eulogizes the role of women in Vietnam's history of repelling foreign aggression in order to strengthen national identity and legitimize the war effort, popular conceptions and ritual practices related to death and remembrance have buttressed the con-struction of more intimate narratives that deal with personal grief, distress, and conflict in everyday life. These narratives exemplify processes of appropriating and transforming official history, and illustrate how national heroes may become efficacious deities that constitute a living presence rather than a glorified memory (Lauser 2008a, 2008b).

Renovation, Economic Growth, and Ritual Revivification

When Vietnam was unified under communist rule after 1975, the "neo-Stalinist" command economy and international isolation soon led to an economic crisis that propelled the war-torn country even deeper into poverty. Ten years later, at the Sixth Party Congress in 1986, the Socialist Republic of Vietnam's leadership initiated the adoption of a "renovation" policy that became known as *đổi mới*. Responding to growing pressures from below (Fforde and de Vylder 1996; Kerkvliet 2005), Vietnam followed the example of China and embarked upon the transition to a market-based economy. Since that time, Vietnam's economy has prospered rapidly and continuously.[5]

Alongside economic restructuring there has been a profound (re)invigoration of commemorative practices, both at the national and individual level. Sacred sites that had been neglected due to the state's restrictive attitudes towards popular religion were reclaimed by local communities as places of worship and ritual practice. Funds were raised for the renovation of village communal houses (*đình làng*), Buddhist pagodas (*chùa*), and temples dedicated to the countless gods, goddesses, heroes, and saints who inhabit the Vietnamese supernatural realm. Village ritual festivals (*lễ hội*) were reorganized (see Endres 2000), and rites of passage such as weddings and funerals were again celebrated with much grandeur (Kleinen 1999; Malarney 2001). Lineage halls (*nhà thờ họ*) were (re)built to honor the ancestors of the patrilineage, and rice fields became dotted with ornately constructed tombs and newly renovated graves of deceased family members. War cemeteries and other monuments for the dead of the revolutionary war were built in nearly every district and commune across the country, their columns or plaques inscribed with the words "The fatherland remembers your sacrifice" (*tổ quốc ghi công*),[6] and "Eternally remember our debt to the heroic martyrs" (*đời đời nhớ ơn các anh hùng liệt sĩ*). Moreover, the "commemorative fever" that seemed to have seized the country resulted in the construction of numerous memorials, museums, war theme parks—such as the infamous Củ Chi Tunnels—and other "monuments to the worship of the past" (Huệ-Tâm Hồ Tài 2001a: 1; Schwenkel 2009). Before turning to the Vietnamese politics of commemoration, we will take a brief look at the basic moral and ideological precepts that underlie commemorative practices and provide some background for the reader who is not completely familiar with the field.

The Ethics of Moral Debt and Remembrance

The veneration of ancestors (*thờ cúng tổ tiên*), which at the individual level is also known as *nhớ ơn ông bà* (remembering the moral debt to the grandparents), is the most common religious belief in Vietnam, and, for the most part, even transcends affiliation with various institutionalized creeds (see Đặng Nghiêm Vạn 1996, 1998). The Confucian concept of filial piety (*hiếu*)—that is, respect, obedience, gratitude, and the obligation to repay the moral debt (*ơn*) to past generations—is inseparably intertwined with the belief that the ancestors depend on the living for their well-being in the other world. Since the realm of spirits and ancestors is imagined to mirror the human world, the ancestors are thought to require the same daily necessities as mortals (see Nguyễn Thị Hiền 2006). Besides incense and food offerings, ancestors are presented with votive paper offerings representing modern luxury items such as fully furnished multi-storey houses, dishes, televisions sets, motorbikes, cellphones, and so on. Whereas edible gifts are retrieved for consumption after the act of veneration, the paper offerings are sent to the other world by committing them to the flames. These sacrificial transactions are a constitutive part of the reciprocal relationship between the living and the dead: the ancestors look after their descendants but expect culinary and other treats, and the living dutifully present food and votive offerings but ask for ancestral benevolence and "blessed gifts" (*lộc*) in return.

A much cited Vietnamese phrase says "wealth gives birth to ritual form" (*phú quí sinh lễ nghĩa*), which in common usage means that ritual expenditures depend on each person's economic means.[7] In a recent article, Kate Jellema describes the case of a village woman named Thúy who had taken great pride in her parents' new grave that she and her siblings had built in order to honor their memory and repay their moral debt. Thúy explains that there are "no hard and fast rules" for the amount of money to be spent on these matters and that each person should contribute according to their ability: "If you're rich, then make [your parent's grave] beautiful and big. If you're poor, make it small. If there are many children who can contribute a lot, then make it big. If there are few children who can only contribute a little, make it small. That's it. ... It's a question of economic means" (cited in Jellema 2007: 477). A poor person who does not have the means to present the ancestors with more than a stick of incense and a bowl of rice thus shows no less "filial piety" than a rich person who offers an opulent meal to the deceased (see also Malarney 2002: 10). However, if a wealthy person neglects his or her parents' graves and does not celebrate their death anniversaries (*ngày giỗ*) with proper sumptuousness, then he or she would be looked upon as an unethical person who lacks filial piety (*bất hiếu*) and "heart" (*tâm*).

In a larger social context, this ethics of moral debt and grateful remembrance also extends to those who have rendered a meritorious contribution (*công*) to the community. In pre-revolutionary Vietnam, this may have been a village founder, a high dignitary who had lived a virtuous life, or the ancestor who first introduced the craft that emerged as a principal means of livelihood for villagers. These moral exemplars belong to a category of ancestors that Malarney has described as the "exceptional dead," defined as "those who are deemed by the living to have been in some way apart from the ordinary and who possessed extraordinary qualities that differentiate them from other dead" (Malarney 2007: 517). In many cases, these meritorious personalities were posthumously deified and worshipped as guardian deities for the benefits they had brought to the community—an obligation best expressed in the popular adage "when you drink water, remember its source" (*uống nước nhớ nguồn*). Among these exceptional dead are also those who had rendered exemplary services to the whole country (*có công với đất nước*), such as the great legendary male and female warriors who defended the nation against Chinese domination. Some of these military heroes have been attributed with supernatural qualities and are believed by the people to have been "living gods" (*thần sống*) who had descended to earth in order to rescue the Vietnamese (Malarney 2001: 47). After the French colonial regime was ousted from Vietnam in 1954, the new socialist state defined these deities as national heroes (*anh hùng dân tộc*) and capitalized on their veneration among the people by constructing them as symbols of patriotic struggle and selfless devotion. Their ranks were soon swelled by a new category of exceptional dead whom the Vietnamese communists characterized as "revolutionary martyrs" (*liệt sĩ, anh hùng liệt sĩ*) (Malarney 2007: 519; see also Tréglodé 2001). This appellation applied to individuals who had gloriously sacrificed (*hy sinh*) their lives on the battlefield for the revolutionary cause.

War, Gender, and Patriotic Commemoration

The official Vietnamese narrative of the war highlights Vietnam's history of repelling foreign aggression and ennobles death in war as meaningful, even sacred. Self-sacrifice in the service of the country, the people, and the revolution, so Malarney states, "was a test of true revolutionary mettle and integrity" (Malarney 2001: 50). In order to incite an even stronger willingness to sacrifice one's life for the noble cause, the state propaganda machine drew upon the imposing example of Vietnam's great and famous military heroes. General Võ Nguyên Giáp who masterminded the French defeat at Điện Biên Phủ and continued to play an important role as a military strategist during the American War, once declared:

> The contemporary ideas of our party, military, and people for the offensive struggle cannot be separated from the traditional military ideas of our people. During our history, all victorious wars of resistance or liberation, whether led by the Trung Sisters [first century], Ly Bon [sixth century], Trieu Quang Phuc [sixth century], Le Loi [fifteenth century], or Nguyen Trai [fifteenth century] have all shared the common characteristic of a continuous offensive aimed at casting off the yoke of feudal domination by foreigners. (Cited in ibid.: 48)

It is, however, important to note that the writing of Vietnamese history and national identity as "a narrative of patriotic endeavour" (Huệ-Tâm Hồ Tài 2001b: 172) did not promote warfare as a cult of masculinity, where men rushed to the battlefield and women remained in the relative safety of their homes. Instead, war was seen as "an evil necessity that must be endured by all" (ibid.: 172). Moreover, women had always been integrated into the war effort, and patriotic historiography glorifies not only male military heroes but female heroes as well. The Vietnamese adage "when war comes, even women must fight" (*giặc đến nhà, đàn bà cũng đánh*) refers to a long history of women fighters. The Trưng Sisters, for example, are highly revered as national heroes who led the first revolt against Chinese domination in AD 39. Just like the famous general Trần Hưng Đạo, who successfully repelled Mongol invaders in the thirteenth century, the Trưng Sisters are considered as "saints" (*thánh*) and worshipped at both the local and national level (Malarney 2001: 47). Another military female hero was Lady Triệu (AD 225–248), a 19-year-old woman warrior who in the third century managed to set up her own army and successfully (at least for some time) defended her territory against Chinese rule. In the twentieth century, Vietnamese women fought alongside men during the war of resistance against French colonial rule as well as during the American War. The total number of women who were on active duty in the regular army of North Vietnam, the militia, and local forces, as well as in various volunteer units, is estimated at approximately two hundred thousand (see Turner 1998; Taylor 1999). Besides serving in combat platoons, they operated underground communication networks, ran jungle liaison stations and ammunition depots, treated the wounded, carried supplies, or served as village patrol guards. The total mobilization of the population for the defense of the homeland against the invading aggressor also made possible what Huệ-Tâm Hồ Tài (2001b) describes as "the feminization of war." Traditionally charged with maintaining the household and protecting the well-being of their families, "duties that call for skills worthy of a battle-hardened general" (ibid.: 174), women shoulder the burden of domestic responsibilities (see Gammeltoft 2001). The strategy of guerrilla warfare, then, "blurs the distinction between the front line and the rear, between combatants and civilians, between the masculine battlefield and the feminine domestic space" (Huệ-Tâm Hồ Tài 2001b: 175; see also Yuval-Davis 1997: 95). In order to "save the country and defend independence," the organization of a nationwide Volunteer Youth (*Thanh Niên Xung Phong*) was enthusiastically embraced by both young men and women across North Vietnam.[8] In this sense, the Ten Girls of Đồng Lộc Junction are not exceptional. But the fact that they died together as a group of young and unmarried girls in one single incident makes them a powerful symbol of revolutionary heroism (*biểu tượng của anh hùng cách mạng*).[9] Moreover, as "vulnerable young girls at the mercy of cruel fate" (Huệ-Tâm Hồ Tài 2001b: 173), they serve as a potent metaphor for the country as a victim of imperialist aggression.

However, a brief look at the narrative construction of their biographies reveals that the image of the "fighting virgins" does not question conventional gender ideologies predicating female virtues of chastity and appropriate behavior, self-sacrifice and resourcefulness, family and motherhood (Gammeltoft 2001). Instead, images of the dutiful daughter and chaste heroic virgin on the one hand, and of the faithful, hardworking wife and loving mother on the other, continue to be upheld as the moral ideal of the virtuous woman in public discourse. The Ten Girls are generally presented as stereotypically dedicated, assiduous daughters who performed their daily duties with optimistic light-heartedness (see CYO 2004: 34–49).[10] Their personalities are described in glowing terms as open-minded, honest, impartial, modest, compassionate, and brave. All of them decided to join the Volunteer Youth unit out of revolutionary zeal. While some of them looked back on a long revolutionary family tradition (Võ Thị Tần, Nguyễn Thị Xuân, Trần Thị

Figure 6.2: Grave of Võ Thị Hợi, Đồng Lộc Junction. Photograph by Kirsten W. Endres, 2006.

Hường), others were orphans or came from deprived backgrounds marked by war (Hồ Thị Cúc, Nguyễn Thị Nhỏ, Trần Thị Rạng). Some of them had left their lives behind to fight for their fatherland as 17-year-old teenagers (Trần Thị Rạng, Võ Thị Hà).

Only the oldest among them were involved in romances or already promised in marriage (Võ Thị Tần, Dương Thị Xuân, Nguyễn Thị Xuân), but had put off their wedding until the country was liberated. All ten girls are described as having sacrificed a perspective of fulfilled femininity—that is, marriage and motherhood—for the revolutionary struggle. The inscription on the memorial reads:

> On this piece of sacred land, at 4 o'clock on 24 July 1968, a squad of ten female youth volunteers heroically sacrificed their lives. They had fully devoted their youth to the task of defending the two arterial roads that connected the rear lines with the front lines in order to achieve complete victory. The names of the ten girls will forever be remembered by our people and by friends all over the world as they refer to a heroic achievement of the heroic Vietnamese nation.

As mentioned above, the official commemoration of revolutionary martyrs was one of the prime concerns of the Vietnamese state, because "[t]he dead soldier was one of the greatest threats to the legitimacy and authority of the Democratic Republic of Vietnam (DRV) in the first three decades of its existence" (Malarney 2001: 46).[11] Besides dotting the landscape with war cemeteries and memorials, an official memorial service was created to honor the contributions of the war dead on a more individual level. Dedicated solely to the glorification of dead soldiers' contribution to the noble cause of national independence and reunification, however, these ceremonies do not address the one issue that is most crucial in Vietnamese cultural ways of conceptualizing and dealing with death: the fate of a dead person's soul.

Rituals for the Living, Offerings for the Dead

The tremendous loss of young, unfulfilled lives not only brought untold sadness and grief to the survivors, it also created a great deal of anxiety for those left behind. According to Vietnamese mortuary conceptions, dying under violent circumstances causes the soul to remain trapped in the memory of mortal agony, a condition Kwon describes as "grievous death" (*chết oan*): "The human soul in this condition of self-imprisonment does not remember the terror as we the living normally would, but relives the violent experience repeatedly. Memory of death for the tragically dead, in other words, is a living memory in its most brutally literal sense" (Kwon 2006: 14). Cast as "the quintessential bad death" (Malarney 2002: 179), losing one's life on the battlefield entailed the precarious possibility for the human soul of being unable to make the transition to the other world, instead be-coming a—potentially malevolent—hungry ghost. The novelist Bảo Ninh vividly describes the eerie desolation of the jungle haunted by the souls of dead soldiers whose bodies had been blown apart by heavy artillery in Vietnam's central high-lands: "They were still loose, wandering in every corner and bush in the jungle, drifting along the stream, refusing to depart for the Other World … The sobbing whispers were heard deep in the jungle at night, the howls carried on the wind. Perhaps they really were the voices of the wandering souls of dead soldiers" (Bảo Ninh 1996: 6).[12] The hungry souls of these fallen soldiers, most of whom died in the prime of their lives, their bodies mutilated beyond recognition and without descendants to respect and worship their memory, are believed to remain caught in the negative emotions of grief and to "angrily roam the earth looking for any food and care they can find" (Malarney 2002: 180). It is for this reason that so many popular Buddhist-Daoist rituals are concerned with propitiating the souls of the deceased and ensuring their safe transition to the other world. One of these rituals is the *Lễ Mông Sơn*—the ritual Mrs Thiền had organized with the help of Master Hiền at Đồng Lộc Junction. Its overall aim is to invoke all the Buddhas, Bodhisattvas, and Saints to facilitate the soul's salvation (in terms of escaping the cycle of rebirth and attaining nirvana). According to spirit priest Hiền, this ritual also applies well to the wandering souls of the war dead:

> All those who died during the war, those who died a grievous death, can-not reach salvation. Many of these souls become a nuisance (*quấy rối*) … but if they walk right on the path of religion they will reach salvation (*siêu thoát*). Then they can be reincarnated into another human, they will no longer be desolate, they will no longer wander around and no longer bear grudges against anyone.

One important precondition for a soul (*hồn*) to rest in peace is a proper burial of its mortal remains. Since the soul is believed to dwell where the bones are, a dead war martyr is unable to receive the care of the living if the remains lie buried in an unmarked grave in the wilderness or in a remote war cemetery far away from home (see Schlecker 2007). This is why it is of utmost concern to the families to locate the grave of missing soldiers and return their bones to their homeland for reburial. The sheer number of Vietnamese combatants missing in action suggests that this is not an easy task.[13] With growing prosperity in the "renovation" era, it became even more pressing for the relatives and families of missing soldiers to push ahead with the search for their remains: after the needs of the living had been attended to, it was time to tend to the dead who had sacrificed their lives so that the survivors would live in peace and prosper. Soul-callers (*người gọi hồn*) with the alleged capacity to contact or "channel" the souls of the ancestors, and psychics (*nhà ngoại cảm*) and other people with "special capabilities" (*khả năng đặc biệt*), suddenly saw themselves confronted with the task of finding the graves of the missing war dead. Formerly regarded as fraudsters and dupers by the socialist state, their apparent success gave them such credibility that a semi-official grave-finding service was established in the mid 1990s.[14] Two cases gained widespread publicity even if most media reports were cautious not to mention the engagement of psychics. In the first case, the remains of eminent novelist Nam Cao (1915–1951) who died during the war against French rule were apparently located by a group of psychics in 1996. The second case was even more spectacular, as it involved one of the founding fathers of the Vietnamese Communist Party (later the Indochinese Communist Party). Trần Phú, the first secretary-general of the party from 1930, was arrested in Saigon by the French in 1931 and died a few months later at Chợ Quán hospital at the age of twenty-seven. In 1999, his family hired a renowned psychic who identified an unmarked grave on the grounds of the former hospital cemetery as Trần Phu's last resting place.

In particular cases and under particular circumstances, the death of a young person may also be thought to be of particularly sacred potency.[15] If, for example, an innocent child or a virgin girl died an untimely, violent, or voluntarily heroic death, or if death occurred during a "sacred hour" (*giờ thiêng*), it is believed that the soul will ascend straight to heaven and become the servant of powerful deities.[16] Some may even become a deity themselves. Heonik Kwon's work provides us with two lively ethnographic examples that describe the transformation of two young female spirits. Whereas in the first case the metamorphosis from a wandering soul (*cô hồn*) to a goddess had already been completed, it was still ongoing in the second. Both cases, Kwon relates, are similar in sharing "a common metahistorical plot of tragic early death, improper burial, and absence of ritual commemoration, and further, separation from origin, reburial, and regeneration as a trans-local deity after a generation's lapse of time since physical death" (Kwon 2008: 119).[17] In a similar vein, Philip Taylor has pointed out that the tales woven around efficacious goddesses most often relate that "they lived socially truncated lives and died abject deaths," thus leaving their potential in their human existence largely unrealized (Taylor 2004: 201). The memory of their unfulfilled lives, however, also makes them extremely responsive to human attention: "Like the hungry ghosts, the goddesses are considered to be full of unrequited lusts, sensual appetites, moods, and memories and hence unusually grateful to those who can satisfy them" (ibid.: 201). The potential of the Ten Girls fits well with the above conception that assumes a divine potency in connection with certain types and circumstances of death. It is hence not surprising that they are assumed by many to have (almost) achieved sainthood (*hiển thánh*).

The above conditions also apply to many of the deities in the pantheon of the Four Palaces (see Chauvet, this volume). These deities manifest themselves in (male or female) spirit mediums (*bà đồng* or *ông đồng*) during elaborate possession rituals known as *lên đồng* or *hầu bóng*. Mrs Thiền has been a practicing adherent of the Four Palaces religion for almost ten years. In 2001, she established a private shrine on the top floor of her narrow townhouse in Hanoi's Cầu Giấy district. Three years later, she started operating as a master medium (*đồng thầy*). As such, she performs initiations into the ritual practice of spirit mediumship and holds *lên đồng* rituals sponsored by her followers and supporters, during which she presents the Four Palaces deities with intricate paper offerings (*vàng mã*) and files petitions (*sớ*) in her followers' names. Besides her religious activities, she is employed in the administration of a national university. Partly because of this proximity to the sciences, but even more so because Mrs Thiền always prepares her rituals very thoroughly, some of her followers call her "the scientific medium" (*bà đồng khoa học*). Mrs Thiền feels "destined to save and cure" (*căn cứu chữa*) other people, and with this purpose she serves the spiritual needs of her followers (*con nhang đệ tử*), the majority of whom are well-educated professionals involved in the private sector or work in government offices, research institutes, and banks.

Mrs Thiền has established herself firmly within the bustling world of mediums in contemporary Hanoi by skilfully combining her entrepreneurial and networking skills with religious and spiritual aims. Her dense network of contacts with other ritual specialists enables her to broker a wide range of ritual services that Mrs Thiền is not qualified to carry out. These include, for example, protective rites at the beginning of the new lunar year (*lễ giải hạn*), the ritual cutting of a karmic bond that may hamper marriage prospects in this life (*lễ cắt tiền duyên*), rites for settling a karmic debt (*lễ trả nợ tào quan*), as well as rites relating to the souls of the ancestors (*lễ gia tiên*). For these rituals, Mrs Thiền usually employs the expertise of Master Hiền, the spirit priest mentioned earlier.[18] Other spiritual experts in her network are diviners (*thầy bói*) and soul-callers (*người gọi hồn*) who act as vessels for the souls of the deceased.

In October 2006, Mrs Thiền attended a grand meeting of the Association of Hà Tĩnh Natives (her husband's native province) that took place in Ho Chi Minh City. The meeting had been organized with the aim of raising funds for the refurbishment of the memorial at Đồng Lộc Junction.[19] The event featured a photo exhibition and praised the heroism of those who died in the bombings of the junction in songs and poems. Mrs Thiền felt particularly moved by the speech of Nguyễn Thị Hường, the only surviving member of the group of young female volunteers. Besides listening to these official tales, Mrs Thiền also learned that every month the soul of the Võ Thị Tần, the team leader of the female volunteer unit, would express itself through a famous soul-caller operating in Thanh Hoá province. During one of these sessions, Võ Thị Tần had apparently conveyed the message that the Ten Girls had ascended to the Heavenly Realm and become servants of the Mother Goddesses. During the meeting, Mrs Thiền also met Mrs Hồng, a Hà Tĩnh native herself. Mrs Hồng successfully operates a land development business in Hanoi and describes herself as a person whose 'heart is close' to Buddha as well as to the saints and ancestors. She regularly visits pagodas and temples and earns merit (*công đức*) by leaving generous donations. When a few weeks later Mrs Thiền told her about her plans for organizing a *Lễ Mông Sơn* at the war memorial dedicated to the Ten Girls, Mrs Hồng eagerly offered to support the endeavor.

As we have already indicated above, the relationship between economic prosperity and religious revival points to fundamental moral concerns. This "preoccupation with the moral dimensions" (Hefner 1998: 27) of the ongoing social and economic transformation has been observed across Asia and is therefore not unique to Vietnam. The ways in which people try to "remoralize their wealth" (ibid.: 28) are neither uniform nor do they merely point to the hold of "tradition" in the face of modernity. Rather, people reconcile their modern lifestyles and ambitions with their moral values and religious ethics in various creative ways. In the case of Vietnam, the "new rules of the game" still need to be defined, and the question of "what is fair, just, and good in this transitional society, still ruled by the Communist Party yet increasingly marked by the accumulation of personal wealth, a widening income gap, exploding consumption, and the privatisation of public assets" (Jellema 2005: 233) has likewise remained unresolved. Ann Marie Leshkowich (2006) has analyzed the case of a south Vietnamese female entrepreneur who describes her economic success as a direct result of her devout adherence to Buddhism. Her argumentation is too complex to discuss here, but an important point Leshkowich makes is that her protagonist uses Buddhism as a morally superior strategy for making profit (vis-à-vis both the social relationship approach of male entrepreneurs and the "superstitious" spiritual practices of market women). In doing so, Leshkowich argues that this female entrepreneur "seeks to assert membership, as a woman, in the successful entrepreneurial class ... not by abandoning tradition in favour of Western modernity, but by building on that tradition to craft a specific kind of modern Vietnamese cultural economy" (ibid.: 304). The case of Mrs Thiền, Mrs Hồng, and the Ten Girls of Đồng Lộc Junction is quite different from the one described by Leshkowich, but it essentially addresses the same issue: the construction of an alternative Vietnamese modernity, a modernity that attends to the concerns of both Party state officials and those of hungry ghosts (which are not all that different), to the desires of accumulating personal wealth and conforming to the ethics of filial piety, to dealing with the vicissitudes of life and the horrors of death.

"They Are Now Serving in Heaven"

Upon her return from the meeting in Ho Chi Minh City, Mrs Thiền started to ponder what she could contribute to repaying the debt of gratitude (*đền ơn đáp nghĩa*) owed to the revolutionary war martyrs of Đồng Lộc Junction. Master Hiền advised her to stage a *Lễ Mông Sơn* at the memorial. This, he argued, would not only facilitate the salvation of the war martyrs' souls, but also smooth the process by which the Ten Girls turned into benevolent deities (*biến thành những vị thiên thần*). The total cost of the ritual, so he estimated, would amount to approximately ten to fifteen million dong (€500–750).[20] In the following weeks, Mrs Thiền enthusiastically devoted herself to raising funds through her network of sponsors, followers, friends, and colleagues. She prepared and distributed a printed notice that described the noble cause and the merits of commemorating the war dead in poetic language. Soon enough, she had accumulated more than eighteen million dong, of which Mrs Hồng had generously contributed one third. In addition, she had offered one of her company cars to transport offerings and participants to Đồng Lộc Junction, approximately 350 kilometers from Hanoi.

Mrs Thiền's journey in commemoration of the Ten Girls and their comrades who died on the battlefields along this part of the Ho Chi Minh trail started during the night of 11 November 2006. At three o'clock in the morning, the group of twenty participants, including ourselves, gathered at the entrance to Mrs Thiền's narrow lane. Everybody helped to pack the huge mountain of votive paper offerings that Mrs Thiền had bought for twelve million dong (€600) into Mrs Hồng's Mercedes van. Whereas the van headed straight for Hà Tĩnh province, the remaining two cars took the group from Hanoi on a pilgrimage to eight different temples before reaching Đồng Lộc Junction at six o'clock in the evening. Master Hiền, his eight apprentices, and one monk would make the journey by night train and arrive in the early hours of the following morning. They therefore missed the official welcome given the group by the Đồng Lộc memorial management board.

The Đồng Lộc memorial site covers the whole area around the junction and consists of several monuments, of which the one in honor of the Ten Girls is the most important.[21] The "historical site" (*khu di tích*) is administered by a management board (*ban quản lý*) responsible for its maintenance as well as for receiving visitors and providing them with information about the site's history. Upon arrival, our group was ushered into the main reception room. Photographs of high-ranking government officials visiting the memorial and lacquered panels with excerpts from their speeches adorned the walls. The tables were arranged around a huge glass showcase containing a model of the former combat zone. The front wall was covered with a red curtain, and a white plaster bust of Hồ Chí Minh looked down from a podium. In front of it stood a vase, a plate for offerings, and a ceramic incense holder—common items if a bust or image of the highly revered "father of the modern Vietnamese nation" is placed on an altar in a temple, but very unusual in an official setting like this. Next to the podium was a television set complete with video and karaoke equipment sponsored by a leading electronics company. When everybody had taken their seat, Mrs Thiền briefly introduced the group as a staff delegation from her university eager to learn more about the site's history from the management board. After a short welcome by the management board director, the floor was given to a charismatic young cadre named Tuấn. What now followed was an expertly crafted commemorative performance consisting of heart-breaking narratives, poems, and patriotic songs. Tuấn masterfully manipulated the emotions of his audience and evoked both painful and glorious memories of war. When Tuấn read the last letter of the Ten Girls' team leader to her mother, most female members of the group were moved to tears.

Struggling to keep her composure, Mrs Hồng then stood up and said what many participants felt at this moment: "We are like members of the same family, and we are all deeply indebted to the war heroes who sacrificed their lives so that we can live today." It is everyone's duty to repay at least a small fraction of this immense debt, Mrs Hồng continued, and therefore "we will pray for the peace of the Ten Girls' souls in order to assure that they have a safe journey to heaven." All this was done with the hope that the virgin war martyrs would continue to protect the nation and ensure its prosperity. Mrs Hồng concluded: "I hope that all of them will help our country in the open-door period, and especially now that we have just gained admission to the World Trade Organization."[22] The lingering sadness finally transformed into cathartic exhilaration when Tuấn turned on the karaoke soundtrack of a well-known patriotic song. The official welcome ended with the whole group clapping their hands in rhythm and joining the cadre in singing "We are marching down the Trương Sơn Road" (that is, the Ho Chi Minh trail).

In the wee hours of the following morning, the group gathered at the memorial and started preparing for the ritual. First, the votive paper offerings were carefully arranged in front of the monument. The Ten Girls were each allocated one two-storied house, three sets of clothes, one box of adornments, one flat palm hat (*nón quai thao*) and one traveling case in which to store everything. Mrs Thiền had also thought of two other groups of female fighters who had died in bomb attacks— eight girls from Quảng Bình and twelve girls from Nghệ An—and had prepared a slightly reduced set of items for them too. For the other revolutionary martyrs (*liệt sỹ*) of Đồng Lộc Junction, Mrs Thiền had bought a total of 1,000 paper shirts with matching ties, 1,500 meters of patterned paper fabric for all ordinary war dead of the area, and 1,000 sets of paper pyjamas for all other hungry souls roaming in the vicinity whose deaths were not related to the tragedy of war. When Master Hiền and his apprentices arrived they brought with them an astounding assortment of colorful Buddhist-Daoist decorations and ornaments. The memorial management board had provided a canvas cover that served as a canopy, shielding the ritual officiants from the glare of the sun, as well as some wooden desks from the meeting room that were arranged to form a makeshift dais for the monk.

The transformation of a national memorial into a religious structure, however, was not met with approval by the local security police, who suddenly turned up and started to voice strong reservations against the memorial's altered facade. The plain-clothes officer expressed his concern that the ritual would interfere with the tour program of visiting groups, and argued that the visitors wanted to see the memorial in its original appearance—that is, not adorned with colorful Buddha images and banners. After a short but fierce discussion, Mrs Thiền gave in to the cadre's order that these should be removed from the memorial without delay and obligingly assured him that the ritual would last no longer than an hour.

In fact, however, the ritual was to last much longer. Each of its several constituent parts pertained to the overall goal of bringing peace to the hungry souls of the war dead and leading them onto the path of salvation. Each part began with a lengthy recital of names from the long list of contributors to the ritual endeavor.

Figure 6.3: Blessing the votive paper garments offered to the war martyrs. Photograph by Andrea Lauser, 2006.

For almost three hours, the spirit priests chanted liturgical texts while the monk performed symbolic acts of purification and worship. With each passing hour, the members of the memorial management board watched the scene with growing nervousness. Occasionally, a group of visitors was ushered around the monument rather quickly. As the heat of afternoon came to its climax, the cameraman Mrs Thiền had hired to film the ritual was slowly losing his focus. Yet the spirit priests continued chanting unperturbed without showing any obvious signs of fatigue. At one point, Mrs Thiền led one of her female followers to one of the graves. Together, the two of them invoked the help of the young war heroine to change "the follower's [apparently errant] husband's attitude." The *Lễ Mông Sơn* finally ended with the burning of the votive paper offerings: each item was carefully unwrapped (the plastic foil collected by poor village women for recycling) and thrown into the crackling fire. While the flames engulfed €600 worth of gaudy paper, Master Hiền and his apprentices started to remove the decoration and quickly returned the memorial to its original state, leaving no trace of its temporary transformation except for the four black-and-white parallel phrases written in calligraphic *quốc ngữ*[23] that expressed—in a more poetic way than the memorial plaque—that the Ten Girls' heroic sacrifice would forever be gratefully remembered.

This, however, was not yet the end of the story. A month later, Mrs Thiền organized another ritual with the aim of applying for the Ten Girls' official recognition in the higher echelons of the spirit world. This honor-conferring ritual

Figure 6.4: Circumambulating the graves. Photograph by Andrea Lauser, 2006.

took place at a temple dedicated to the pantheon of the Four Palaces. Master Hiền presented petitions (*sớ*) to the gods and read out the honor-conferring edict listing the names of the Ten Girls. In order to supplement the offerings sacrificed during the *Lễ Mông Sơn*, Mrs Hồng and another woman now contributed a set of more feminine votive paper outfits that also included ten glamorous paper lingerie sets, embellished with scintillating sequins, and matching high heeled strappy sandals. Among the participants was also Mrs Quyền, a female soul-caller whom Mrs Thiền often refers her clients to in case a ritual requires establishing contact with the souls of the ancestors. When the honor-conferring rite had ended, Mrs Quyền suddenly became possessed by Võ Thị Tần, the team leader of the female volunteer unit. The brief conversation that unfolded between the (mostly female) participants and the soul of the virgin war hero was interspersed with heart-breaking sobs, bright smiles, and the occasional military salutation. Mrs Thiền finally invited Võ Thị Tần to descend into the soul-caller's body on another day, at Mrs Thiền's private temple. This encounter was scheduled for the sixth day of the eleventh lunar month. Space does not permit us to repeat in detail the rich exchange that ensued on that day (see Endres 2008). Most importantly, the soul representing the Ten Girls gratefully acknowledged having received the offerings and pleaded with Mrs Thiền to consider the organization of more such rituals for the war martyrs' souls at other national cemeteries and memorials, where whole armies of hungry ghosts still remained uncared for. Moreover, the girl's soul attended to a variety of concerns raised by the attendees—such as marital conflicts, family issues, and illness. In this sense, Mrs Thiền had successfully integrated the Ten Girls into her "supernatural network" of divine beings that could be approached by humans for their assistance and advice.

A Convergence of Different Worlds

As our ethnographic example shows, the memorial site of Đồng Lộc Junction is a multivocal arena in which socialist-nationalist and global-neoliberal trajectories of modernity intersect and interact with the realms of popular religious belief, human creativity, and economic prosperity. On the level of national-patriotic discourse, the fighting spirit and heroism of the Vietnamese people have certainly become the most important signifiers of national identity, if not to say the nation's civic religion. In a rather ambivalent way, this political discourse intersects with (or is challenged by) the spiritualized (or religious) discourse that has gathered new strength and momentum over the past two decades. In actual fact, Mrs Thiền's ambitions as a spirit medium are still very close to what has hitherto been labeled "superstition." Therefore, if she wants to have her activities seen as completely justifiable and legitimate, she must organize them under the theme of heroism and ancestor worship. The moral-economic discourse of the post-"renovation" era, in turn, not only legitimizes the pursuit of wealth but almost declares it a moral duty toward the heroic ancestors and martyrs who sacrificed their lives so that others could (one day) enjoy peace and prosperity. At the same time, however, the comprehensive development goal of the country, to build a "rich people, strong country, civilized and equal society," also raises concerns about the moral principles that (should) guide individuals in their personal pursuit of wealth. It is in this complex multivocal arena that our (predominantly female) actors construct their lives and imbue them with meaning and significance.

Let us again take a short look at who our actors are. First of all, as outlined in the Introduction to this volume, the Ten Girls must be seen as "part of the agentive network." As revolutionary war martyrs (*liệt sĩ*) they are, in actual fact, not exceptional. What makes them special is that they were ten in number when they sacrificed their lives in one single stroke (ten is seen as a perfect number that implies completeness), and that their bodies were found intact and undamaged by the bombing. Their innocence—and thus the tragic, or "unjustness" of their death—is heightened by their female gender and the fact that they are believed to have died as virgins. While the Ten Girls represent (a kind of) an archetypal ideal in the state cult of remembrance and the official pantheon of patriotic heroes, their commemoration also feeds the contrapuntal discourse that emerged at the dawn of "renovation" policy in 1986. This "counter-memory" in the Foucauldian sense evokes the darker side of heroism and the high price that had to be paid for the country's "liberation" (*giải phóng*) (Huệ-Tâm Hồ Tài 2001b: 180; see also Bradley 2001). At the same time, the idea of their "unjust death" also facilitates the conceptualization of young female heroes as powerful spiritual beings who are receptive to the attention of their propitiants.

Second, Mrs Thiền is a master medium and spiritual broker who offers her followers and supporters a wide range of ritual services and remedies (see also Endres 2011: 149–55). Strictly speaking, she is not a businesswoman and therefore depends on her followers' and supporters' donations and contributions in order to finance her ambitious ritual projects. Mrs Hồng, in turn, is a highly successful female entrepreneur concerned with the moral dimension of the new economy. As a woman who was born in the same time period as the Ten Girls, she feels under pressure to remoralize her wealth. The question for her (as for many others who belong to Vietnam's emerging class of newly rich) is, therefore, "how to be at once wealthy and good" (Jellema 2005: 235). Our human female actors represent a generation of women who reinvent and position themselves in various engendered spaces that mark the transformational dynamics of late socialist Vietnam. Whereas Mrs Thiền creates her space of action and power in the religious realm and gathers rich followers in order to pursue spiritual projects, Mrs Hồng seems eager to use (a small portion of) her wealth in order to bring her feminine spiritual needs (which might also be called "superstitions" by some) in line with patriotic sentiments. Finally, the ritual acts intended to appease the Ten Girls' souls condense the whole scenario into a complex network of mutual obligation and reciprocal relations in which women entice the souls of the war dead with conspicuous offerings, and the spirits gratefully return the attention by bestowing happiness and prosperity.

Notes

1. The so-called Ho Chi Minh trail ran through the rugged borderlands of Vietnam, Laos, and Cambodia. It was not a single route, but rather a complex web of jungle paths, truck routes, and river transportation systems that enabled North Vietnamese communist troops to infiltrate the South and ensure a steady flow of supplies for the military effort. The Vietnamese refer to the trail as the Trương Sơn Road (Đường Trương Sơn).
2. All personal names used in this chapter are pseudonyms.
3. According to the official Đồng Lộc memorial site publication (CYO 2004), between April and October 1968 this less than twenty kilometer long section of the road system underwent at least two thousand air bombardments with nearly fifty thousand bombs dropped day and night (ibid.: 21). This publication is the official brochure of the historical site of Đồng Lộc Junction and the National Volunteer Youth, issued by the Communist Youth Organisation of Hà Tĩnh Province.
4. Hirschman, Preston, and Vu Manh Loi (1995) estimate the numbers of Vietnamese war dead at one million. It is important to note that the nationwide commemorative effort excludes those who died while serving in the army of the Republic of Vietnam (South Vietnam); only those who fell fighting the French or fighting for the North are commemorated.
5. From 1997 to 2004, economic growth averaged 6.8 per cent per year, even against the background of the Asian financial crisis and a global recession; see http://www.index-mundi.com/vietnam/economy_profile.html, retrieved 7 January 2009.
6. The translation follows Malarney (2001: 57); a more literal translation would be "the land of the ancestors records your work" (ibid.).
7. A similar idiom is "offerings depend on financial means" (*tuỳ tiền biện lễ*), which is a more literal rendering of the same idea.
8. The district administration of Can Lộc, for example, requested four hundred youth volunteers and received over three thousand applications (CYO 2004: 15).
9. The slogans of the Volunteer Youth eulogize military spirit and romantic solidarity, e.g., "all for the frontline" (*tất cả cho tiền tuyến*), and "the enemy destroys one, we multiply by ten" (*địch phá một, ta làm mười*). See CYO (2004: 13).
10. This image of the Ten Girls is also conveyed in Nghiêm Văn Tân's memoir (Nghiêm Văn Tân 2006) and the feature film *Ngã ba Đồng Lộc* (dir. Lưu Trọng Ninh 1997).
11. After the official unification of the country under communist rule in 1976, the name was changed to the Socialist Republic of Vietnam (SRV).
12. The English translation was extensively revised and adapted to American War jargon. This is why some Vietnamese place names have been distorted; for example, that of the *gọi hồn* marshes in the central highlands. While the meaning of *gọi hồn* is "calling the souls of the dead," the translation in Bao Ninh's novel reads "Jungle of Screaming Souls"; see Kleinen and Cao Xuan Tu (1998).
13. The number of Vietnamese missing in action are estimated at three hundred thousand.
14. The service operated under the rubric of the "scientific experiment into the finding of graves by special capabilities" (*chương trình khảo nghiệm khoa học tìm mộ từ xa bằng khả năng đặc biệt*). Its mission was to test and verify the success rate of people with unusual abilities (*khả năng đặc biệt*), and to establish hypotheses to explain them. Today, various institutions take on a similar task—e.g., the Center for Research into Human Capabilities (*Trung tâm nghiên cứu tiềm năng cua con người*). Whereas some

psychics (i.e., people with extra-sensory perception) are affiliated with such official or semi-official services, others work independently. Psychics apply different methods in their search, as illustrated by the impressive BBC2 documentary *Psychic Vietnam* produced by Joe Phua and broadcast on 18 May 2002 (see http://news.bbc.co.uk/2/hi/programmes/this_world/4758847.stm). See also Schlecker and Endres (2011).

15. Malarney mentions this possibility but did not encounter any such cases during his fieldwork in Thinh Liet (Malarney 2002: 232 n.5).
16. For example, children who died young are believed to become servants of the Third Princess, *Cô Bơ*, who is part of the Four Palaces pantheon and belongs to the Water Palace.
17. Interestingly, the process of deification involved a time of study and apprenticeship "in an other-world academic institution" while gaining a reputation by possessing new spirit mediums or soul-callers and transmitting their stories through them.
18. In the case of a complicated concern, she refers her followers to another spirit priest whom she considers even more knowledgeable and skilful (*giỏi hơn*).
19. See http://www.toquoc.gov.vn/vietnam/showPrint.asp?newsId=4612, retrieved 9 July 2007.
20. The average annual per capita income in Vietnam is currently about €1700.
21. Others include a large obelisk with a huge plaque right at the T-junction, another towering monument with a heroic sculpture approximately fifty meters away from the first, a small memorial hall dedicated to the commemoration of the fallen members of the Volunteer Youth, another small hall dedicated to all war dead who died at Đồng Lộc Junction, and a small museum.
22. A few days before this trip, on 7 November, Vietnam had finally been accepted into the Word Trade Organization.
23. *Quốc ngữ* (national language) is the current script for the Vietnamese language based on the Latin alphabet.

References

Ashplant, Timothy G., Graham Dawson, and Michael Roper, eds. 2000. *The Politics of War Memory and Commemoration*. London: Routledge.
Bảo Ninh. 1996[1993]. *The Sorrow of War: A Novel of North Vietnam*. New York: Riverhead Books.
Bradley, Mark Philip. 2001. "Contests of Memory: Remembering and Forgetting War in the Contemporary Vietnamese Cinema," in *The Country of Memory: Remaking the Past in Late Socialist Vietnam*, ed. H.-T. H. Tai. Berkeley: University of California Press, pp.196–226.
CYO. 2004. "Ngã bà Đồng Lộc—Ngã ba anh hùng [Đồng Lộc Junction—junction of heroes]," Hà Tĩnh Province, Vietnam: Communist Youth Organisation.
Đặng Nghiêm Vạn. 1996. "The Cult of Ancestors as a Religion," *Vietnamese Studies* 3: 35–64.
———. 1998. *Ethnological and Religious Problems in Vietnam*. Hanoi: Social Sciences Publishing House.
Endres, Kirsten W. 2000. *Ritual, Fest und Politik: Zwischen Tradition und Ideologie*. Hamburg: LIT Verlag.
———. 2008. "Engaging the Spirits of the Dead: Soul-calling Rituals and the Performative Construction of Efficacy," *Journal of the Royal Anthropological Institute* 14(4): 755–73.
———. 2011. *Performing the Divine: Mediums, Markets and Modernity in Urban Vietnam*. Copenhagen: Nordic Institute of Asian Studies Press.
Fforde, Adam, and Stefan de Vylder. 1996. *From Plan to Market: The Economic Transition in Vietnam*. Boulder, CO: Westview Press.

Gammeltoft, Tine. 2001. "'Faithful, Heroic, Resourceful': Changing Images of Women in Vietnam," in *Vietnamese Society in Transition: The Daily Politics of Reform and Change*, ed. J. Kleinen. Amsterdam: Het Spinhuis, pp.265–80.

Hefner, Robert W., ed. 1998. *Market Cultures: Society and Values in the New Asian Capitalisms*. Singapore: Institute of Southeast Asian Studies.

Hirschman, Charles, Samuel Preston, and Vu Manh Loi. 1995. "Vietnamese Casualities During the American War: A New Estimate," *Population and Development Review* 21(4): 783–812.

Huệ-Tâm Hồ Tài. 2001a. "Situating Memory," in *The Country of Memory: Remaking the Past in Late Socialist Vietnam*, ed. H.-T. H. Tai. Berkeley: University of California Press, pp.1–17

———. 2001b. "Faces of Remembrance and Forgetting," in *The Country of Memory: Remaking the Past in Late Socialist Vietnam*, ed. H.-T. H. Tai. Berkeley: University of California Press, pp.167–95.

Jellema, Kate. 2005. "Making Good on Debt: The Remoralisation of Wealth in Post-revolutionary Vietnam," *Asia Pacific Journal of Anthropology* 6(3): 231–48.

———. 2007. "Everywhere Incense Burning: Remembering Ancestors in Đổi Mới Vietnam," *Journal of Southeast Asian Studies* 38(3): 467–92.

Kerkvliet, Ben Tria. 2005. *The Power of Everyday Politics: How Vietnamese Peasants Transformed National Policy*. Ithaca, NY: Cornell University Press.

Kleinen, John. 1999. *Facing the Future, Reviving the Past: A Study of Social Change in a Northern Vietnamese Village*. Singapore: Institute of Southeast Asian Studies.

Kleinen, John, and Cao Xuan Tu. 1998. "The Vietnam War through Vietnamese Eyes: A Review of Literary Fiction and Cinema," *Vietnam Review*, March, 345–68.

Kwon, Heonik. 2006. *After the Massacre: Commemoration and Consolation in Ha My and My Lai*. Berkeley: University of California Press.

———. 2008. *Ghosts of War in Vietnam*. Cambridge: Cambridge University Press.

Lauser, Andrea. 2008a. "Zwischen Heldenverehrung und Geisterkult. Politik und Religion im gegenwärtigen spätkommunistischen Vietnam," *Zeitschrift für Ethnologie* 133: 121–44.

———. 2008b. "Ahnen, Götter, Geister in Vietnam und in der Diaspora: Ein transnationales Forschungsfeld," in *Migration und religiöse Dynamik: Ethnologische Religionsforschung im transnationalen Kontext*, eds. A. Lauser and C. Weisskoeppel. Bielefeld: Transcript, pp.147–72.

Leshkowich, Ann Marie. 2006. "Woman, Buddhist, Entrepreneur: Gender, Moral Values, and Class Anxiety in Late Socialist Vietnam," *Journal of Vietnamese Studies* 1/2: 277–313.

Malarney, Shaun K. 2001. "'The Fatherland Remembers Your Sacrifice': Commemorating War Dead in North Vietnam," in *The Country of Memory: Remaking the Past in Late Socialist Vietnam*, ed. H.-T. H. Tai. Berkeley: University of California Press, pp.46–76.

———. 2002. *Culture, Ritual, and Revolution in Vietnam*. London: Routledge Curzon.

———. 2007. "Festivals and the Dynamics of the Exceptional Dead in Northern Vietnam," *Journal of Southeast Asian Studies* 38(3): 515–40.

Nelson, John. 2003. "Social Memory as Ritual Practice: Commemorating Spirits of the Military Dead at Yasukuni Shinto Shrine," *Journal of Asian Studies* 62(2): 443–67.

Nghiêm Văn Tân. 2006. *10 Cô gái Ngã ba Đồng Lộc: Truyện ký*. [The Ten Girls of Đồng Lộc Junction: A Memoir]. Hanoi: NXB Phụ Nữ.

Nguyễn Thị Hiền. 2006. "'A Bit of a Spirit Favor is Equal to a Load of Mundane Gifts': Votive Paper Offerings of *Len Dong* Rituals in Post-renovation Vietnam," in *Possessed by the Spirits: Mediumship in Contemporary Vietnamese Communities*, eds K. Fjelstad and T.H. Nguyễn. Ithaca, NY: Southeast Asia Program, Cornell University, pp.127–42.

Pelzer, Kristin. 1993. "United States and Vietnam: On the Need for Spiritual Reconciliation," *Buddhist–Christian Studies* 13: 247–57.

Roudometof, Victor. 2003. "Beyond Commemoration: The Politics of Collective Memory," *Journal of Political and Military Sociology* 31(2): 161–69.

Schlecker, Markus. 2007. "Welfare and Wellbeing," unpublished paper presented at the international conference "Modernities and Dynamics of Tradition in Vietnam: Anthropological Approaches," Binh Chau Resort, Vietnam, 15–18 December.

Schlecker, Markus, and Kirsten W. Endres. 2011. "Psychic Experience, Truth and Visuality in Postwar Vietnam," *Social Analysis* 55(1): 2–22.

Schwenkel, Christina. 2009. *The American War in Contemporary Vietnam: Transnational Remembrance and Representation*. Bloomington: Indiana University Press.

Tatum, James. 1996. "Memorials of the America War in Vietnam," *Critical Inquiry* 22(4): 634–78.

Taylor, Philip. 2004. *Goddess on the Rise: Pilgrimage and Popular Religion in Vietnam*. Honolulu: University of Hawaii Press.

Taylor, Sandra C. 1999. *Vietnamese Women at War. Fighting for Ho Chi Minh and the Revolution*. Lawrence: University Press of Kansas.

Tréglodé, Benôit de. 2001. *Héros et Révolution au Viêt Nam*. Paris: L'Harmattan.

Turner, Karen Gottschang (with Phan Thanh Hao). 1998. *Even the Women Must Fight: Memories of War From North Vietnam*. New York: Wiley.

Yuval-Davis, Nira. 1997. *Gender and Nation*. London: Sage.

7

SPIRIT CULTS AND CONSTRUCTION SITES: TRANS-ETHNIC POPULAR RELIGION AND *KERAMAT* SYMBOLISM IN CONTEMPORARY MALAYSIA

Beng-Lan Goh

The brief economic bubble of the early 1990s ushered in a period of relative prosperity and heightened national reimagining in Malaysia as the country joined the ranks of the dragons of the Asia-Pacific economic rim. As the Malaysian economy prospered with its increasing integration into the global market, economic globalization quickly became a nationalist goal. This was marked by the launch of the grandiose National Vision 2020 by the then prime minister Mahathir Mohammad, which aimed to make Malaysia a fully industrialized country by the year 2020.

This new nationalist vision made economic liberalization and cultural reinvention imperative. Capital controls were relaxed in order to stimulate investment. This spate of liberalization had particular effects on the building industry as various policies regarding land, property law, taxation, and investment were relaxed in order to facilitate foreign capital flows into the Malaysian building industry (Goh 2002).

On the cultural front, however, things were a bit more complicated. The National Vision saw the launch of a new "Malaysian nation" (*bangsa Malaysia*) which envisioned a breed of sophisticated, technologically informed, and globally oriented citizenry. However, this spate of cultural reimagining was accompanied by an escalating official anti-Western rhetoric whereby elements of "tradition" and "Islam" were valorized and re-envisioned, and grandiose urban building projects were undertaken that expressed new national sensibilities responsive to market instrumentalities (see ibid.: 51ff.). In the context of Malaysia's multi-ethnic body

---

Endnotes for this chapter begin on page 160

politic, this cultural reimagining had contradictory consequences. On one front, the envisioning of a "Malaysian nation" challenged existing boundaries between the cultural core (Malays, indigenous groups) and citizens (non-Malays), and enabled a move away from a narrow or exclusive definition of a Malay nation. This inclusionary imagining of the Malaysian nation at the official level encouraged active debate at the everyday level, whereby demands for equal rights and opportunities for all were made at various intersections of ethnicity, class, gender, and so on. Given the Islamism of Malaysian public life since the 1980s—in which the Malaysian state and the Islamic opposition party (PAS) had been locked in a battle to out-Islamize each other (Mohamad 2001)—the valorization of Islam as a counter-cultural idiom by the state only helped consolidate Islam as a formidable, emotive and pre-eminent force of Malay identity. As a significant identity marker of Malayness in Malaysia, the expansion of Islam beyond the framework of Malay nationalism into a global political force served to fragment the Malay community itself, besides widening tensions between Malay Muslims on the one hand and non-Malays and non-Muslims on the other. This complicated identity politics resulted in highly ethnicized discourses about the country's economic, urban, and technological achievements during the 1990s (Goh 2002: 52–62).

In an ethnographic study of urban development in Georgetown, Penang, during this period, I found that urban actors were actively taking on ethno-cultural arguments about the "New Malaysia" originating in official political discourse in order to pursue their goals (ibid.). Amongst them, property developers stood out as the most innovative group as they took the opportunity of a market upswing to tempt the newly rich in Malaysian society into acquiring modern lifestyles. However, at the same time as they aggressively pursued their business ventures, I observed a curious oddity: property developers were devoutly propitiating a Malay Muslim spirit known as *keramat* or its Sinicized version, the *datuk kong* (*nadugong*),[1] a guardian spirit of local sacred places. All property developers whom I studied erected makeshift shrines to venerate the *keramat* at their construction sites, and some even went to great lengths to perform elaborate rituals to appease these Malay Muslim spirits in the course of their development activities. Some of these makeshift shrines became permanent structures of the urban landscape of modern Penang, being rebuilt at inconspicuous corners within the compounds of new residential estates, shopping and commercial complexes, hotels, other recreational resorts, and so on.

Engaging with anthropological perspectives on spirit cults, this chapter explores the symbolic significance of *keramat* worship amongst property developers in terms of its conjuncture with capitalist modernity and ethno-religious nationalism in Malaysia. It argues that the *keramat* cult is not merely a medium which negotiates the contradictions of capitalism but also serves as a repository of the deep structures of trans-ethnic cosmologies and shared socio-moral orders within local society despite their erasure by modern bureaucratic powers.

Understanding Capitalist Sacralization

Modern spirit cults have generally been studied in terms of subaltern resistance against capitalist oppression and commoditization in recent anthropological works. Seen as symbolic orders which express capitalist tensions and contradictions, a wide spectrum of supernatural practices and cosmologies have been treated as idioms through which powerless groups express, wrestle with, contain, and maneuver themselves in relation to the exploitation, commoditization, and contradictions of capitalist relations (see, e.g., Lewis 1971; Nash 1979; Taussig 1980; Comaroff 1985; Ong 1987; Kitiarsa 2008). As a result, we have learnt a great deal about local conceptions of power and morality under modern conditions, in particular how subaltern identity constructions and resistance within capitalist processes are embedded in and mediated by supernatural activities and framed by various indigenous cultural logics.[2] The involvement of a powerful group of capitalists such as property developers in spirit cults in the course of capitalist accumulation, however, overturns these usual links between sacralization and capitalism. It raises questions about the connections between powerful capitalist actors and religious symbolism which have remained under-explored in anthropological studies. This under-exploration may in part be due to a common assumption that capitalist accumulation is essentially a productivist and desacralized activity. Capitalist actors, we often assume, are rational actors who only accommodate alternative moral logics into their practice when compelled by forces outside the capitalist process. For instance, capitalist actors may at times have to bow to pressure or resistance by marginalized groups who may resort to cultural resistance or political lobbying as a means to curb capitalist powers. However, there is no assurance that economic power alone guarantees political and cultural domination. Pragmatically speaking, like all other social actors, powerful capitalists may for a variety of reasons voluntarily embrace alternative logics in the course of pursuing their economic goals.

My findings suggest that *keramat* worship amongst property developers in Penang, Malaysia, is precisely such an example, although dimensions of subaltern resistance may also be associated with this spirit cult when adopted by marginal groups (see Ong 1987).[3] For the purpose of understanding *keramat* propitiation amongst property developers in Malaysia, I find older anthropological studies which approach capitalist sacralization in the context of wider historical, cultural, and moral forces of social reproduction useful. Rather than merely subsuming capitalist sacralization within the logic of capitalist pursuits and contradictions, these studies tie the phenomenon of capitalist sacralization to larger historical processes of socio-moral reproduction (Parry and Bloch 1989). Such perspectives overturn normative assumptions about capitalism as merely a desacralized, individualistic, and accumulative activity. Instead they provide us with a way to view capitalism as being ineluctably entwined with historical socio-moral imperatives of social reproduction. It is the imbrications of capitalism and the historical and socio-moral forces of reproducing society that explain the forces of capitalist sacralization. It is such a framework that I find useful in explaining the conjoining of the *keramat* cult and property development in Malaysian capitalist modernity.

My analysis shows how the phenomenon of *keramat* worship—a symbolic order of supernatural protection and harm from hazardous economic activities and natural calamities—amongst property developers is rooted in the deep structures of cultural hybridity of the maritime Malay world upon which modern Malaysian society is founded. Converging with Chinese supernatural beliefs in the context of increasing bureaucratic controls over Islam in Malaysia, the *keramat* cult has become a potent idiom for expressing and negotiating tensions inherent in a highly speculative industry and an ethnically charged political economy. Only by understanding the complex coming together of deep maritime historical structures of pluralism, capitalism, and Malaysian ethno-religious nationalism can we better understand the logics that accompany this peculiar capitalist sacralization.

Beyond the usual interpretations of subaltern resistance, the phenomenon of the Malaysian *keramat* cult compels those who study modern capitalist sacralization to address its complicity with the politics of ethno-religious nationalism and its role as a vehicle which reinstates deeply rooted socio-moral orders which cannot be simply erased by the forces of modern bureaucracy and social organization. In addition, I argue that the trans-ethnic and trans-cultural symbolism displayed in this cult offer competing definitions of Islam and ethnicity to those produced by Malaysian state discourses, challenging their enforced rigid boundaries and narrow meanings of ethnicity and religion.

In what follows, I first offer an overall picture of *keramat* propitiation amongst property developers amidst a situation of rapid but precarious capitalist growth and a changing political arena in Penang and wider Malaysia. I then delineate the relationship between this instance of popular religion and larger historical and political-economic transformations in Malaysia to explain the cult's popularity amongst property developers. These insights provide the background in relation to which the ritual symbolism of *keramat* worship amongst property developers is analyzed.

The *Keramat* Cult and Property Developers in Penang

I first became aware of *keramat* propitiation amongst property developers in Penang when I was doing research on urban development in Penang in the early 1990s. I had initially studied twenty property development companies which were aggressively transforming Penang's cityscape. The analysis provided here is based upon data collected during this early research as well as subsequent research conducted in recent years into transformations of this Malay Muslim spirit cult.

All the companies studied, with the exception of one joint Indian–Chinese venture, began as Chinese investments, of which five took on Malay partners along the way. During my fieldwork, it was possible for property development companies to be wholly foreign owned for the first five years of operation.[4] This situation came about following the liberalization of the National Land Code in 1988 which allowed 100 per cent foreign equity in new hotel and tourist construction projects. Of the companies I studied, five began as local–foreign joint ventures which involved Japanese, Taiwanese, Kuwaiti, and Sino-Indonesian capital; only one company was wholly owned by Taiwanese. The capitalization nature of these companies demonstrates that all the developers felt compelled by Malaysia's nationalist ideology to incorporate Malay partners from the off despite the five years' leeway allowed.

There was a pragmatic reason for foreign investors to take on Malay partners. Developers told of how having Malay partners, especially those who are politically connected, made it much easier for their companies to obtain the necessary permits and safeguarded their projects from compulsory land acquisition by the state. Section 3(b) of Malaysia's Land Acquisition Act (1960) provides state authorities with the power to acquire land on its own behalf from a corporation undertaking work of public utility.

Government controls over the property development industry are exercised in the form of legislations at national and state levels.[5] These regulations aim to standardize the industry, protect consumers as well as compel developers to contribute to nationalist development goals. In addition, property developers are compelled by government rulings to conform to various nationalist development agendas. For instance, in 1991 the Ministry of Housing and Local Government imposed a ruling requiring developers to adopt Malay names for their projects. Developers are, however, known to circumvent this ruling by using Malay names when they apply for advertising permission from the Ministry but then switch to non-Malay names when promoting their projects. At the state level, local planning rules also require developers to contribute to nationalist goals. In Penang, which has a Chinese-majority population which holds much of the state's economic power, fulfilling nationalist objectives becomes ever more imperative.

All of the developers studied speculated heavily in high-cost condominiums and commercial properties which came into vogue in Malaysia during the 1990s. As we know, property development is a highly volatile industry characterized by short cycles of boom and bust. The property upturn of the early 1990s, stimulated by the relaxation of foreign equity stipulations under the New Economy Policy, was the fourth of a series of property booms to occur in Malaysia after it gained independence (Lim and Pang 1991: 88; Salih 1991: 5).[6] One of the greatest challenges in the industry is for a developer to know when to step up construction activities during economic upturns and when to stop or slow down prior to a downturn. An inability to read the market correctly can lead to disastrous consequences, as demonstrated in the severe downturn in property development during the mid 1980s alongside a nationwide recession in Malaysia which forced many developers into bankruptcy.

As property developers actively reshaped the urban landscape, they inevitably faced resistance by community and squatter groups affected by their activities. I found that while property developers were most effective in negotiating impediments posed by urban squatters and tenants standing in the way of their projects, they were less successful in rejecting the demands of certain Indian and Chinese "gods" or deities evoked by their devotees for the relocation of their shrines within their development sites. However, the most puzzling thing to me was the active and voluntary propitiation of *keramat*s—a Malay Muslim guardian spirit— at their construction sites. Of the twenty companies studied, all reported to have participated in *keramat* propitiation in the course of their activities. In fact two companies which were owned by born-again Christians[7] also carried out *keramat* propitiation, although these developers explained that they had only allowed it as their contractors and workers would not carry out work if the *keramat* spirit was not first appeased.

For most developers, *keramat* propitiation rituals were held at the beginning and ending of construction activities. It was also common that an additional propitiation ritual would be held if construction activities coincided with the "hungry ghost" festival celebrations observed by the Chinese community in Penang during the seventh lunar month. Usually two other Chinese spirits or ghosts—Tua Pek Kong (Dabogong) and Ho Hia Ti Kong (Hao Xiongdi Gong)—would be propitiated along with the *keramat* during the "hungry ghost" month.

Commonly, propitiation rituals were quick and simple. In most cases, small three-dimensional zinc structures were erected at construction sites prior to ground breaking for the propitiation rituals. These structures were painted red, and Chinese-style urns, believed to embody the *keramat* spirit, were placed inside these shrines. These shrines were usually removed after the completion of the project. Noticeably, only in projects located in the foothills adjacent to forested terrain were makeshift shrines rebuilt as permanent structures and relocated to corners within the compounds of completed projects. In one case, the company built a shrine on a 5,000 square foot plot of land at the back of its condominium project. Interestingly, the shrine shared the spot with a popular Chinese deity— Tua Pek Kong (Dabogong)—who is supposed to guard pioneer settlements.[8] I was told that the company spent about RM 30,000 on the shrines,[9] a larger sum than that which most developers were prepared to use to compensate urban squatters during the period of my study.

Propitiation rituals mimic practices found in Chinese popular religion. Typically, in simple and quick rituals, the *keramat* were offered white candles, joss sticks, water, coffee, or tea, and worship items known in the Hokkien dialect as *datuk kong liao* (*nadugong liao, ji pin*). These ingredients typically included benzoin (a type of incense), flowers, betel leaves, quick lime, and flakes of areca nut. In construction projects located near to hills or on sites originally associated with *keramat* presence, or those which encountered accidents upon starting work, more elaborate propitiation rituals were held. These rituals would typically involve food offerings of *nasi kunyit* (turmeric rice), chicken or mutton curry. Significantly, though, *keramat* offerings are strictly halal—that is, the food must follow Islamic law regarding the killing and preparing of meat: animals must be slaughtered according to Islamic rites, and the food must not contain pork, nor be cooked with utensils that have ever touched pork or lard. In these elaborate *keramat* propitiations, nearby communities were invited to partake of the food offerings after the rituals. Because of the requirement that the food be halal, property developers had to obtain ritual offerings from Malays. In Penang there are a few renowned Malay Muslim shops and stalls which specialize in providing food for *keramat* propitiation.

Some of these elaborate propitiation rituals displayed overt religious eclecticism, drawing on popular Islamic and Indian religious elements besides the predominant aspects of Chinese popular religion. One company whose development was located near a hill in the predominantly Malay suburb of Sungei Ara engaged a Malay *pawang* (shaman) and Chinese spirit medium *kitong* (*jitong*) for its propitiation ritual. During this ritual, the *pawang* first recited Koranic verses (*baca doa*) which was followed by a ritual and a seance by the spirit medium.

When I asked developers why they bothered with the *keramat*, the two commonest explanations I received were: for the sake of work safety; and to ensure that construction activities ran smoothly without delays. Mixed sentiments of reverence and fear indicated by desires to appease or avoid punishment, avert work disruption, and secure agreement and blessings were evident from responses gathered. One of the property developers, a born-again Christian, explained that he did not want to have anything to do with *keramat* propitiation given his Christian beliefs, but he had had to give permission to his contractors to carry out the ritual. He finally gave in to pressure from his contractor who persistently nagged him about allowing *keramat* worship at the company's construction site. The contractor, the property developer explained, cited several mishaps at the worksite as well as repeated disturbing dreams about the *keramat*'s unhappiness as grounds for his demand.[10] The developer told me that although he finally allowed a *keramat* propitiation to be held on his project site, he had told his contractor not to provide him with any details about the ritual as he did not want to know anything about it. He explained that he had only given approval on the basis that no shrine was to be erected at the construction site.

The rationales provided by property developers point to a prevalent belief in the power of the *keramat* amongst this group of capitalists who saw their construction activities as transgressing sacred spaces guarded by this Malay Muslim supernatural being. Yet at times a pragmatic attitude towards the *keramat* could also be observed, particularly with regard to the removal of the shrine upon completion of construction activities. The once-sacred temporary shrines were often callously dismantled after the last appeasement ritual. Even the urns, said to embody the *keramat* and hence a sacred object that should not be destroyed even when shrines are demolished, were also casually removed by workers and placed at various Chinese and Indian temples. Developers often could not care less about where the urns went:

> When we dismantle the shrine when everything is completed, a ritual is done to remove the shrine. The urn [is] removed to a Chinese or Indian temple. The temples are paid money for it. The temples place the urns in front of their various deities or anywhere in the temple. I don't really care or know much about what the temples do with the urns.

Amongst the companies studied, I only found one company which continued to carry out weekly *keramat* propitiation activities even after completion of its project. This company had built a permanent *keramat* shrine behind its condo-minium-cum-hotel project in Batu Ferringhi, northern Penang. The *keramat* propitiated at this site is known to be one of the most powerful in Malaysia, the Panglima Hitam (Black Warriors). Panglima Hitam refers to a group of seven brothers whose mythic origins can be traced to Melaka, the state associated with the founding of the Malay polity and civilization (see Ng 1977). Recent field visits to this *keramat* indicate that propitiation rituals are still being carried out. However, there is a new addition: a photograph of Ganesha, the Hindu elephant god,

Figure 7.1: Shrine of Panglima Hitam and Ganesha in Batu Feringghi, Penang. Photograph by Beng-Lan Goh, 2004.

is now placed beside the urn, which holds seven flags, said to embody the spirit of the Panglima Hitam.

The overall picture of *keramat* propitiation amongst property developers in Penang shows that this group of capitalist actors were compelled by a popular belief in the supernatural power of the *keramat* as the guardian of local grounds. Developers had gone to great lengths to conduct propitiation rituals and build permanent shrines, believing that these efforts were necessary to protect their workers and ensure smooth work operations. Clearly the dangers, competitiveness, and volatility of the construction industry in part explain the concurrence between property development and the *keramat* which has long been a symbolic order through which the uncertainties and perils associated with dangerous or risky economic activities are negotiated. It could be argued that the propitiation of the *keramat* stemmed in part from the developers' desire to avoid ill luck, work accidents, and failure in a highly unpredictable economic sector where circumstances are often outside of their control.

Yet, beyond economic risk, the imperative to propitiate the *keramat*, a Malay Muslim guardian spirit, when a wide array of other guardian spirits who perform similar functions of protection are found in local folk religions,[11] points to the significance of Malay Muslim politics which comprise a central feature of Malaysian nationalism. The common perception amongst developers that their construction activities transgressed the sacred boundaries guarded by a Malay Muslim guardian spirit that they needed to appease reflect their anxieties about state power. The regulatory powers of the state and its ethno-religious ideologies are clearly everyday realities faced by property developers. Given the powerful political control exercised by the Malaysian state and its agencies, symbolic orders are often more efficient safety valves through which creative ways of coping with or overcoming state powers can take place. The worship of *keramat* or *datuk kong* could be read as a metaphor of Malay Muslim political dominance. It is interesting to note that amongst property developers, who are predominantly ethnic Chinese, the identity of the Muslim *keramat* is strongly associated with Malayness, whereas *keramat*s are also known to be associated with other Arabic saints amongst the Malay-Muslim population in Malaysia (see Mandal 1997).

We could read *keramat* worship by developers as representing both respect and a desire to curtail, appease, or circumvent the Malaysian state and Malay Muslim power. The propitiation rituals display reverence for the power of the *keramat* over the land, in part seen through the observance of Muslim food customs. Yet, a pragmatic attitude is observed in developers' veneration of the *keramat* in the way that they could not care less what happened to the urns which are said to embody the spirit as long as the necessary propitiation rituals are carried out prior to their removal. This attitude is similarly reflected in the business strategies of developers as they take on Malay partners in order to overcome state controls.

Yet the amorphous cosmology associated with this Malay Muslim cult, which accommodates different religious beliefs of the various ethnic groups in Malaysia, as indicated by the eclectic religious symbolism displayed, raises questions about the multiplicity of meaning in a trans-ethnic and trans-cultural context. A two-way diffusion of Malay, Chinese, and Indian beliefs and practices is observed in the *keramat* rituals. On the one hand, this Malay folk institution is Sinicized into the *datuk kong* cult, and Chinese patterns of worship are adopted with the veneration of Chinese folk deities alongside the *keramat*. On the other hand, a "Malay-sianization" of Chinese ritual patterns is observed in the specific observation of halal food offerings to the *datuk kong*. The cosmology of *keramat* propitiation and belief among property developers suggests a supernatural congruence of Malay, Chinese, and Indian folk beliefs in this local Muslim guardian saint.[12]

Clearly, these peculiar trans-ethnic manifestations of the *keramat* order stand in stark opposition to prevailing ethno-religious discourses in contemporary Malaysia, whereby rigid and clear boundaries between ethnic groups are enacted and policed by the state. How do we make sense of these contradictions posed by *keramat* symbolism? The answer, I argue below, lies in understanding how the *keramat* order is engendered by both the connections and tensions within the deep structures of cultural hybridity that are part of the Southeast Asian maritime world and Malaysian nationalist ideologies.

Keramat, Animism, and Islam in the Malay World

The cult of saints is common throughout the Islamic societies of Southeast Asia, the Middle East, and North Africa.[13] The worship of innumerable pious Muslim men and women, including rulers and founders of settlements, who are believed to have achieved saint (*wali*) status, possess magical abilities, and the power to influence events and ensure peace, harmony, and the safety of particular localities, is universally found among Islamic societies (Endicott 1970: 90).

Muslim saint worship in Malaysia, Singapore, and Indonesia is known by the word *keramat*, a Malay term derived from the Arabic *karamat*, which refers to a "miracle worked by a saint" (Reeves 1995: 310). Introduced through the arrival of Islam in Southeast Asia, which coincided with the spread of Sufism,[14] the *keramat* cult has its origins in the syncretism of Malay and Indian-derived Shia beliefs, as well as the mysticism (*tasauf*) of Sufism (Abdul Kahar et al. 1974: 14). Exemplifying the creative localization of Islam in the region, which drew upon established animistic and cultural traditions in maritime Southeast Asia, Muslim saint worship incorporates Malay animistic notions of souls (*semangat*) throughout the natural world. It is commonly believed that *keramat* spirits can appear and disappear at their will, and can sometimes manifest themselves in living entities—such as trees, butterflies, snakes, and tigers—and in inanimate objects—such as unusual looking mounds, stones, earth, rocks, and graves. It is therefore not surprising that these objects are worshipped and shrines are often erected over or near to them. The *keramat* is thought to be an amoral force which can be petitioned for both good and bad purposes; nevertheless, its influence is not subject to the wishes of the petitioner alone, and *keramat*s may intervene even when not specifically called upon. Overall, relations between the *keramat* and human beings are seen to be ambiguous, and the spirit can oscillate between mild mischievousness and utter malevolence when neglected or offended. In order to appease or keep *keramat*s from interfering in human affairs, appropriate rituals of propitiation must be held (Endicott 1970: 53).

Hybrid practices have characterized the spread of this syncretic Islamic cult in maritime Southeast Asia. The French scholar Chambert-Loir has noted that mauso-leums of Muslim saints were built upon Savaite temples and Buddhist stupas in Java as early as the fifteenth and sixteenth centuries (Chambert-Loir 2002: 138). The hybrid nature of the *keramat* cult was still evident during the colonial era: Salmon shows "cultural symbiosis" in the spread of this cult across Java and on an island off Aceh during the beginning of the eighteenth century (Salmon 1993: 284). An example is that of the Islamic holy tombs across the island of Java ascribed to Zheng He, the Chinese Muslim commander-in-chief of the Ming fleets.[15]

In colonial Malaya, this religious practice equally displayed the deep regional structures of cultural hybridity. Originally associated with a rural Malay practice, es-pecially amongst Malay fishermen and peasantry (Winstedt 1924; Firth 1946; Skeat 1967; Endicott 1970), *orang asli* (indigenous peoples) and Chinese rural commu-nities were also observed venerating the *keramat* in British Malaya (Cheu 1992: 383; 1996: 17). *Keramat* propitiation amongst Malays, indigenes, and Chinese rural communities in colonial Malaya was linked to the desire to reduce misfortune and uncertainty arising from hazardous economic activities such as fishing and logging. While rituals vary in various localities, a central principle of *keramat* propitiation lies in appeasing specific guardian spirits, receiving protection against natural ca-lamities, and/or ensuring abundant harvests (Cheu 1996: 65f.).

The adoption of *keramat* worship as part of Chinese popular religion in urban Malaysia was only observed during the 1970s and 1980s (ibid.: 17). Its transfor-mation into an urban popular religion must be understood in terms of the increas-ing constraints placed on trans-cultural and trans-ethnic spaces within the highly ethno-religiously charged political economy of Malaysia. It is to these forces that we next turn.

Keramat, Islamic Bureaucratization, and Malaysian Political Economy

As a society with roots in the hybrid maritime history of Southeast Asia, modern Malaysia was the product of an awkward modification of the Western ideal of a unitary nation-state bound by one language, religion, and culture. In order to find a way to incorporate all of Malaysia's ethnic groups within this nation-state framework, a distinction was made between a cultural core—the *bangsa Melayu*, "Malay and indigenous races"—and a legalistic definition of citizenship (*warganegara*) for non-Malay and non-indigenous communities.[16] Hence, *bangsa* (nation, race) is not used for nationality in the case of the modern Malaysian nation-state (see Harper 1996: 241). Rather, there is a modified conception of the nation-state, one which combines the idea of a cultural core along with ideals of common citizenship, political struggle, and shared territory, institutions, and language. In this modified nation-state model, equality does not necessarily equate to sameness. Rather, nationhood operates with a precarious notion of ethno-cultural differentiation which makes a distinction between a Malay cultural core and certain ethno-cultural others, but offers equal opportunity and treatment to all members of national society. Theoretically, the legalistic definition of citizenship enshrines the right of all communities to identify themselves as citizens of the nation. Nonetheless, pragmatically, this model of national integration suffers from serious tensions and contradictions, the most important of which concern state hegemony and equal rights to economic and social opportunities between the Malay cultural core and other ethnic groups. These tensions have erupted into ethnic riots, the most severe of which were the 1969 race riots, which resulted in the New Economic Policy (NEP), and which, between 1970 and 1990, positively reinforced the socio-economic position of Malays.

However, by the 1980s, the ethnically determined ideology of the NEP had come under critical pressure from an increasingly differentiated society and a politically resurgent Islamic movement which further complicated inter- and intra-ethnic tensions. As Islam, an important marker of Malayness, became implicated in a widespread global religious struggle, the Malaysian government, supposedly safeguarding Malay interests, became increasingly challenged by Malaysia's Islamic groups who pushed for religious orthodoxy. This situation saw an increasing Islamization of government bureaucracy which exacerbated both inter- and intra-ethnic tensions, resulting in the heightened political and cultural fragmentation of Malaysian society (Kahn and Loh 1992).

Within the Malay community, the rise of orthodox Islam, which rests on a more universalistic rather than localized conception of the religion, led to an emptying-out of local Malay cultural influences (*adat*). Inevitably, hybrid Islamic practices such as *keramat* propitiation came under increasing attack. This practice was criticized for being out of step with orthodox Islam, and the eastern states of Kelantan and Trengganu, controlled by the Islamic opposition party (PAS), even banned *keramat* worship (Rashid and Karim 1984: 65). The overt push for a pristine Islam in Malaysia gradually forced the Malay community to abandon *keramat* worship. Rashid and Karim (ibid.) have pointed to how rural Malay communities who observed *keramat* worship were increasingly pressured to abandon the practice, defined as *syirik* (proscribed), as urban middle-class civil servants, such as school teachers, imposed their reformist, orthodox interpretations of Islamic doctrines on rural areas.

Interestingly, there was an equivalent religious resurgence among non-Malays in response to Islamic revivalism in Malaysia. This involved the revival of other religious traditions such as Christianity, Hinduism, and Buddhism during the 1980s. So widespread was this religious fervor in Malaysian society that the 1980s has been called an era of religious revivals (Ackerman and Lee 1988). These revivals have been analyzed within the framework of ethno-religious nationalism in Malaysia. To take a case in point, the continued practice of Chinese popular religion in Penang at this time has been interpreted by DeBernardi (2004) as an important means of sustaining collective memories of shared struggle and pride in Chinese cultural traditions. This continued religious expression was thus critical to Chinese identity at a time when this ethnic group became increasingly marginalized by the postcolonial identity politics involving Malay dominance (*ketuanan Melayu*).

What is often left under-explored in analyses of religious revivals in Malaysia, however, are the trans-ethnic and trans-cultural dimensions. Despite the growing rigidity of ethnic boundaries in Malaysian official discourse, the religious revivals of the 1980s displayed trans-ethnic and trans-cultural characteristics. For instance, alongside Islamism, the urban middle-classes among the Chinese, Indian, and other ethnic communities significantly turned to evangelical Christian movements, such as Pentecostalism (Ackerman and Lee 1988). In folk religions, meanwhile, inter-ethnic dynamics could also be observed: Chinese devotees worshipped at Indian temples, and Indian devotees would adopt Chinese patron saints as their deities. Nevertheless, a reverse trend appears to characterize current Malaysian Islamism. Certainly, there has been conversion to Islam among the non-Malay communities of Malaysia, but such trans-ethnic trends have dramatically diminished since the 1980s given the increasing conservatism and bureaucratization of the religion.

As an Islamic practice with hybrid origins, the *keramat* cult came under increasing scrutiny with the increased policing of Islamic doctrine. Frowned upon and even banned in some states, many Malay Muslim devotees were coerced into abandoning the cult during the 1980s (Rashid and Karim 1984; Cheu 1992, 1996). It is within this context that Chinese and Indians gradually took over the worship of *keramat*s, bringing it into the urban terrain. A study by Rashid and Karim (1984) noted an interchange of *keramat* worship between Malay and Chinese fishing communities in the village of Teluk Kumbar in Penang. The village's Malay fishermen had long propitiated a legendary powerful sea spirit known as Pak Hitam on a small island near the village.[17] The Malay villagers, however, began to abandon *keramat* worship when they came under pressure from Malay teachers and government officials to stop the proscribed practice. This abandonment led Chinese fishermen in the community to take over the worship of the spirit as they feared Pak Hitam's wrath and its consequences for their activities in the vicinity of the spirit's island. Rashid and Karim show how trans-culturalism occurred at the ritual and economic fronts as the Chinese took over the worship of Pak Hitam. The Chinese fishermen became "ritualized" and came to believe that "Malay animism" was the "original and the best" way to ensure Pak Hitam's protection (ibid.: 65). In addition, a new social group of "ritual entrepreneurs" emerged amongst the Malay community, some becoming ritual mediators while others started halal food businesses, as the Chinese devotees sought to provide the proper food to Pak Hitam (ibid.: 64).

Studies by Cheu (1992, 1996) also provide us with a nationwide picture of the spread of a Sinicized form of *keramat* in the form of the *datuk kong* cult—that is, the very Malay Muslim spirit adopted by property developers mentioned above. Particularly popular amongst the urban Chinese working and middle classes, as well as among small- and large-scale entrepreneurs, the *datuk kong* cult became an urban phenomenon in the late 1970s. The term *datuk kong* is composed of two synonyms, *datuk* and *kong*, meaning "grandfather" in Malay and Chinese respectively (Cheu 1996: 8). *Datuk* is also an honorific title conferred on politicians, famous business personalities, and community leaders by either the federal or state government in Malaysia. The word *kong* also means saint and is an honorific conferred on a range of Chinese deities. Cheu notes that the *datuk kong* and *keramat* cults have gained in popularity amongst the Chinese population alongside an

Figure 7.2: Three of the seven figurines wearing Malay Muslim costumes and caps in a Panglima Hitam shrine in Kimberley Street, Georgetown, Penang. Photograph courtesy of Gwynn Jenkins (2004).

increase in entrepreneurial and speculative economic activities, including gambling (ibid.). In this urban context, *keramat* worship has become linked to a desire for lucky windfalls and protection against unpredictable capital investments.

With the popularity of the *datuk kong* cult, a proliferation of shrines can be found all over Malaysian urban centers, such as in new housing estates, commercial and factory complexes, bridges, and even beside expressways. Cheu (ibid.: 31) points out that some of the *datuk kong* shrines even incorporate traditional Malay hut-shaped structures with the characteristic horn-shaped roofs of Minangkabau architecture.[18] Furthermore, in some states, such as Selangor and the Federal Territory, the star and crescent (a symbol of Islam and the thirteen Malaysian states, as found on the Malaysian flag) are found in *datuk kong* shrines (ibid.: 31). Indeed, the adoption of Islamic symbolism in the *datuk kong* cult is now a common nationwide feature. Often, *datuk kong* figurines don *haji* prayer caps, the headwear associated with Islamic ulema or pious men; and my own recent survey of *datuk kong* shrines in Penang revealed that beside Malay-looking figurines, *kain pelekat* (sarongs worn during Islamic prayers) are also placed in some shrines.

Quite clearly, religious symbolism associated with the *datuk kong* cult mirrors the nature of ethnic power relations in Malaysian society. The adoption of *keramat* and the assimilation of Malay and Islamic symbolism in a Sinicized version of the *keramat* cult in the form of the *datuk kong* reflect the acceptance of dominant Malay Muslim power in this land. Noting this point, Cheu argues that in this context *keramat* symbolism must be read as the Chinese "desire to reconcile their sense of being and belonging to a multi-ethnic nation" (Cheu 1992: 381). Yet Cheu's studies also point to how the curtailment of the *keramat* cult by orthodox Islamists has caused other ethnic communities such as the Chinese and Indians to adopt the cult, which has seen it spread to Malaysian urban centers.

I would argue that the trans-ethnic and trans-cultural symbolism of the *keramat* cult can be read as a register of the articulation between the deep structures of the ethno-cultural hybridity of the *keramat* cult—which reflects historical realities of a fluid and plural maritime world upon which modern Malaysia was built—and the recent ethno-religious identity politics that have been prompted by the rise of Malay nationalism. The versatile display of trans-ethnic symbolism in the *keramat* cult shows that Islamic orthodoxy and bureaucratization in modern Malaysia cannot erase the deeper maritime legacies of porous trans-ethnic cosmologies. It is therefore pertinent for us to consider how, beyond being an effective medium for channeling anxieties and risks faced by the property development industry, the phenomenon of *keramat* worship amongst developers is undoubtedly also connected to the undercurrents of ethno-religious politics. The *keramat* cult could be interpreted as a channel which brings together the connections and contradictions between the deeper historical structures of ethno-cultural hybridity and the nature of modern ethno-religious nationalism in Malaysia. While it is evident that we can link *keramat* worship to the exigencies of a highly speculative industry, the trans-ethnic and trans-cultural symbolism found in the *keramat* cult also reminds us of past shared ethno-cultural cosmologies which have been increasingly erased by narrow official discourses about religious and ethnic divides in Malay nationalism. The persistence of symbolisms alluding to the deep trans-ethnic and trans-cultural past suggests a counter-cultural impulse in the *keramat* cult. Memories of shared ethno-cultural cosmologies from a deeper and fluid maritime world have refused to go away and instead find expression in the unregulated spaces of this popular religion. *Keramat* symbolism may not change society but it nonetheless represents a form of power outside of formal politics in that it serves as a vehicle to remind us about alternative ethno-religious narratives and social-cultural orders which have, otherwise, been silenced or forgotten. They constitute part of an ongoing dialogue of remembering the past and challenging the mainstream interpretations of ethnic and religious identifications imposed by official discourse.

Conclusion

This chapter has argued that the symbolism of *keramat* worship amongst property developers can be read as an ongoing expression of deeper historical realities. Furthermore, I have suggested that the contemporary *keramat* cult is implicated in the economic and ethnic anxieties and (dis)locations involved in the complex entwinement of property development and ethno-religious nationalism in Malaysia. These symbolic expressions may not be conscious political acts in themselves, but they nonetheless powerfully reveal contradictions within the economy as well as the social, ethnic, and moral orders of the day. In addition to these economic dimensions, *keramat* symbolism reflects the underlying historical reality of shared ethno-cultural worlds in modern Malaysian society that have been erased by current political and cultural discourses. It offers us a way to speak about the possibilities of transcending ethno-cultural differences and finding commonalities rooted in a shared socio-cultural legacy. In addition, the particular conflation of the *keramat* cult with Malay Muslim identity, and the amorphous character of *keramat* cosmology, which speaks of trans-ethnic and trans-cultural accommodation, potently disrupt dominant and narrow imaginings of ethnicity and Islam in contemporary Malaysia.

The particular meeting of the *keramat* cult and a group of powerful capitalist actors such as property developers dispels monolithic conceptions of capitalism as a secular, individualist activity and reveals instead its imbrication within wider historical, collective, and socio-moral orders and impulses. The resilience of the *keramat* cult as an imaginative horizon for negotiating connections and contradictions arising from deeper historical realities and modern formulations of political economy in Malaysia provides us with the grounds to rethink more commonplace interpretations of spirit cults in terms of the subaltern resistance to capitalism and commodification.

Notes

1. All Chinese terms are cited in Hokkien, a common Chinese dialect used in Penang. Romanized transcriptions of standard Mandarin equivalents are provided in parentheses.
2. In Aihwa Ong's work on spirit possession amongst female factory workers in Malaysia, she argues that spirit possession is a temporary means of resistance and an expression of powerlessness as workers destroyed factory machinery instrumental to their exploitation during periods of possession (Ong 1987). Others, like Taussig (1980), show how landless mine workers in Bolivia reflect on and cope with the power, danger, and immorality of the new capitalist economy through folklore and shamanic practices.
3. In Aihwa Ong's work, she points out how a *datuk* was amongst the spirits which possessed factory girls in Malaysia (Ong 1988: 32). My own work on urban development has shown how urban squatters used the power of *keramat*s as a means of contesting property developers (Goh 2002).
4. Malaysia's Industrial Coordination Act (1975) requires at least 30 per cent Malay or *bumiputera* (sons of the soil) equity ownership for manufacturing companies with shareholders' funds of at least RM 2.5 million or those which employed at least 75 full-time employees.
5. In Malaysia, property developers are controlled by two sets of regulations. The Housing Developers (Housing and Licensing) Regulations (1989) require property developers to: obtain licenses from the Ministry of Housing and Local Government before they engage in development activities; procure advertising permits from the Ministry before they advertise and sell their projects; and enter into contracts of sale with purchasers in the form of the Sales and Purchase Agreement. In addition, the Housing Developers (Housing Development Account) Regulations (1991) were introduced to prevent housing developers from absconding with the purchasers' payments.
6. Property booms occurred in Malaysia during the following years: 1963/64, 1973/74, 1981–1983, and between 1989 and the early 1990s. There is a theory among economists and property consultants that the property development cycle in Malaysia peaks every eight years unless events disturb the cycle, in which case the gap lengthens to ten or twelve years (see Salih 1991; Marbeck 1993).
7. Ackerman and Lee (1988) and Nagata (1995) have written about the revival of Christianity amongst urban-based non-Malay populations in Malaysia during the 1980s, and argue that the Christian revival is part of a non-Malay response to Islamization in Malaysian society.
8. Tua Pek Kong refers to the spirit of the Chinese pioneer, Chang Li, a political refugee from the Hakka district of southern China who arrived in Penang prior to the British presence. According to DeBernardi, the Southeast Asian Tua Pek Kong has been identified by some as equivalent to the Chinese "God of the Earth" or Tho Te Kong (Tudi Gong) (DeBernardi 2004: 149).
9. Equivalent to US$7,896; at the time the Malaysian ringgit (RM)/dollar exchange rate was $0.2632.
10. Muslim saints are known to work through the power of dreams (see Reeves 1995; Werbner 2003).
11. Other local guardian saints include the Chinese Tudi Gong or "God of Earth" (see DeBernardi 2004: 149), which protects locality, and Muneeswaran, a guardian of local places in popular Hinduism in Malaysia and Singapore, which offers protection to devotees (see Sinha 2003, 2005).
12. Sinha (2005) has pointed to the merging of different beliefs in Chinese and Hindu popular religious practices in Malaysia and Singapore.
13. For an example of the dynamics associated with Muslim saint worship in an Egyptian town, see Reeves (1995).
14. Anthony Johns (1961) has noted that the expansion of Islam in Southeast Asia coincided with the spread of Sufism—characterized by mystic literature and practices—in

Mecca, Medina, and northern India. Southeast Asian responses to Sufism were not merely derivative but complex and creative, as reflected in the writings of Islamic intellectuals in the region.
15. Zheng He is also commonly worshipped as Sam Po Kong, a Chinese deity, amongst Chinese communities in Southeast Asia.
16. The Malays form the largest of three officially designated *bumiputera* (indigenous) groups. Other *bumiputera* groups are the *orang asli* of peninsular Malaysia and the Malay-related groups of the states of Sabah and Sarawak.
17. I suspect that the Pak Hitam in Rashid and Karim (1984) is similar to Panglima Hitam, the Seven Warrior Brothers mentioned earlier.
18. In Malaysia, the Minangkabau people are found in the state of Negeri Sembilan. Minangkabau architecture is characterized by roofs shaped like buffalo horns and this feature has been incorporated into modern architecture to produce a popular neo-modern urban form in contemporary Malaysia.

References

Abdul Kahar bin Yusoff, Abu Bakar bin Shariff, Abdul Razak bin Mohamed Sultan, Ahmad bin Kasmar, Joseph Casimer Fernandez, Suleiman bin Hassan, and W. William. 1974. "Historical Survey of the Mosques and Keramats on Penang Island," research paper. Penang: Malayan Teachers College.

Ackerman, Susan, and R. Lee. 1988. *Heaven in Transition: Non-Muslim Religious Innovation and Ethnic Identity in Malaysia.* Honolulu: University of Hawaii Press.

Chambert-Loir, H. 2002. "Saints and Ancestors: The Cult of Muslim Saints in Java," in *The Potent Dead: Ancestors, Saints and Heroes in Contemporary Indonesia*, eds. H. Chambert-Loir and A. Reid. Honolulu: University of Hawaii Press, pp.132–40.

Cheu, Hock Tong. 1992. "The Datuk Kong Spirit Cult Movement in Penang: Being and Belonging in Multi-ethnic Malaysia," *Journal of Southeast Asian Studies* 23(2): 381–404.

———. 1996. "Malay Keramat, Chinese Worshippers: The Sinicization of Malay Keramats in Malaysia," Research Paper No.26. Singapore: Department of Malay Studies, National University of Singapore.

Comaroff, Jean. 1985. *Body of Power, Spirit of Resistance: The Culture and History of a South African People.* Chicago: University of Chicago Press.

DeBernardi, Jean. 2004. *Rites of Belonging: Memory, Modernity, and Identity in a Malaysian Chinese Community.* Stanford, CA: Stanford University Press.

Endicott, Kirk Michael. 1970. *An Analysis of Malay Magic.* Oxford: Clarendon Press.

Firth, Raymond. 1946. *Malay Fishermen: Their Peasant Economy.* London: Routledge and Kegan Paul.

Goh, Beng-Lan. 2002. *Modern Dreams: An Inquiry into Power, Cultural Production and the Cityscape in Contemporary Urban Penang, Malaysia.* Ithaca, NY: Southeast Asia Program Publications, Cornell University.

Harper, T.N. 1996. "New Malays, New Malaysians: Nationalism, Society and History," *Southeast Asian Affairs 1996*, pp.217–37.

Johns, Anthony. 1961. "Sufism as a Category in Indonesian Literature and History," *Journal of Southeast Asian History* 2: 10–23.

Kahn, Joel S., and K.W. Loh, eds. 1992. *Fragmented Vision: Culture and Politics in Contemporary Malaysia.* Sydney: Allen and Unwin.

Kitiarsa, Pattana, ed. 2008. *Religious Commodifications in Asia: Marketing Gods.* London: Routledge.

Lewis, I.M. 1971. *Ecstatic Religion: An Anthropological Study of Spirit Possession and Shamanism.* Harmondsworth: Penguin.

Lim, Linda Y.C., and Eng Fong Pang. 1991. *Foreign Direct Investment and Industrialization in Malaysia, Singapore, Taiwan and Thailand.* Paris: Development Centre of the Organization for Economic Cooperation and Development.

Mandal, Sumi. 1997. *Hadhrami Traders, Scholars, and Statesmen in the Indian Ocean, 1750s–1960s.* Leiden: Brill.

Marbeck, Aloysius B. 1993. "Investing in Residential Property," *Property Malaysia*, June/July, pp.57–63.

Mohamad, Maznah. 2001. "Women in the UMNO and PAS Labyrinth," in *Risking Malaysia: Culture, Politics and Identity*, eds. M. Mohamad and W.S. Koon. Bangi: Penerbit Universiti Kebangsaan and Malaysian Social Science Association, pp.112–38.

Nagata, Judith. 1995. "Continuity and Change in World Religion: The Intersection of the Global and Parochial in Malaysian Buddhism," in *Managing Change in Southeast Asia: Local Identities, Global Connections*, eds. J. DeBernardi, G. Forth, and S. Niess. Alberta: Canadian Council for Southeast Asian Studies, University of Alberta, pp.207–25.

Nash, June. 1979. *We Eat the Mines and the Mines Eat Us: Dependence and Exploitation in Bolivian Tin Mines.* New York: Columbia University Press.

Ng, Cecelia Siew-Hua. 1977. "Sam Poh Neo Neo Keramat: A Study of a Baba Chinese Temple," unpublished paper. Singapore: Department of Sociology, National University of Singapore.

Ong, Aihwa. 1987. *Spirits of Resistance and Capitalist Discipline: Factory Women in Malaysia.* Albany: State University of New York Press.

———. 1988. "The Production of Possession: Spirits and the Multinational Corporation in Malaysia," *American Ethnologist* 15(1): 28–42.

Parry, Jonathan P., and Maurice Bloch, eds. 1989. *Money and the Morality of Exchange.* New York: Cambridge University Press.

Rashid, Mohd Razha, and Wazir-Jahan Karim. 1984. "Ritual, Ethnicity, and Transculturalism in Penang," *Sojourn* 3(1): 62–77.

Reeves, Edward B. 1995. "Power, Resistance, and the Cult of Muslim Saints in a Northern Egyptian Town," *American Ethnologist* 22(2): 306–23.

Salih, Kamal. 1991. "The Malaysian Economy in the 1990s: Alternative Scenarios," in *Beyond 1990: International and Domestic Perspectives*, eds. L.K. Hock and S. Nagaraj. Kuala Lumpur: Persatuan Ekonomi Malaysia, pp.41–58.

Salmon, C. 1993. "Cults Peculiar to the Chinese in Java," in *Chinese Beliefs and Practices in Southeast Asia*, ed. C.H.T. Petaling Jaya: Pelanduk Publications, pp.279–305.

Sinha, Vineeta. 2003. "Merging 'Different' Sacred Spaces: Enabling Religious Encounters through Pragmatic Utilization of Space?" *Contributions to Indian Sociology* 37(3): 459–94.

———. 2005. *A New God in the Diaspora? Muneeswaran Worship in Contemporary Singapore.* Singapore: Singapore University Press.

Skeat, Walter. 1967. *Malay Magic: An Introduction to the Folklore and Popular Religion of the Malay Peninsula.* New York: Dover Publications.

Taussig, Michael. 1980. *The Devil and Commodity Fetishism in South America.* Chapel Hill: University of North Carolina Press.

Werbner, Pnina. 2003. *Pilgrims of Love: The Anthropology of a Global Sufi Cult.* Bloomington: Indiana University Press.

Winstedt, Richard. 1924. "Keramat: Sacred Places and Persons in Malaya," *Journal of the Malayan Branch of the Royal Asiatic Society* 2(3): 264–79.

8

BEING A SPIRIT MEDIUM IN CONTEMPORARY BURMA

Bénédicte Brac de la Perrière

The Taungbyon Brothers are among the most popular spirits belonging to the pantheon of the Burmese spirit possession cult. They are the tutelary spirits of Taungbyon, a village in central Burma, north of Mandalay, where a festival is celebrated in homage to them every August. In 2007, I was returning to Taungbyon after a long absence when I saw Myat Lay Wadi Nwe.[1] I could not help but be captivated by her outstanding allure, dressed in surprisingly luxurious and brown *yogic* attire,[2] her hair neatly tied in a topknot, her bright face graced by a large smile. She was sitting on a platform at the very place where my friend, a deceased spirit medium, used to sit next to the most packed doorway of the temple housing the Taungbyon Brothers. Her stance, full of dignity, was striking in the midst of the excited crowd of pilgrims and spirit mediums arriving from across Burma to pay homage to the spirits of Taungbyon. I joined the human flow to meet this newcomer on the scene of Burmese spirit possession and ask her how she had ended up in this place.

With her sophisticated urban way of speaking, Myat Lay Wadi Nwe told me how she arrived at Taungbyon for the first time four years before, the year following the death of my friend. She insisted that she came on her own, moved only by the voice of one of the spirits of the place, the Younger Brother instructing her to come. Then she met the daughter of one of the temple custodians, who happened to have been her schoolmate and who arranged for her to sit on this platform, where she was frequently passed by the many pilgrims. Her description of being called by the spirits and receiving their signals as if they were radio waves was in contrast to that of other spirit mediums, as was her appearance as a *yogi*. Not merely a newcomer, in her appearance and her behavior she had brought something new to Burmese spirit possession.

Endnotes for this chapter begin on page 181

Spirit mediums get their first training in spirit possession under the guidance of a master who identifies their main spirit. New mediums usually come to festivals under their master's tutelage, staying at his camp together with other disciples and clients; their participation in festivals is framed by this obligation. In this regard, Myat Lay Wadi Nwe's claim to have come to Taungbyon of her own accord was clearly distinctive. Later on, I learned that she was actually connected to the spirit mediums' network that is linked to the place she occupies at Taungbyon. Furthermore, thanks to this network, she had come through the main ritual procedures by which one becomes a spirit medium. Nevertheless, her narratives and practices mark a clear departure from those found among other Burmese spirit mediums. Indeed, her narratives and practices are a manifestation of her own sophisticated Burmese urban middle-class background. In other words, they are a clear expression of the way modern trends operating in Burma find their way into ritual practices usually understood as "traditional."

In no way are Myat Lay Wadi Nwe's ways of performing a uniquely idiosyncratic departure from a fixed set of traditions. In fact, the opposite is true: more than twenty-five years of inquiry into Burmese spirit possession has shown me the extent to which these practices are and have always been responsive to changing contexts. However, Burmese certainly do see these practices as pertaining to their identity, which they perceive as originating in an immemorial past. More precisely, they see them as coming from their pre-Buddhist past. In this chapter, I focus on contemporary spirit possession performances that demonstrate that, far from being instances of mere "superstition," these practices are deeply ingrained in their sociological environment and reactive to current socio-economic transformations in Burma. Nevertheless, the image displayed by Myat Lay Wadi Nwe at Taungbyon was bewildering precisely because it was not simply a reaction to changes. By presenting herself as an independent, modern woman at a local festival to the spirits, she was actually embodying tensions inherent in spirit possession in Burma. My analysis will show that new trends in contemporary spirit possession are the result of current visions of the world active in the ritual setting. Moreover, these interactions between new perceptions and traditions are part of a process whereby the reproduction of spirit possession gives space to forms of modernity. Indeed, Myat Lay Wadi Nwe's image was an image of Burmese modernity, although an alternative one.

The Burmese Spirit Worship Setting

In Burma, spirit worship is primarily addressed to a pantheon of spirits known in English as "the Thirty-seven Lords." Together, they form the pantheon of the Burmese cult of spirit possession. "Spirit possession" here refers to the ritual practice of making the spirits enter the body of the practitioner or medium. This is "positive" spirit possession, implying identification with and the voluntary incorporation of the spirits, as opposed to "negative" spirit possession, implying rejection of the spirits and exorcism (Heusch 1971; Rouget 1985). The main expression of positive spirit possession in the Burmese cultural context is dancing. The *nat*s—as the spirits are known in Burmese—manifest themselves through, as well as being propitiated by, their mediums through dancing. Mediums are known as *natkádaw*, or *nat* "spouses." The consecration of a new *natkádaw* is conceived of as a marriage to one of the *nat*s belonging to the pantheon. Thus, *natkádaw* become mediums through a process of being called upon by a specific *nat*, a common feature of this kind of possession cult. The vocation is elective and evolves in groups of mediums that are conceived of as *nat* "families." We may conceptualize these "families" as "schools of possession." As spirit possession specialists, *natkádaw* are a professional group performing privately sponsored ceremonies to the thirty-seven *nat*s (ceremonies known as *nat kánà bwè*), mainly for an urban clientele.[3]

*Nat*s belonging to the spirit possession pantheon are also the object of local cults in the domains they belong to, and of huge annual public rituals in these places. The festival of Taungbyon is an instance of such a public ritual. The populations of these domains propitiate the spirits individually as a form of traditional, bonded ritual obligation to a tutelary spirit. The ritual configuration taken as a whole is thus a nationwide cult legitimated through spirit possession, which in turn comprises a collection of local cults legitimated through "tradition" (*yòya*). Performances range from privately organized ceremonies called *nat kánà bwè* to huge local annual gatherings involving pilgrimage—such as the Taungbyon festival—celebrating individual spirits in their own domain. These festivals thus integrate the local into the national.

Today, this linkage between local cults and a nationwide institutionalized cult of spirit possession depends principally on the participation of spirit mediums (*natkádaw*) at festivals. The latter are specialists of the cult of the thirty-seven *nat*s. Most of them live in main urban centers in Burma (Yangon, Mandalay…) and, three times a year, they all converge on the main festivals of central Burma. In this way, festivals work as a framework for dialogical exchanges between local and more central identities. If only in the domain of the rituals, spirit mediums' participation in the festivals brings standardization to the local events by infusing them with the mediums' standardized urban practices while the latter are enriched by local idiosyncrasies. It is important to note here that this ritual configuration also sets up an endless confrontation between localities and spirit mediums acting as agents of wider Burmese society. Recently, these exchanges between the local and the national have taken diverse forms according to the relative positioning of groups of spirit mediums, local caretakers of ritual institutions, and local communities. In some cases, power struggles of the spirit mediums have allowed for ritual segmentation in existing festivals resulting in the presence of concurrent ritual institutions in the same locality. In other cases, forgotten local rituals were reinvigorated to the benefit of local caretakers. Issues at stake are manifold, from the local economy and regional development to the reproduction of spirit mediums as a profession (see Brac de la Perrière 2005, 2007).

The Autonomization of Spirit Possession

This articulation of local cults in relation to the cult of the thirty-seven *nat*s appears to be a specific characteristic of Burmese spirit possession. On the whole, practices of spirit possession are known in all the religious systems of the lowland societies of mainland Southeast Asia, either as part of annual public rituals for tutelary spirits or as part of therapeutic cults.[4] However, from Laos to northern Thailand, with its possibly distinctive matrifocal cults; from Cambodian communal *neak ta* to T'aï principalities *lak muang*, nowhere do we encounter in reports of mainland Southeast Asian traditions such an integration of cults into one centralized pantheon of figures, except in the northern Vietnamese cult of the Four Palaces.[5] The integration of the different functions of spirit possession in the cult of the thirty-seven *nat*s, in which spirit possession is the dominant ritual form, appears definitively as a striking characteristic of the Burmese cult.

However, the origins of the Burmese cult are uncertain. The foundation myth of the cult suggest its origins lie with the inception of Burmese Buddhist kingship under King Anawratha (1044–1077). Indeed, this myth is crucial to understanding how the spirit possession cult is framed within Burmese Buddhism, and needs to be understood as a historically produced narrative in parallel with the standard national history.[6] On the one hand, the introduction of Buddhism and the establishment of Buddhist kingship in Burma have a much more complex development than is implied in the myth, on which we are not in a position to elaborate here. On the other hand, the current cult of the thirty-seven *nat*s and its singular configuration has evolved through continuous interactions between central ritual institutions of the disappeared Buddhist monarchy and local ritual practice. The cult may be said to have evolved from the rituals that the monarchy formerly performed to the main tutelary spirits of the kingdom. The first reference to a list of guardian spirits deserving a royal cult is to that fixed under King Pindale of Ava (1648–1661). From such existing lists, we may say that the current pantheon has emerged progressively from the combination of different configurations of city guardians and of the group of *Min Mahagiri nat*s that were the object of a more ancient royal cult.[7]

The specialists of this royal cult were court officers depending on royal patronage. During the second half of the nineteenth century, a new policy of local rituals was implemented that led to more standardization and the creation of an independent profession of ritual specialists. It is significant that these developments occurred in the context of the intensification of Western interference in Burma during the nineteenth century, and finally of the breakdown of the monarchy in 1885. However, these developments explain the continuation and even expansion of the cult after the collapse of Burmese royalty. My hypothesis that the collapse of Burmese kingship had an impact on the formation of the contemporary ritual institutions of the cult of the thirty-seven *nat*s parallels that of scholars of Buddhist studies concerning a similar impact on the development of contemporary Buddhist institutions, such as the *Shwegyin* branch of the *Sangha* and practices such as lay meditation. These hypotheses shed light on the dramatic changes brought about in Burmese society and culture because colonial authorities did not assume the traditional role of the Buddhist kings as keepers of the cosmos and patrons of religions.

In the field of the cult of the thirty-seven *nat*s, British neglect of religious institutions during the colonial period involved a series of displacements. Suddenly, the court officers' traditional offerings to the main tutelary spirits of the kingdom were discontinued. However, the cult of the thirty-seven *nat*s did not disappear but evolved outside of the kingship context relying increasingly on spirit mediums' elective possession for its legitimacy. The result is a cult in which possession by the thirty-seven *nat*s is now concentrated in the hands of ritual specialists for a theoretically limited pantheon of spirits. These specialists, formerly part of the Burmese court, now operate on their own in an increasingly urban context (Brac de la Perrière 2006b). This is a process of transformation through which spirit possession loosely scattered in local cults of tutelary spirits of the Buddhist kingdom became the main ritual expression in a cult of a national pantheon of spirit possession figures. I propose calling this process the "autonomization" of spirit possession in the Burmese religious field.

The increased autonomy of spirit possession does not mean that it stands apart from the overall religious system. On the contrary, one of the aspects of autonomization is that the cult is both in constant interaction with, and is normatively separated from, Buddhism. More precisely, this constant interaction is built on the physical separation of ritual institutions.[8] To start with, like most Burmese, spirit mediums are lay Buddhists and spend significant parts of their earnings on religious donations to monks. But as a rule, no ceremony for the thirty-seven *nat*s is held in a Buddhist monastery or in the precincts of a pagoda, except as part of the foundation rituals for a new pagoda. Communal shrines for the *nat*s are usually located close to a monastery, but outside of it. Moreover, there is a conflict between the status of monks and that of spirit mediums: a spirit medium who enters a monastery for a certain period of time, as is the habit of Burmese men, loses all ritual qualification as a medium. Monks cannot assist in a ceremony for the *nat*s, according to their *vinaya* rules, although they can bless it before it starts. They cannot be possessed and are not supposed to worship *nat*s because monks are of a higher status. In fact, they are not affected by spirits' actions. In this capacity, they may, at least a few of them, practice exorcisms for people suffering attacks by spirits, either *nat*s or, more typically, ghosts.

The distinction between Buddhism and the spirit cult is accentuated by the striking integration of practices within the cult of the thirty-seven *nat*s at every level, from individual and family to local and regional, in such a way that it coalesces in a field of its own. It is important to emphasize that the physical separation between the spirit cult and Buddhist practices serves to differentiate the two domains within the Burmese religious sphere. This construction has a very specific function: to maintain hierarchy by keeping Buddhism separate, pure, and superior. It is mainly a normative separation.

In the time of the monarchy, this hierarchical relation was maintained by the overarching institution of Buddhist kingship, in which kings were both patrons of religion and keepers of the cosmos, as mentioned above. As such, kings were both pre-eminent donors to the community of Buddhist monks and patrons of rituals dedicated to the tutelary spirits. This is not to say that Buddhism was a state religion: while the king was a Buddhist, he also allowed any religion to be practiced in his kingdom.

Until today Buddhism has not been a state religion in Burma although it is largely dominant. During the parliamentary period that followed independence in 1948, under the leadership of Prime Minister U Nu—a pious Buddhist as well as a recognized devotee of the *nats*—religious matters took on a growing importance that led to the formation of the influential Department of Religious Affairs and to the convening of the fifth Theravadin Synod at Yangon in 1955. But U Nu's proposition during the 1960 elections to make Buddhism the state religion was one of the causes of the military upheaval that led General Ne Win to seize power in 1962. Under Ne Win's socialist regime, Buddhism was restored as the religion of the majority with a more distant involvement of the authorities in religious matters. However, control of religion and particularly of monks was still a critical issue. The same development can be observed in the cult of the thirty-seven *nats*: while U Nu is known to have donated magnificent statues of spirits during his time as prime minister,[9] General Ne Win's takeover ended official participation in the cult. A famous episode concerning the banning of a movie showing the story of a female spirit, Saw Mon Hla, the Shwezayan Lady, occurred in 1963, a timely illustration of political changes regarding the cult (Ferguson 2008). In essence, these changes meant an end to public displays of devotion among officials, whose recognized involvement in the cult mainly centered on the control of spirit mediums.

However, the increased autonomy of spirit possession meant that the cult of the thirty-seven *nats* managed to sustain itself without a central cult institution and without explicit official support. If not specific to Burma in mainland Southeast Asia, the autonomy of spirit possession in the overall religious system occurred relatively early here and seems to have resulted in its ongoing reproduction despite the political turmoil of the twentieth century. By contrast, in other parts of Southeast Asia there were calls following independence for a halt to diversified practices linked to spirit possession. In Laos, for example, spirits (*phi*) were reported to have been sent to re-education camps; in Cambodia, the displacement of local communities caused spirits (*neak ta*) to disappear; in Vietnam, the ban placed on the cult of the spirits of the Four Palaces forced it into clandestine practice; and in northern Thailand, matrifocal cults vanished as traditional gender relationships were affected by the transformation of rural ways of life. But these declines in traditional spirit cults were short-lived, and new developments have led to a burgeoning of spirit possession cults in modern, urban contexts across mainland Southeast Asia. Thus, Rosalind Morris (2000) provides an illuminating analysis of contemporary formation of spirit possession cults in Chiang Mai, northern Thailand, in the context of state-building and modernization. Other recent descriptions of contemporary religion in contexts of urban migration and growing globalization provide plenty of evidence of the reinvigoration of spirit possession practices. If only in the field of Vietnamese studies, numerous analyses demonstrate the resurgence of spirit cults in the era or "renovation" (*đổi mới*).[10] Philip Taylor (2004), for instance, describes the emergence of a goddess in southern Vietnam that gives a hitherto unseen translocal quality to Kinh practices of spirit worship, and Karen Fjelstad has documented a case in a transnational context (Fjelstad and Nguyễn Thị Hiền 2006). All these new developments tell of spirit possession cults which build on traditional religious practices and are redeployed in relatively large segments of contemporary society.

Contemporary Trends

The autonomization of spirit possession seems to have occurred earlier in Burma than in other countries of continental Southeast Asia, except possibly in Vietnam. Although spirit possession in Burma has not been affected to the same extent as it has in Vietnam by post-independence history, increasingly urbanized spirit possession practices backed by local ritual practices have proved, here as elsewhere, to be very responsive to contemporary socio-economic changes. Urban society is undergoing significant changes that have had an impact on the religious field. In particular, the economic growth experienced in the 1990s, even in Burma, has resulted in the intensification of spirit worship and in the further segmentation of ritual institutions (Brac de la Perrière 2005, 2007). Increased wealth was at this time ostentatiously displayed in spirit possession performances as evidence of the spirits' efficiency. This tendency came to an end with the financial crisis of 1997 and the subsequent political, economic, and social developments in Burma.

At the political level, the Department of Religious Affairs has gained in importance under the current military government. The authorities have also taken steps to try and compensate for their lack of legitimacy by extensively patronizing religious institutions, particularly by involving themselves in the renovation and building of pagodas. As for the cult of the thirty-seven *nat*s, they do not publicly recognize their participation, although it is common knowledge that wives of high-ranking military officers are followers of the most influential spirit mediums of today, as they were before. The cult is not supported officially on the grounds that the practices involved are mere "superstitions" allowed to continue as "tradition." These practices are, however, more and more strictly controlled by the authorities, with differentiated objectives according to the context involved: big festivals in central Burma are monitored in order to maximize benefits accruing from fairs as well as ritual offerings, while ceremonies involving the thirty-seven *nat*s are put under growing surveillance.

Changes in the composition of the urban population, as well as increasing disparities of wealth, combined with severe inflation, are factors that deprive the spirit mediums of their main source of income, namely the organization of the *nat kánà bwè*, which became too expensive for their usual clients. Burmese wholesale trade in the main market of Yangon, a main source of spirit mediums' clientele since the 1970s, is on the point of changing completely due to the concentration of the market into the hands of a few business families with different origins and backgrounds. Even more significant, influential monks have recently voiced strong criticism of the alleged rapacity of spirit mediums, which resonates with current feelings among the population about being harassed by the predatory behavior of the government and other institutions.

Furthermore, official permission to undertake *nat kánà bwè* is required from the local authorities, just as it was under General Ne Win's rule. But that permission is becoming more and more difficult to obtain. Nowadays, the registration of mediums' schools as performers' groups under the aegis of the Department of Culture is a prerequisite for organizing spirit possession performances. The administration of mediums by the Department of Culture rather than Religious Affairs is based on formal similarities between spirit possession ceremonies and other traditions of performing arts in Burma, mainly dance, music, and drama (known as *zat pwè*). But this ignores the decisive ritual orientation of *nat kánà bwè*, which is what separates spirit possession ceremonies from other performances.

The local office of the Department of Culture makes its decisions on the basis of the degree to which ritual specialists conform to traditional practice. The office has the capacity to interrupt any event that displays Western dress, dance, or song. Moreover, the office grants permission for ceremonies to be held only after ritual specialists have approached various other municipal and local offices of departments said to be concerned, mainly the departments of Immigration, Religious Affairs, and Internal Security. To my knowledge, permission is no longer granted for performances in downtown Yangon, where numerous ceremonies used to be performed in the 1980s. The only one I have heard about recently was a celebration organized in November 2007 on a small island in Kandaw Gyi Lake, right in the heart of Yangon, by one of today's most influential mediums. The ceremony was held to celebrate the return of the mayor of Yangon to his position after he had been suspended following his management of the monks' demonstrations in autumn 2007. The celebration was a private one, an exceptional event to enact the restoration of order in relation to this high-ranking official.

The present context means that spirit mediums who rely solely on the organization of ceremonies for the thirty-seven *nat*s, as they used to do in the 1990s, are now facing difficulties. In a performance organized collectively by a local community in Yangon, a local astrologer who was once a spirit medium went to dance for the *nat*s and, when possessed by the *nat* U Min Kyaw, made this public apology to him: "Dear Father, forgive your son. Today, the Burmese spirit mediums can no longer live on serving the *nat*s. That is why I had to quit the *nat*s' line to follow that of the astrologers."[11] This particular spirit medium chose to stop performing, although it is said that the vocation of spirit possession cannot be abandoned. Others have chosen different strategies to cope with the scarcity of opportunity for undertaking performances, in particular by making changes in the cult configuration that allow them to attract more affluent clients. These strategies will be presented here with the aim of seeing what they mean regarding the autonomy of spirit possession.

The Increasing Fame of *Bòbògyì* and *Thaik* as Pagoda Guardians

Changes undertaken by spirit mediums in their performances have produced what appears to be a blurring between normatively separated aspects of Burmese religion. I have already mentioned Myat Lay Wadi Nwe's appearance on the scene of spirit possession, dressed in the brown color that is the mark of *yogi* in Burma. Before examining what this might mean, we have to look at congruent phenomena, such as the entrance into some performances of a series of figures, called *bòbògyì* and *thaik*, who are not usually summoned at the *nat kánà bwè*. *Bòbògyì* and *thaik* are generic appellations identifying categories of beings mainly linked to pagodas and, in the case of *bòbògyì*, sacred trees (Sadan 2005). Although these categories encompass a wide range of figures, those embodied in performances may be specifically qualified as pagoda guardians. Indeed, *bòbògyì* and *thaik* used to be invoked at the beginning of the ceremonies for the thirty-seven *nat*s, together with a number of spiritual figures inhabiting the cosmological world of the Burmese Buddhists. But this calling was considered a way to inform them of the ritual occurrence and as a rule they were not ritually incarnated nor summoned on this occasion.[12] The question then is how these generic figures associated with the protection of a Buddhist sanctuary rather than with the list of the thirty-seven *nat*s came to be present in the context of *nat kánà bwè*.

Bòbògyì, which actually means "grandfather," are considered male, and they are conceived of as spirits of places that have been converted to Buddhism when Buddhism was first institutionalized locally through the foundation of a pagoda. The most famous *bòbògyì* is settled in the Sule pagoda located in the middle of downtown Yangon. *Thaik* are linked to treasures, especially pagodas, treasures, or relics; they are usually imagined as beautiful young ladies dressed in fancy, glittering green clothes. Any pagoda might have such guardian figures, but they were not necessarily identified or represented until recently, precisely because they were generic figures.

Those incarnated during the *nat kánà bwè* are on the contrary carefully designated and named, like Myat Nan Nwe, the *thaik* of Bottataung pagoda, also situated in downtown Yangon. They may have narratives told about them and have had images of them located for a relatively long time in the precincts of the pagoda of which they are in charge, such as that of Sule *bòbògyì*.[13] His statue is that of a standing old man, dressed in white and signaling his dedication to the religion. He points his index finger towards Shwedagon pagoda because he took part in its foundation by pointing out its place.

Most of the pagoda guardians, however, have emerged or re-emerged quite recently. One can easily verify this through a tour of pagodas, where the numerous shrines to *thaik* dressed in green and *bòbògyì* dressed in white, with freshly painted and flashy images, have been recently refurbished, if not newly founded. This is the case, for instance, of the *thaik* Myat Myat Sein. Myat Myat Sein was already a well known imaginary figure belonging to the cohorts of *thaik* ladies but did not have a physical representation of her own at Shwebontha pagoda, the historical pagoda facing Prome, on the opposite bank of Irrawaddy river, of which she is in charge. This came to an end when the almost abandoned pagoda was refurbished under the supervision of Khin Nyunt on the occasion of the building of a new bridge there. I was told that a donor from Mandalay made an offering of a brand-new magnificent image of the *thaik*. This is rather typical of what happened everywhere in Burma during the 1990s whenever there were new infrastructure developments: the refurbishing of pagodas and a proliferation of iconographic representations obtained through donations of well-to-do civilians said to have a "belief" (*yonkyi hmú*) in the figure represented.

What can be inferred from these rather schematic stories is that at the time of the call for private funds for the renovation of Buddhist monuments, lay men and women were urged to support parts of Burmese cultural heritage of which they were not aware. According to Burmese Buddhist conceptions, to support a religious foundation is an outstanding way to get religious merit: the reward expected is no less than progression on the karmic path towards nirvana. This is how businessmen or women become strongly committed to the particular religious monuments they agree to finance. They are prone to develop a sense of a predestined link with the spiritual founding figures attached to the place, which they bring to light through their contributions. This attitude explains their particular devotion and offerings to these figures, beginning with the commissioning of representations of *thaik* and *bòbògyì* in their pagodas. In the case of Myat Myat Sein, pilgrims have now become numerous, and thanks to the new bridge they come to present specific offerings—green heeled sandals—to her new image. Thus, mental figures of *thaik* and *bòbògyì* which are thought to have always been present in the pagodas are made more tangible through the multiplication of images.

However, from a more strict Buddhist point of view, the devotion to religious guardians inside pagodas is a mark of relaxed practice, and consequently controversial. Boards of trustees of pagodas usually tolerate the devotion and accept donations of new images of these figures on the grounds that they are obliged to allow lay men and women to make merit according to their own conceptions. But in some cases, the exponential growth in this kind of devotion has caused trustees to take action against it. This is how Myat Nan Nwe of Bottataung pagoda, who previously had a small image on the platform of the pagoda, came to be ousted from it and established in a brand new temple opposite the pagoda entrance and, at the same time, graced by a new, taller, and fancier sculpture. Her fame had grown in such a way that her cult was no longer tolerable inside the Buddhist sanctuary precincts. In other words, devotion to her had grown on a par with the lowering of her status in Buddhist terms. Eventually, the devotees began to offer her nun's robes, especially during the Buddhist retreat, as a demonstration of her religious status.

Thaik, *Bòbògyì*, and the Spirit Possession Pantheon

The emergence of *thaik* and *bòbògyì* on the scene of spirit possession occurs in the context of recent developments in their figurative representation in the pagodas, which further fuels general devotion to these figures. These newly represented characters, which appeal to the imagination of today's public, are precisely those who happen to be embodied during spirit possession performances. Ritual embodiment of a spiritual being seems to require its material representation. Indeed, to be embodied, spirit entities need to be identified and credited with physical and behavioral characteristics: these characteristics are displayed in the spirit images.

If the growth of devotion to *bòbògyì* and *thaik* allows for them to be embodied during spirit possession performances, their time and place in the ceremony reveals that a separation is still maintained between the pagoda guardians and the thirty-seven *nat*s. As for the *thaik*, it is notable that they are the first entities to arrive during performance; this timing grants them a higher position than any other figure in spirit possession and ensures that they do not mix with the *nat*s. Not only are they separated from the *nat*s according to this temporal sequence, but usually there are no figurative images of them within the scene of spirit possession, though there may be representations of them within the precinct of the pagoda of which they are guardian. Moreover, they are not presented with specific food offerings while they are present in the body of a medium, which signals them as definitively different from the *nat*s. This is also the case of the *bòbògyì*, for, as one spirit medium explained, they are not beings that experienced a violent death as the *nat*s are but older spirits who voluntarily converted to Buddhism as soon as they encountered it.

Thus, in the context of spirit possession performances, the higher status of pagoda guardian spirits seems to be deliberately preserved through acts which differentiate them from the thirty-seven *nat*s, while within pagoda precincts the growing fame of guardian spirits exposes them to more controversies. They actually fill an interstitial space in the Burmese cosmological hierarchy of beings that allows them to be called upon as figures of devotion in different spheres of Burmese religion. Their rising fame affects the practice of spirit mediums willing to satisfy the devotional demands of their clients, even more so as the difficult economic context leads them to reposition themselves in the religious marketplace. On the one hand, as spirit mediums try to attract new wealthy clients that are able to sponsor *nat kánà bwè*, they encounter the devotees of such figures. On the other hand, at a time of change, when affluent city people are less connected to rural roots and influenced by the criticisms voiced by popular modern monks against *nat* worship, spirit mediums may also seek a revalorization of their practice through the co-optation of these higher-status figures. A brief review of how some spirit mediums in Yangon have come to incorporate pagoda guardian figures into their spirit possession practice will throw light on what is involved here.

U Thein Lwin is an established spirit medium who claims a special relationship with *thaik*. He explains this as having to do with his Shan origins, the same ethnic identity as that attributed to Saw Mon Hla, a spouse of King Anawratha who became the prototypical feminine pagoda guardian spirit. Thanks to this special relationship, U Thein Lwin has started to invent new *thaik* figures. He speaks readily of how he saw a female entity in a dream asking him to have a representation of her made. He fulfilled her wish, ordering a figure of the *thaik* from a sculptor that would match the vision he had of her in his dream. The resulting image has to be regarded as an original representation of a pagoda guardian. As a consequence, he explained, he could not set up the image in his shrine at home. That is why he ended up establishing it in a monastery in the ward where he and his wife, also a medium, have a few clients who now sponsor the cult of this *thaik*. Another client, an engineer working on a dam project, then asked him to install a representation of the *thaik* of the pagoda attached to the irrigation project. In this way, we can say that U Thein Lwin has developed a specialization in the worshiping of *thaik*.

Other moves undertaken by U Thein Lwin and his wife demonstrate that they are both experimenting with new ways to alter their practice, allowing for the reproduction of their ritual speciality in a time of hardship. Together with a group of spirit mediums eager to create a more accessible ritual, they have taken part in the creation of a new festival in the Irrawaddy delta, where no member of the thirty-seven *nat*s was previously settled, shortcutting the established hierarchies. The festival is devoted to an alternative figure of U Min Kyaw, an eminent member of the thirty-seven *nat*s. The alternative figure is named Talaing Kyaw, and is supposed to have lost his life on the spot where the new festival has been established. The ritual specialists responsible for this innovation may be seen as trying to create new locales for spirit possession.

As for U Hla Kyi, he has established himself as a spirit medium in Thamaing, the ward in Yangon where he grew up, and he is concerned with the local *bòbògyì*. Thamaing *bòbògyì* is a duplicate of Hmawbi *bòbògyì* and is connected to the Shwedagon pagoda by having pointed out its location, as is Sule *bòbògyì*. Thamaing *bòbògyì* dwells in a small sanctuary located between two neighbouring pagodas. U Hla Kyi is the custodian of the shrine, which he inherited from his father, and he lives there. Eventually, he also became a fully fledged spirit medium and developed his clientele by building on his strong links to the local community. Taking advantage of these circumstances, he organizes ceremonies for the thirty-seven *nat*s for his clients in the temple. Thus, the human-size image of the *bòbògyì* stands in the middle of the shrine with the medium's collection of images around it. It happens that U Hla Kyi embodies the *bòbògyì*, although not too often, because, he comments, "the *bòbògyì* is not like a *nat*."

Finally, U Win Hlain is one of the few spirit mediums known to be able to attract enough sponsors to organize the two performances a month that permit a comfortable standard of living. A brilliant dancer, he has developed a way to perform ceremonies that is more like a show than a ritual. Building on the fact that the same practices are involved in performances involving the thirty-seven *nat*s (*nat kánà bwè*) and other performing arts (the aforementioned *zat pwè*), he tends to highlight the aesthetic aspects of performance rather than the lively ritual exchanges between devotees and spirits that can make spirit possession ceremo-

Figure 8.1: U Hla Kyi as a spirit medium in Yangon. Photograph by Bénédicte Brac de la Perrière, 2007.

nies unpredictable. This aesthetic dimension of his practice is very much in favor among the current urban public, and it explains how he was chosen by a French cultural broker to take part in the first public performance of a Burmese spirit medium abroad, at the Quai Branly Museum in Paris in March 2008. Leaving aside issues such as the potential commodification of Burmese spirit possession, I would like to underscore here that his invitation abroad indicates how much U Win Hlain is riding the wave of contemporary trends, ready to step into the global market.

U Win Hlain performs at home, in front of a glittering row of shrines. At the end of the shrines, slightly separated from the rest, he has settled glamorous representations of the most famous *thaik*s he embodies during the first part of his seances. The beginning of his performances is thus a show of the main feminine pagoda guardian figures. Besides his special taste for *thaik* incarnations, U Win Hlain is also repositioning his practice as a ritual specialist. For instance, dressed in the brown dress of *yogi*, a category of religiously dedicated individuals, he organizes Buddhist rituals for devotees of the thirty-seven *nat*s who usually sponsor his spirit possession ceremonies. Rather than a mere spirit possession specialist, this tends to position him as a general ritual specialist for his clients.

For these three mediums, their connection with the pagoda guardians is just part of a set of strategies for coping with the novelty of their socio-economic context. It fills the need for new avenues of spirit possession practice, satisfying a new demand among the diverse public they seek to attract in the contemporary urban setting, and enabling them to resist the criticisms of superstition and constraints exercised by the authorities. These strategies bring spirit mediums into contact with other religious developments in contemporary Burma, such as the fame of pagoda guardians, a by-product of current government's politics of religious legitimization. Indeed, spirit possession is concerned by the more general transformation of the religious scene.

The Connection between Pagoda Guardians and *Weikza* Devotees

One interesting feature the three spirit mediums mentioned above share is that they belong to a category that has been in touch with different sectors of Burmese religion, particularly those connected with a kind of religious virtuosi called *weikza*. *Weikza* are human beings who are supposed to have escaped the karmic cycle although they are still present in a disincarnated form to help humans. Their devotees engage in religious practices and adopt ascetic ways as they enter into a cult group. As more and more *nat* devotees do, all of the three mediums mentioned above go to the annual celebration of the disappearance of Bomingaung, the most famous *weikza*, at Mount Popa. This religious event, which celebrates the *weikza*'s disappearance, has gained in fame since its fiftieth anniversary in 2002. Bomingaung used to practice meditation and other ascetic practices at Popa, which has long been the main holy site in Burma. His grave is located at the base of the peak but is supposed to be empty. Standard representations of him have burgeoned along the slopes of the mountain since 2002. Devotees come to celebrate his disappearance and his success in his quest for *weikza*-hood. On Popa, "everybody turns to the brown dress of religiously devoted persons," as one spirit medium said, meaning that spirit mediums turn into *weikza* followers for the time

Figure 8.2: U Hla Kyi as a *weikza* devotee at Mount Popa. Photograph by Bénédicte Brac de la Perrière, 2007.

of the anniversary celebration. This indicates a temporary change of vocation—or "line," as Burmese say, using the English word—implied by their participation in an event related to the *weikza* sphere of Burmese religiosity.

It is in this context that we can return to Myat Lay Wadi Nwe, the spirit medium dressed in brown clothes at the Taungbyon festival that I introduced at the beginning of this chapter, and seek to understand how different religious spheres are articulated as "lines" in Burma. After having first encountered her at Taungbyon, I went to the woman's home, a comfortable house in a remote suburb of Yangon, isolated in semi-rural surroundings befitting her family business. There, she has imposed her quasi-ascetic way of life on her family. Dressed in brown on an almost daily basis, monopolizing part of the house to tend her elaborate shrines (*dat khan*)—which combine altars to the thirty-seven *nat*s, pagoda guardian figures, and the *weikza* buddha—from time to time she holds fully fledged spirit possession ceremonies (*nat kánà bwe*) in a special pavilion. Having been through all of the requirements that lead to becoming a medium (*natkádaw*)—particularly marriage to her main spirit, the Younger Brother of Taungbyon—Myat Lay Wadi Nwe is indeed a spirit medium, although of a special kind. A quick sketch of her life and her spiritual career will be enough to make the point.

Before moving to her current home in 1999, Myat Lay Wadi Nwe had never been inclined to spirit worship. She had always lived in downtown Yangon, where her parents were wholesale traders. As a professional, she worked for the customs department while her husband was employed in overseas trade. Brought up as a 'pure' Buddhist, she only practiced meditation. She says that her neighbors at that time would think her a fool if they knew about her present day practices. Eventually, she and her husband earned enough money to buy the land where they now live and start a business there. Significantly, it was this move away from government employment and an urban way of life that led to her spiritual transformation. Like many other Burmese from the urban middle class who have to engage with their country's current administration, the price she had to pay involved compromises, tension, and frustration. In this context, early retirement and the start of an independent family business in a suburban milieu was a move similar to withdrawal from the world, a kind of withdrawal signaling a turn to religious life in a Buddhist context.

According to Myat Lay Wadi Nwe, she appreciates the peace of the place she lives in, which allows for the spirits, any sort of spirits, to come. As soon as she arrived there, she undertook the fulfilment of ascetic vows and meditated following the *weikza* path. Subsequently she began to hear the voices of spirits coming to tell her what to do, and discovered a part of her karmic destiny: she had been a *naga* in a previous life before being reborn as a human. *Naga* are a kind of serpentine being pervasive in Burmese cosmology, and are linked to the protection of pagodas, together with the *bòbògyì* and the *thaik*. Myat Lay Wadi Nwe then started to look for her *naga* family by touring the main pagodas which had *naga* as guardian figures. After a long search, she found that she was the sister of the Shwesattaw pagoda *naga*, Nammada. When the Younger Taungbyon Brother, one of the thirty-seven *nat*s, asked her to be his "wife," meaning his medium, she first resisted. But unable to stand the "guilt" of having rejected him, she joined the practice of an established spirit medium who married her to the spirit.

This is how she became a *natkádaw* while already being a Bomingaung devotee, and how she began to run a *nat* shrine (*nat kánà*) in parallel with a *weikza* shrine (*dat khan*). Interestingly enough, she distinguishes between forms of spirit possession according to the kind of spiritual figure manifesting itself in her, comparing possession by the *weikza* to radio waves. Her practice of spirit possession is informed by her meditation, allowing different categories of spiritual beings to come and talk to her and advise her about what she should do. In worshipping the thirty-seven *nat*s she actually follows such advice rather than obeying the instructions of an established specialist, as is the norm among spirit mediums. However, she had to rely on spirit possession masters to have the consecration rituals performed, especially her marriage to the Younger Taungbyon Brother. But, she insists that she actually performed it by herself, organizing everything and having to do it twice because she did it wrong the first time. Both of the masters who officiated at her consecration ceremonies died shortly afterwards, she told me, implicitly suggesting what is understood in this context: that an early death of a ritual specialist is a spiritual punishment for ritual deficiency. Incidentally, it also allows her to be independent of a master. Myat Lay Wadi Nwe readily explains that she obtained most of her statues of the *nat*s by purchasing them from these deceased spirit mediums' heirs; as a rule, cult specialists are supposed to get them from their clients or inherit them from their master. In every regard, Myat Lay Wadi Nwe proclaims the singularity of her spiritual career, a singularity that could account for her desire to be distinguished from ordinary spirit mediums, as her brown clothes demonstrate.

Her singularity is actually linked to the fact that she came to spirit possession through her previous practice of meditation, following the *dat* "line" as a *weikza* cult devotee. Among spirit mediums, one often hears the statement that the *dat* "line" (connected with the *weikza*), *thaik* "line," and *nat* "line" are three separate "lines" that one cannot cross or combine. Observation of actual practice, however, demonstrates that the practitioners bridge these "lines" according to their relative ranks in the overall Burmese Buddhist symbolic system. Thus, *dat* specialists are supposed to be able to control the *nat*s, and some *dat* specialists, taking advantage of this capacity, make plans to organize spirit possession ceremonies (*nat kánà bwè*) for their clients. However, to do so they need the cooperation of a *natkádaw* who is the real specialist of spirit possession. As the *natkádaw* would say, *dat* specialists do not know how to bring the *nat*s. For instance, as they are not supposed to drink alcohol, *dat* specialists are not in a position to satisfy the *nat*s who are fond of drinking. However, *natkádaw* cannot organize *dat* ceremonies. But, as we have seen with U Thein Lwin, U Hla Kyi and U Win Hlain, those among them who become involved with the *weikza* cults gain a "religious" dimension that seems to make them able to attract to their ceremonies figures closer to Buddhism, such as pagoda guardians.

However, in Myat Lay Wadi Nwe's experience, inspiration by pagoda guardian spirits, here the *naga* Nammada, is central. Hence, on her way to master her life and the world surrounding her, Myat Lay Wadi Nwe experiments for her own sake, taking a spiritual path that reverses the trend observed in the practice of some spirit mediums. U Thein Lwin, U Hla Kyi, and U Win Hlain seek a revalorization of their practice through adding pagoda guardians to their pantheon of spirit possession figures, having access to them possibly through their familiarity with the *weikza* path; while Myat Lay Wadi Nwe came into contact with the thirty-seven *nat*s through her practice of meditation and her predetermined link with pagoda guardians. Whereas spirit mediums turn to brown clothes to attend the *weikza* festival, Myat Lay Wadi Nwe keeps her brown clothes on for the *nat* festival.

Conclusion

The congruent developments of representing the spiritual founding figures of pagodas in the form of statues and of embodying them during spirit possession performances demonstrate that, far from being independent, spirit worship and more Buddhist-oriented practices are actually connected. The true interstitial character of pagoda guardians, allowing for a switch from one sphere of religiosity to another, does not necessarily mean that the normative separation between spirit possession and Buddhist practice we have underscored is on the way to becoming blurred. Rather, what I have called the autonomization of spirit possession seems still to be at work in these processes of sustaining hierarchy. The processes we have been accounting for may actually be said to be part of the dialogical process involved in the delimitation of the domains of practices in the religious sphere. Building on current trends of religiosity in which they take part—namely the fame of pagoda guardians and the growth of *weikza* cults—urban spirit mediums are actually attempting to renegotiate their position in the overall Buddhist religious scene.

In this manner, modern trends find their way into the ritual sphere. The ritual configuration of the cult of the thirty-seven *nat*s, by articulating spirit possession to local rituals, allows for interactions between new trends and "traditions." But the autonomous character of spirit possession not only facilitates strategies whereby specialists adapt to changing conditions. It also provides a niche for alternative modernities, a place for bricolage, where outstanding characters such as Myat Lay Wadi Nwe may attempt to master their world in a context of daily oppression and political impotence.

Notes

1. The fieldwork on which this chapter is based was conducted during a stay in Yangon (Rangoon) as a representative of École Française d'Extrême-Orient between February 2007 and August 2008. I am grateful to the spirit mediums who shared their experience with me. All the mediums mentioned in this chapter are referred to by their real name, except for Myat Lay Wadi Nwe, who requested that I use a pseudonym according to her choice. Finally, special thanks to Owen Wrigley and Patrick McCormick for help with my use of English at different stages.
2. In Burmese, *yogi* designates a category of people having made vows pertaining to Buddhist practice. They wear brownish clothes as a sign of their (sometimes temporary) asceticism, which distinguishes them from the usual Buddhist lay men and women. However, they do not have the status of religious men, such as monks gain through proper ordination; the latter follow a stricter and fixed set of rules compared to the voluntary and fluctuating vows of the *yogi*. Spirit possession, as a ritual specialization, is separated from this kind of asceticism, and spirit mediums who are Buddhist do not as a rule dress as *yogi*.
3. For more details, see Spiro (1967) and Brac de la Perrière (1989).
4. For a synthetic approach of spirit possession in mainland Southeast Asia, see Condominas (1976), and Brac de la Perrière (2000).
5. On territorial cults in Laos, see Archaimbault (1972) and Condominas (1975); for Cambodia, Forest (1992); among the T'aï, Maspéro (1971) and Formoso (1996); and for Thailand, Tambiah (1970). On matrifocal cults in northern Thailand, see Cohen and Wijeyardene (1984). On therapeutic cults in Laos, see Hours (1973) and Pottier (1974). Finally, on the Vietnamese cult of the Four Palaces, see Durand (1944) and Chauvet (this volume).
6. It was not until 1831 that this standard national history came to be fixed in the *Glass Palace Chronicle*, a royally sponsored synthesis of previous royal and local chronicles (see Luce and Pe Maung Tin 1923).
7. On the list of the Thirty-seven Lords (*nat*s), see Temple (1906). See also my analysis of the manuscript of Kawi Dewa Kyaw Thu, who was a court ritual officer during the nineteenth century (Brac de la Perrière 2006b).
8. On the articulation of Burmese spirit cults and Buddhism in the shape of a normative hierarchy, see particularly Brac de la Perrière (1996, 2006a).
9. On U Nu's position concerning the cult of the Thirty-seven Lords, see Nu (1989).
10. See Keyes, Kendall, and Hardacre (1994), Malarney (2002), Chauvet (2004), Fjelstad and Nguyễn Thị Hiền (2006), Endres (2007), DiGregorio and Salemink (2007), and Kwon (2008). For Cambodia, see also Marston and Guthrie (2004).
11. The speaker used the English word "line" in his speech. On the Burmese use of the word "line" to mean a spiritual and vocational path (Burmese *lan*), see below. Significantly, this public apology reveals that a "line" follower is bound with strong links and feelings.
12. Things are more complex in the case of the *thaik*, for a *thaik* may actually be held responsible for accidental wild possession occurring in the possession pavilion later on, during a seance. However, in this kind of case the *thaik* are unidentified female dragons, not a pagoda guardian, and to deal with the situation would not imply ritual possession by this being.
13. There has been a representation of the *bòbògyì* in the Sule pagoda since at least 1906, as is evident from a picture in Del Mar (1906: 30 *en face*). I am grateful to Don Stadtner for this reference.

References

Archaimbault, Charles. 1972. *Les courses de pirogues au Laos: un complexe culturel*. Ascona: Artibus Asiae.

Brac de la Perrière, Bénédicte. 1989. *Les rituels de possession en Birmanie: du culte d'état aux cérémonies privées*. Paris: Association pour la Diffusion de la Pensée Française.

———. 1996. "Les naq birmans entre autochtonie et souveraineté," *Diogène* 174: 40–52.

———. 2000. "Chamanisme et bouddhismes en Asie," in *La politique des esprits: chamanismes et religions universalistes*, eds. D. Aigle, B. Brac de la Perrière, and J.-P. Chaumeil. Nanterre: Société d'Ethnologie, pp.17–24.

———. 2005. "The Taungbyon Festival: Locality and Nation Confronting in the Cult of the 37 Lords," in *Burma at the Turn of the Twenty-first Century*, ed. M. Skidmore. Honolulu: University of Hawaii Press, pp.65–89.

———. 2006a. "Les rituels de consécration des statues de Bouddha et de naq en Birmanie," *Purushartha* 25: 201–36.

———. 2006b. "A Presentation of a Parabaik Written by the Kawi Dewa Kyaw Thu, Ritual Officer at King Mindon's Court," *Myanmar Historical Commission Golden Jubilee Conference Proceedings*, Vol.2. Yangon: Yangon University Press, pp.215–41.

———. 2007. "To Marry a Man or a Spirit? Women, the Spirit Possession Cult and Domination in Burma," in *Women and the Contested State: Religion, Violence, and Agency in South and Southeast Asia*, eds. M. Skidmore and P. Lawrence. Notre Dame, IN: University of Notre Dame Press, pp.208–28.

Chauvet, Claire. 2004. "Du commerce avec les esprits des Quatre Palais: étude d'un culte de possession à Hanoi," Ph.D. dissertation. Nanterre: University of Nanterre.

Cohen, Paul T., and Gehan Wijeyardene, eds. 1984. *Spirit Cults. Mankind* (special issue) 14(4): 249–360.

Condominas, George. 1975. "Phiban Cults in Rural Laos," in *Change and Persistance in Thai Society: Essays in Honor of Lauriston Sharp*, eds. G.W. Skinner and A.T. Kirsch. Ithaca, NY: Cornell University Press, pp.252–73.

———. 1976. "Quelques aspects du chamanisme et des cultes de possession en Asie du Sud-Est et dans le monde insulindien," in *L'autre et l'ailleurs: mélanges offerts à Roger Bastide*, eds. J. Poirier and F. Raveau. Paris: Berger Levrault, pp.215–32.

Del Mar, Walter. 1906. *The Romantic East: Burma, Assam and Kashmir*. London: Adam and Charles Black.

DiGregorio, Michael, and Oscar Salemink. 2007. "Symposium on Living with the Dead: The Politics of Ritual and Remembrance in Contemporary Vietnam," *Journal of Southeast Asian Studies* 38(3): 433–40.

Durand, Maurice. 1944. *Technique et panthéon des médiums viêtnamiens (dong)*. Paris: École Française d'Extrême-Orient.

Endres, Kirsten. 2007. "Spirited Modernities: Mediumship and Ritual Performativity in Late Socialist Vietnam," in *Modernity and Re-enchantment: Religion in Post-revolutionary Vietnam*, ed. P. Taylor. Singapore: Institute of Southeast Asian Studies, pp.194–220.

Ferguson, Jane. 2008. "Blasting the Past, or What Happens When the Silver Screen Promotes Burman-centric History Amongst Ethnically Diverse Viewers", unpublished paper presented at the Asian Studies Conference, Atlanta, GA.

Fjelstad, Karen, and Nguyễn Thị Hiền, eds. 2006. *Possessed by the Spirits: Mediumship in Contemporary Vietnamese Communities*. Ithaca, NY: Cornell University Press.

Forest, Alain. 1992. *Le culte des génies protecteurs au Cambodge: analyse et traduction d'un corpus de textes sur les neak ta*. Paris: l'Harmattan.

Formoso, Bernard. 1996. "La cosmologie des T'aï et l'empreinte du bouddhisme," *Diogène* 174: 53–71.

Heusch, Luc de. 1971. "Possession et chamanisme," in *Pourquoi l'épouser? Et autres essais*. Paris: Gallimard, pp.226–44.

Hours, Bernard. 1973. "Possession et sorcellerie dans un village du sud Laos," *Asie du Sud-Est et le Monde Insulindien* 4(1): 133–46.

Keyes, Charles F., Laurel Kendall, and Helen Hardacre, eds. 1994. *Asian Visions of Authority: Religion and the Modern States of East and Southeast Asia*. Honolulu: University of Hawaii Press.

Kwon, Heonik. 2008. *Ghosts of War in Vietnam*. Cambridge: Cambridge University Press.

Luce, Gordon H., and Pe Maung Tin. 1923. *The Glass Palace Chronicle*. Rangoon: Burma Research Society.

Malarney, Shaun Kingsley. 2002. *Culture, Ritual and Revolution in Vietnam*. Honolulu: University of Hawaii Press.

Marston, John, and Elizabeth Guthrie. 2004. *History, Buddhism and New Religious Movements*. Honolulu: University of Hawaii Press.

Maspéro, Henri. 1971. "La société et la religion des Chinois anciens et celle des Tai modernes," in *Le Taoisme et les religions chinoises*. Paris: Gallimard, pp.221–76.

Morris, Rosalind C. 2000. *In the Place of Origins: Modernity and Its Mediums in Northern Thailand*. Durham, NC: Duke University Press.

Nu, U. 1989. "Nats," *Crossroads* 4: 1–12.

Pottier, Richard. 1974. "Notes sur les mediums et chamanes de quelques groupes thai," *Asie du Sud-Est et le Monde Insulindien* 4: 99–110.

Rouget, Gilbert. 1985. *Music and Trance: A Theory of the Relation Between Music and Possession*. Chicago: University of Chicago Press.

Sadan, Mandy. 2005. "Grandfather, Bless this Nissan," in *Burma at the Turn of Twenty-first Century*, ed. M. Skidmore. Honolulu: University of Hawaii Press, pp.90–111.

Spiro, Melford. 1967. *Burmese Supernaturalism: An Explanation in Reducing Suffering*. Philadelphia: Institute for the Study of Human Issues.

Tambiah, Stanley J. 1970. *Buddhism and the Spirit Cults in North-East Thailand*. Cambridge: Cambridge University Press.

Taylor, Philip. 2004. *Goddess on the Rise: Pilgrimage and Popular Religion in Vietnam*. Honolulu: University of Hawaii Press.

Temple, Richard C. 1906. *The Thirty Seven Nats, a Phase of Spirit Worship Prevailing in Burma*. London: W. Criggs.

9

RECONFIGURING *MANORA RONGKRU*: ANCESTOR WORSHIP AND SPIRIT POSSESSION IN SOUTHERN THAILAND

Alexander Horstmann

Introduction

Religion in Thailand today is characterized by contradiction: while conventional Theravada Buddhism seems to have lost much appeal with the younger generation, Buddhism is also being revived in new forms. The worship of Buddhist saints, the booming cult of Buddhist amulets, and the presence of "magic monks" show that a reconfigured Buddhism is able to thrive in particular niches in modern urban society (Jackson 1999; Taylor 1999, 2008; Kitiarsa 2005b). While the capitalist economy and the growing nation-state have weakened ancestral traditions and traditional authority in rural areas, the same forces have also propelled the dramatic expansion in, and presence and visibility of spirit mediums in urban areas who are possessed by royalty and who speak to a diverse clientele, including the highest members of the political elite (Morris 2000; Tanabe 2002; Kitiarsa 2005b). These urban spirit mediums coexist with, and draw upon elements of Theravada Buddhism. Although processes of modernization, rationalization, and globalization have put a lot of pressure on "traditional" society, its institutions have not disappeared; rather, they have reappeared in new configurations, satisfying the social needs of modern people. Rosalind Morris (2000) ties the rise of spirit possession in contemporary Thailand to the political economy of the modernist Thai state, which has commodified spirit possession, repackaging it through its electronic mediation on video and television as an object of desire and longing. Morris shows that the process of mediation through new media technologies is crucial for the new configurations of spirited modernities.

Endnotes for this chapter begin on page 198

In this chapter, I will focus on the example of *manora rongkru*—a three-day ceremony of ancestral vows—to illustrate the coexistence and intertwining of spirit possession, Theravada Buddhism, and Islam, as well as the resilience and revitalization of spirit beliefs and possession, in southern Thailand.[1] Peter Jackson argues that the modern phase of Thai religion involves doctrinal rationalization accompanied by organizational centralization and bureaucratization, whereas the postmodern one is characterized by a resurgence of supernaturalism and an efflorescence of religious expression at the margins of state control, involving a decentralization and localization of religious authority (Jackson 1999).

I argue that people in southern Thailand, like others in the country, seek communication with the spirits to come to terms with the challenges and ailments of modern life. They hope that the spirits can influence their lives in favorable directions. Communication and interaction with spirits is facilitated and enacted by professional mediums who are possessed by specific deities. The second reason for the resilience of the spirits, I argue, is resistance against the growing orthodoxy of both Theravada Buddhism and Islam. While Theravada Buddhism preaches awakening from ignorance through mindfulness, people are more attracted to the sacredness and power of the Buddhist saints, which they see as the highest spirits in the spirit hierarchy. Villagers use Buddhist festivals, such as the festival of the tenth lunar month (*ngan deun sip*), to remember and provide offerings to beloved ancestors. Meanwhile, Islam is rapidly globalizing, and Muslims have become involved in transnational movements, and consume Islamic images produced by the transnational flow of global media, such as the internet (Horstmann 2007). However, Muslim villagers still believe in ancestor spirits. For example, they believe that the ancestor spirits visit them after Ramadan and they offer their communal meal to them after prayer. Lambek calls this co-existing expression of religion "polyphony" (Lambek 2000: 70). Villagers of both religions thus "navigate among the various claims that either ancestral power or modern religion makes upon them and in which they are not in a position to make a decision in favour of one or the other" (ibid.: 70).[2] Along with Lambek, I would argue for a reflexive position that recognizes the need of people to belong to religions whose canon has developed a negative stance toward spirits. While Buddhism removes itself from the ghostly sphere, villagers are interested in building congenial relationships between humans and spirits (*phi*). Beliefs create a bridge between the living and their own ancestors. The term *phi ta yai* (spirits of great grandparents or ancestor spirits) refers to the good and benevolent ancestors who stay in the heavenly realm, are not yet reborn, protect the living, watch over them, and provide assistance to good people and punish the bad. Not all dead persons achieve ancestor status, and only very powerful people who have accumulated a lot of merit can achieve the status of great ancestors. People who committed a lot of sin in their lives are degraded to the status of hungry ghosts. There is a large variety of offerings to ancestor spirits, ranging from simple family reunions to the elaborate *manora rongkru*.[3]

Manora Rongkru, the Ancestral-vow Ceremony

A central form of interaction and communication with the spirits in southern Thailand is the *manora rongkru* ceremony—also known as *nora rongkru*, or simply *nora*—in which designated spirit mediums or members of the community become possessed by the great grandparents' (*ta yai*) ancestor spirits. *Manora* or *nora* designates both the dancer of the genre as well as the art form itself (Jungwiwattanaporn 2006: 377). While the word *nora* reflects its Indian Buddhist *jataka* origin, it is important to note that the Suthon-Manora dramatic plot, which depicts a folk story containing a creation myth, is almost absent in the actual *nora* performance (Ginsburg 1972). In this myth, which exists in a number of local variants, a princess known as the Lady of White Blood (white signifying the sacred) is sent from the King's palace and set adrift in the ocean on a bamboo raft for becoming incestuously pregnant by her brother while training in the *nora* dance. Lady White Blood is saved by a peasant couple and gives birth to a son, Si Sata, and she teaches him how to dance *manora*. Si Sata is the first male teacher of the *manora* dance and performance genre. Out of gratitude for saving her life, Lady White Blood donates gold she finds in the forest to Takura temple, where it is used to make a Buddha figure.[4] At the climax of the *nora* vow-fulfilment ceremony, the ancestor spirits of the dead descend into the mediums' bodies and possess them.

Figure 9.1: *Nairong manora* in Ban Dhammakhot, Songkhla, Thailand. Photograph by Alexander Horstmann, 2006.

Once possessed, family members are able to laugh and cry with their loved and lost ones, and receive wisdom and advice from the ancestor spirits.

In the grand ceremony of *manora*, entertainment, performance art, ancestral tradition, creation myth, and spirit possession all intermingle. This is because the *manora* master, called *nairong manora* (alt. *nairong*), a bird-winged shaman and dancer, uses dance and verse to call the *manora* ancestors (Nunsuk 1980). The grand *manora* ancestors were the first teachers of the art of *manora* and are commonly venerated by southern Thai villagers, who host vow ceremonies in order to placate the powerful deities. The *nairong manora* embodies the wisdom and knowledge of the first teachers, who are venerated as mythological figures. The *nairong*—usually male—possesses supernatural power and calls the great ancestors to help him heal and exorcise black magic (*sayasart*).[5]

The term *nora rongkru* literally means "*manora* stage teacher," and the dances performed by the possessed spirit mediums are also called vow dances (Butsararat 1992, 2003; Hemmet 1992: 276; Isaradej 1999). The cycle of a full vow ceremony, the *manora rongkru*, lasts three days and takes place on a make-shift stage that is constructed only for the duration of the ceremony and dismantled after it ends. During the ceremony, the *nairong* invites *manora* as well as non-*manora* ancestor spirits to descend from the heavenly realm to witness the ceremony and join the stage. The *manora* ancestors are elevated to the highest status of teachers and honored in a special ceremony (*piti wai kru*). The *nairong* seeks intensive preparation with the family hosting the *nora*, which is indispensable for the success of the ritual, especially its ancestor part. He thus enquires about every single deity and ancestor spirit of the house. The host aims to counter misfortune by hosting a full vow ceremony and exorcising the influence of black magic. The host makes a vow to the first teachers of the *manora* and shows gratitude by returning an offering to the great ancestors. The host will most likely promise to host a *manora rongkru* every year, depending on the vow made to the ancestors. As *manora* have become very expensive—due to the cost of the food and drink and elaborate offerings that have to be provided—some families have to wait as long as nine years to hold another *manora rongkru*. If the host does not keep to the vow made to the ancestral spirit, the ancestor spirits may exercise serious punishments.

These vow ceremonies are different in size. In the past, crowning ceremonies for the leading *nairong* took place in the oldest and most sacred Buddhist temples. Some of the most spectacular ceremonies nowadays take place in temples where the great *manora* ancestors are supposed to stay or in temples that are associated with the *manora*'s mythological figures. These open ceremonies constitute a public space in which people are attracted to the power of the great *manora* ancestors. In these, people anonymously seek to attach themselves to the benevolent power of the great *manora* ancestors and not to the ancestors of the personal house or community.

In the following, I focus on the ways in which today's *manora rongkru* sheds light on communication with the ancestor spirits in southern Thailand. I argue that the growth in spirit mediums is a reflection of social, political, and economic changes in Thailand in the media age, and that religious practices of participation in spirit cults have responded creatively to the social transformation of every-day life. Modern media technologies are constitutive of the religious imagination about spirits and render present the transcendental realm to which it refers. Media are opening up new registers of mediation (Van De Port 2006: 445). The record-ing of *manora* through video technology contributes to the commodification of the ritual, which partly explains its current growth in popularity and its prominent place in the public sphere. Following Meyer and Moors (2009), I argue that the aesthetics of the performance of *manora* contribute to the sensationalization of the tradition and thus to its current revitalization.[6]

The performance of *manora* articulates with and is embedded in the multi-re-ligious situation in southern Thailand. While *manora* has always been closely as-sociated with Theravada Buddhist temples, and while Buddhist ordination used to be a condition for the graduation of the *nairong*, *manora* had no religious restric-tion to Theravada Buddhism. Yet, participants increasingly tend to see the *manora* as a Buddhist tradition. Marlane Guelden (2007) argues that *manora* adjusted to the religious needs of different ethnic and religious groups, while Jungwiwat-tanaporn (2006: 375) follows Isaradej (1999) in arguing that *manora* functions like a family court in settling conflicts within the family and creates the feel-ing of "communitas" by bringing together the realms of the living and the dead. Therefore, seen from this perspective, *manora* seems to have made a substantial contribution to managing religious difference and mediating between Theravada Buddhism and Islam by integrating both religions into an encompassing value system of local ancestral beliefs. In the following, I am interested in testing this assumption against the current development of *manora*. Being a multi-religious ritual, in which offerings include both Buddhist and Islamic sacred objects, it is interesting to ask if *manora* functions to integrate Buddhists and Muslims into a common belief system or if *manora* just functions to subjugate Islam to the he-gemony of Buddhism.

Religious forms are not static phenomena, but have reacted with flexibility to the conditions of dislocation, rapid social change, and social uncertainty that have led to the development of niches in the religious market that cater to the poor, the lower middle class, and also to the very wealthy (Morris 2000; Guelden 2007). Buddhism is by no means a united front against which *manora rongkru* posi-tions itself. My thesis is that conventional Buddhism in southern Thailand aims to regain lost territory through its appropriation of *manora* festivals in the public domain. I aim to show that *manora*'s increasing dependence on Buddhism and the state creates the conditions for the subordination of *manora* to the civilizing influence of Buddhist morality. The increasing co-optation of *manora* by Bud-dhism marginalizes the participation of Muslims in the ceremony and has led to the withdrawal of most of them from the multi-religious rituals such as *manora*.

While both Buddhism and *manora* benefit from the latter's commodification, the subordination of *manora* is never complete and tensions and contradictions between orthodox religion and religion as everyday practice prevail. But before looking more closely at the *manora* ceremony, a few words on the regional context are necessary to understand how people in southern Thailand speak about religion and spirit beliefs.

The Local Context

It is not uncommon in the Lake Songkhla area to observe a multi-religious ritual in which spirit possession blends with Theravada Buddhism and Islam (see Horstmann 2004). The *manora rongkru* ceremony is a unique institution that has developed according to the social needs of the people of the mixed community on the eastern banks of Lake Songkhla, where Buddhists and Muslims live together in closely-knit neighborhoods and kinship networks. People in southern Thailand feel they are part of an imagined community, as they are all considered descendents of the first *manora* teachers. People and houses, and sometimes whole villages, are considered of *manora* descent (*trakun manora*).

My own research in the Lake Songkhla area has focused on the provinces of Songkhla, Patthalung, and Nakhonsrithammarat. Located at Lake Songkhla, Tambralinga is one of the oldest kingdoms in Southeast Asia. The Isthmus of Kra on the west coast of southern Thailand was a very important trade route from mainland to insular Southeast Asia, and a cultural crossroads. Both Buddhism and Islam, which have existed in this region for several hundred years, can be considered indigenous religions (Golomb 1978), and over that time they have mutually influenced one another. With the centralization of the Thai state, however, the Lake Songkhla area became dominated by Theravada Buddhism, and the oldest and most sacred temples can be found in the area. These temples played an important role in the process and narrative of state building in southern Thailand, in which Muslims who settled in the Lake Songkhla area as migrants and sometimes as slaves played a very marginal and peripheral role. Consequently, the communities in the region became more clearly separated from each other along religious lines, with Buddhists and Muslims coming to distinguish themselves by adopting more conspicuously religious dress and identity. Nowadays, the population of Songkhla, Patthalung, and Nakhonsrithammarat provinces is mainly Buddhist, and Muslims are in the minority.

Hundreds of years ago, villagers lived in unison with nature and animals and believed in the power of spirits, especially ancestor spirits, and the belief in ancestor spirits still exists today. There are interesting variations in Buddhism and Islam in the Lake Songkhla region, both of which coexist with ancestor spirit beliefs.[7] In southern Thailand, only the most recent ancestors are remembered, except for individual persons who were known to have accumulated a lot of merit.

The anonymous ancestors are conceptualized as a collective who on their way to heaven help the living and keep away malevolent spirits. Only a few receive the title of "great ancestors," among whom are Buddhist saints, Muslim governors, and the first *manora* teachers. These great ancestors are known for their power, charisma, and merit and are remembered by personal name.

Southern Thailand has thus developed a unique ritual culture that combines elements of local religion, Theravada Buddhism, and Islam. However, the influences of the national Buddhist community (*Sangha*) and transnational Islamic missionary movements have divided villagers, sometimes leading them to live contradictory lives. Some religious leaders have continued with old traditions, while also being under the strong influence of forces who claim to represent modernity. People thus find themselves in a situation where traditional beliefs coexist with new and more orthodox ideas. In more recent times, the circulation of media images of the communal violence between Buddhists and Muslims in the three border provinces of Pattani, Yala, and Narathiwat has engendered a heated discussion about the coexistence of Buddhists and Muslims in Thailand. Following this violence, religious and ritual spaces have become more rigidly separated and controlled.

In the following, I want to look at the dynamics of change taking place in the reconfigured practice of *manora*. This is not the first reconfiguration of the *manora rongkru* ceremony, for it has been taken out of its rural context and transformed into a commodity and political ideology before. During the era of Phibulsongkhram, between the 1930s and 1950s, *manora* performers were encouraged to change costumes for European dress and military uniforms. Famous *nairong* were appointed national artists and were summoned to perform for the Thai king in Bangkok. The first to do this was Nora Teum from Trang. He was seen as a civilized and modern *nairong* who also used elements from *lakhorn chatri* (classical Thai dance), *luuk tung* (country folk song), and TV soap opera. There was fierce competition between the *nairong* for fame (Butsararat 2003; Guelden 2005a,b).

A Household Ritual

In May 2006, in the village of Ban Dhammakhot, on the eastern shore of Lake Songkhla, a *manora rongkru* ritual is underway. Designated family members of a household light candles, and their bodies begin to shake. Possessed by their ancestors' spirits, they begin to dance like professional dancers on stage under the guidance of the bird-winged *manora* dancers, who please the ancestor spirits by singing *manora* verses.

A *manora rongkru* ritual will have been prepared for months or even years in advance. It is crucial that all family members are present, and that they complete all associated financial and organizational arrangements. The head of the family sets a date in the period between May and September in consultation with a trusted *nairong*. He calls to the ancestor spirits and controls the harmful spirits who may enter the stage through the back door. During the numerous consultations which precede a performance, the *nairong* inquires about the motivation of the family for inviting the *manora* and organizes the ceremony accordingly. The *nairong* is thus informed about the situation of the host and about all the ancestors and deities who will be present. This information enables him to contact the deities by name during the performance.

The host family places photographs of their ancestors on the ancestral shrine in the house, prepares the offerings, food, and drinks for all the visitors for the three-day event, and builds a temporary stage on a lawn near their house. The stage serves as a ceremonial space as well as a performing area for *manora*. A spirit shrine (*palai*) is placed on a small elevated platform on the right-hand side of the stage. It represents a tall house where only *manora* ancestor spirits reside; the shrine for the host family's ancestor spirits is in the main house. During the ritual, a white sacred string (*saisin*) links the *palai* to the shrine in the host family's house. The *palai* serves as the link between the god-like realm of the *manora* spirits and the host family's ancestors. The performance space for a *manora* varies. Traditionally, it was a makeshift space on the ground, with just four bamboo pillars and a roof signifying the performance space's boundaries. The *manora rongkru* is performed in the intimate compound of a private house and is open only to invited family members, relatives, and good friends. In this sense, then, it is an intimate family affair.

Music plays a hugely significant role in the ritual. A *manora* dancer's costume is layered with a chest piece, a neckpiece, and shoulder ornament, all made from strings of small, colorful plastic beads. Other unique features are a golden crown (*soed*), a silver wing ornament, a birdlike tail, and long, bent fingernail extensions. A *soed* crown is considered sacred; only those who have gone through a *krob-soed* initiation ritual are allowed to wear it.

Ban Dhammakhot, where I observed three consecutive *manora rongkru* ceremonies in the household of Wandi and Leg, is typical of villages in rural Thailand. Relatives arrive from all directions and help to cover the costs of the ritual. In addition to the rich offerings, the food for the guests is plentiful, consisting of southern Thai dishes. The audience comments on the performances of the *manora* troupe and gets into active communication with the dancers, whereby good-humored joshing and joking takes place after the consumption of generous amounts of alcohol.

The local spirit mediums are complemented by professional mediums from the city, and the ritual is used to treat some patients from within the kinship group. The spirit medium becomes possessed by powerful ancestor spirits and moves a burning candle in circular movements over the head of the patient, who sits on a mat on the stage. By this means, the spirit medium aims to remove excess heat, thus exorcising the harmful spirit.

Wandi, the female head of the household, appeared as a medium and embodied the powerful local guardian spirit. Returning ecstatically to the shrine in the house with a candle in her hand, she paid her respect to the deities of the house, moved back to the stage, and then climbed the ladder to the *palai* to venerate the great teachers before returning to the core family group of the household where the spirit met the family members, beginning with the oldest grandfather and proceeding by declining age through to the daughter. With great emotional warmth, she hugged and embraced the family members, and tears were shed because the family members have not seen their loved ones for a long time. The spirit jokes and laughs with family members and the community. The ancestors inquire about the status of the family and provide valuable advice. Very exhausted, Wandi almost loses consciousness; later she awakens as herself.

A Temple Festival

The spectacular public performances of *manora rongkru* at the temples of Wat Takae and Wat Takura are sponsored by the temples themselves, local government, and wealthy business people in the area. These grand rituals are public spectacles which attract thousands of pilgrims and worshipers from all parts of southern Thailand. They come to honor the first teacher of *manora*, Si Sata, the son of Mae (mother) Simala (also called "the great mother of the earth"), who is believed to be a reincarnation of the Hindu god Shiva.

By the time of my research, the *manora rongkru* in honor of the first teacher in Takae and the celebration in honor of the first teacher's mother had become highly commodified festivals. However, these events nevertheless kept the intimacy and spirituality of the original *manora*, in which all people are descendents of the first teachers and thus expected to venerate the great ancestors. Organizing such an event involves what Adam Yuet Chau calls the "coercion of the community" (Chau 2006); that is, the successful imposition of community norms and beliefs in a particular locale.

The ceremony for the veneration of Khun Si Sata takes place every year in the last week of April in the grounds of Wat Takea temple in Patthalung. Six of the twelve founding spirits of *manora* are said to possess spirit mediums at Wat Takae. The *nairong* who has the privilege of performing in the grand ceremony at Wat Takae is regarded as a direct successor of Si Sata and is among the greatest living *manora* teachers in southern Thailand. During the grand *manora rongkru* ceremony at Wat Takae, the successor of the first *manora* teacher is crowned and accepted as a teacher of the grand *manora*. The male *manora* teacher derives his power from the spirit of the first teacher, Si Sata, whose spirit is present and who observes the performance with keen interest.

Si Sata is commemorated with a statue that sits like a Buddha in a small hall (*viharn*) that has been constructed to accommodate him. The pilgrims offer flowers and food offerings to the spirit of Si Sata in the hall. This great ritual is carried out among the extended *manora* "family," which includes all people with *mano-*

ra descent (*trakun manora*). As nearly all households in old villages are *trakun manora*, everybody is called upon to join the ceremony at Wat Takae.

When I witnessed the ritual in 2007, it was a hot day and huge crowds came to the temple. The participants submitted a request to the ancestral spirits and deities and after fulfilment reciprocated by dancing with the hunter's mask in the temple.[8] Dozens of people came in large families to join the party, mingle with the crowds, and visit the many market stalls selling Buddhist amulets, *manora* music, and food, drinks, and other items. The event was organized by a preparation committee, consisting of the temple abbot, local civil servants, and prominent businessmen. The main representatives of the committee represented the *manora rongkru* at Wat Takae as a Buddhist tradition. One particular businessman, involved in construction and engineering and dressed in the traditional white clothes of the spirit mediums, was the main sponsor of the event. This businessman accumulated huge prestige, merit, and the attention of the spirits by sponsoring the ceremony. He was among the designated spirit mediums that participated every year at the Wat Takae ceremony. During the ritual, he was possessed by the ancestor spirits and danced among other mediums in the pavilion.

Entrance to the stage was restricted by the authority of the *manora* teacher. Nevertheless, it seemed that people came and went and that the stage became a very fluid space. A hundred onlookers were allowed to stay close to the stage in the hot sun to observe the spectacle and to comment on it. The music was extremely loud, blasted by loudspeakers across the temple terrain. After the perform-

Figure 9.2: Possessed business sponsor dancing at Wat Takae, Patthalung. Photograph by Alexander Horstmann, 2007.

ance of the *manora* dancers, the stage filled with dancers and people who wore the *manora* ancestral mask of the hunter. Old women who had visited *manora rongkru* regularly for decades joined in and began spontaneously to dance. Spirit mediums in white clothes joined the scene and became possessed by the great *manora* ancestor spirits. The stage was constantly filled with possessed spirit mediums and dancers, until the *nairong* called the dancers from the stage to make space for the ritual.

After a break, the *nairong* granted waiting families the opportunity to enter the stage and to present their babies and children. Some babies suffered from a skin disease that had left terrible red marks on their face. The magical treatment by the *nairong* was a viable alternative to the difficult medical treatment in a modern hospital. This special ritual—called *yiap sen* (stepping on the sore)—has been performed for centuries. From the perspective of *manora*, the illness is caused by a malevolent female spirit, who has selected the child and marked it. According to legend, Si Sata healed this illness and removed the sores from the faces of two hunters by washing his feet in sea water and putting them on the hunters' wounds. The parents brought their babies onto the stage and placed them on a pillow. During his dance, the *nairong* bathed his foot in a bowl of sacred water and betel leaf. He then wrote a mantra in old Khmer on his foot and put it into a flame. The rhythm of the music intensified, and then the *nairong* moved his foot, turned around, and touched the face of the child firmly with his bare foot. The musician beat his drums strongly and increased the drama of the unfolding event. During *yiap sen*, the *nairong* is said to be possessed by the spirit of the first *manora* teacher and uses his power and knowledge in the healing ritual. The authority of the *nairong* in healing the sores is unquestioned and widely known in southern Thailand. At the *manora rongkru* I attended, the ritual was repeated several times as many parents came to the ceremony with their babies full of hope that the malevolent spirit could be domesticated and exorcised.

The climax of the Wat Takae ceremony was the crowning initiation ceremony, in which a new *nairong* is certified to lead a *manora* by wearing the *manora* crown. The assistant of the *nairong*, who was dressed in white clothes during the ritual, was prostrate in front of the *nairong*. There was a concentrated silence at this stage, everybody being aware of this precious moment. The *nairong* placed a crown on the head of his assistant, thereby transmitting the power and knowledge of the *manora* tradition to him. From this point on, the newly crowned assistant is able to adopt the beautiful costume of the *nairong*, and he is free to found his own *manora* group and perform with it. He submits himself to the authority of his teacher for the duration of the ritual, but eventually succeeds him. After the crowning ritual, he carried out his first performance under the auspices of his teacher and the spirit of Si Sata.

During the ritual, the stage was one of the main theatres of action, but in parallel, the image of Si Sata in the small temple building also attracted large crowds who offered candles, flowers, incense, betel leaves, and food in worship of the first *manora* teacher. At the Wat Takae ritual, only the great ancestors were invited to the festival, including the first *manora* teachers, the guardian spirits of the land of Takae, the kings, and Buddhist saints. Spirit mediums and masked dancers felt free to occupy the stage throughout the ritual. Every single ritual, whether in the intimate sphere of the house or in a public space, represents the microcosm of the world and the universe in the understanding of *manora*. The public performance at Wat Takae attracted hundreds of participants and onlookers who hoped to benefit from the presence of Si Sata's spirit and his power to heal.

A Hybrid Festival

In the first week of May 2007, another large ceremony attracted thousands of pilgrims, and families flocked to the temple of Wat Takura in Satingphra to participate in the merit-making activities. The ritual in Satingphra was also organized by a committee consisting of local bureaucrats and the Buddhist abbot of Takura. The ceremony transformed the sleepy village of Ban Wat Takura into the site of a huge feast to which large crowds were attracted by the healing power of the Buddha image that is stored in a box behind two temple doors. The unwrapping of the small Buddha image accompanied by the music of the *manora* musicians was the highlight of the festival.

This particular *manora rongkru* was a hybrid ritual that drew on elements of Theravada Buddhism and *manora* practice. Takura is an important place in the *manora* myth. According to older people, Mae Srimala donated the gold that an elephant found in a bamboo tree to the temple of Wat Takura to distribute among the people. According to another narrative, the gold was donated to the abbot to be transformed into the holy Buddha image. During the festival, the Buddha image was presented in a cage to the pilgrims who waited for hours to sprinkle some holy water on the Buddha image. The unwrapping of the Buddha image was preceded by the intense chanting of Buddhist monks in Pali and drums play by selected *manora* musicians located in the temple hall in front of the door. Male dancers wearing the *manora* mask of the hunter danced wildly in the smaller pavilion.

A special stage was again erected for the *manora rongkru* performance. Hundreds bought a ticket for 50 baht to enter the stage and dance to the music (which was pre-recorded and broadcast by loudspeaker). The dancers wore only individual parts of the *manora* costumes or the hunter's mask. After five minutes, the music stopped, and the *nairong* sent the dancers from the stage as he got ready for the next ritual, the *yiap sen* (mentioned above). Again, people bought tickets for 50 baht, and in this case mothers brought their children onto the stage. Before curing the babies with his foot, the *manora* master asked the mother about the child's illness. Just as at Wat Takae, numerous families flocked to the temple in the hope of a cure.

In addition to the healing ritual, another event had brought people to Wat Takura: the ordination of young women into Buddhist nuns following the fulfilment of a vow they had made to Mae Simala, the mother of the *manora*. In contemporary Thailand, women are marginalized with regard to ordination into the Buddhist *Sangha*. At Wat Takura, women had the special opportunity of being ordained for one day. The young nuns-to-be were eager to perform the ordination ceremony, but because of their sheer number the ceremony was carried out in a very concise form. Every thirty minutes, ten women were ordained together. The young women identified themselves with the female hero of the *manora*. They regarded their ordination to the status of *mee chi* in Takura as a meritful act and as a way of reciprocating their vow to Mae Simala.

On the second day of the festival, a young mother with a black *jilbab* (headscarf) pushed her way through the crowds. She was received by the *nairong*, who nodded to her and instructed her to place her baby on a pillow. He slowly rotated, put his foot into the holy water, then into the fire, and finally, under loud music from the drums, onto the face of the crying baby. In her desperate need for a cure, the young Muslim woman had come all the way from Chumphorn province. Eager to find her way to the *nairong*, she ignored the Buddhist trappings of the event she had sought out. Some Muslim participants at the festival may not have been recognized as Muslims by others because they were not wearing Islamic dress, but because of her veil this woman made her Islamic affiliation known. This case shows that even as a Muslim the woman hoped that the great ancestor spirits, in whose power she clearly believed, would aid her child's recovery.

The sprinkling of water on the Buddha image, the dancing in the temple, the *yiap sen* ritual on the stage, the healing activities of the monks, the mass ordination of young nuns, and a young Muslim woman in search of cure for her child's ailment—these all took place in the atmosphere of a popular festival at which there were a hundred market stalls, selling food, drink, Buddhist amulets, handicrafts, fake hunter masks, and *manora* musical instruments. Nowhere is the postmodern nature of contemporary *manora rongkru*, with its commodification and hybridization, clearer than in the festival I witnessed at Wat Takura.

Concluding Remarks

Contemporary *manora rongkru* is not the tranquil rural ritual that has been described admirably by Isaradej (1999). Through modern media, images of *manora rongkru* festivals have developed a life on their own. They have contributed to enhancing the power and charisma of famous *nairong* and the hosts or sponsors of a ceremony. The crowds come regularly as pilgrims to worship the great *manora* ancestors. They emphasize the importance of the ritual by giving it the attribute 'big' (*yai*).[9] The noise and smells, the entranced mediums and the presence of the deities have transformed the *manora* festivals at Wat Takae and Wat Takura into huge sensoriums, events which—in the multiplicity of their elements—bombard the senses. Many people are attracted by *manora* troupes and the successors to the great *manora* teachers of the past who are considered the greatest in the region. While the reason for individual families hosting a *manora* is more specific, and has to do with submitting specific requests, the reason for the large crowds at grand *manora* festivals is less specific and has to do with the magic of the place where they are held. To explain the contemporary relevance of Thai popular religion, we have to consider the reconfigured function of *manora rongkru* in relation to Thailand's economic boom of the last few decades. I would argue that the decisive factor in the revitalization of *manora rongkru* is the search for magical efficacy and divine benevolence in a context of modernization. The revitalization of *manora rongkru* has taken place against a background of the intensification and individualization of religious experience in southern Thailand. While people have withdrawn from conventional Buddhism and Islam, the search for an individualized spiritual experience in modern Buddhists movements and Islamic revivalist movements is more popular than ever. Communities in southern Thailand are linked to the transnational flow of images by national and global media and, in turn, enter national and global flows themselves. People thus experience a very personal *manora rongkru* that has accommodated itself to meeting their particular spiritual needs.

While both Thai Buddhist and Malay Muslim items are offered to the ancestral deities, Muslims are withdrawing from *manora* in large numbers. For Buddhist participants, the nature of the *manora* ancestor spirits is not of importance, since both Buddhist and Muslim ancestors and deities are invited by the *nairong*, depending on the locality. While *manora* seems to be losing its inter-religious footing, the commodification of *manora* does not make it less authentic or powerful. More people than ever seem to give their trust to the spirits and are willing to invest in them. The role of Buddhism in accommodating the big *manora* spectacles in its temples is part of its spectacular revitalization. While the old *nairong* who played for the Thai king did not see a difference between Buddhists and Muslims, today's representatives on the Buddhist temple's *manora* committees do: they see *manora* as a set of Buddhist beliefs and practices. The distinction between ancestors according to their religion constitutes a real rupture as people in southern Thailand did not previously distinguish between them. The *manora* has become a prosperity ritual in which commodification has contributed to the prestige of its sponsors and may even provide them with incredible wealth. As such, *manora* resembles the Buddhist robe-giving ceremony (*kathin*), which also provides huge prestige to its main sponsor (e.g. Keyes 1995). While the original *manora* idea of advice being given by the caring ancestors is not lost, only wealthy families can afford to host a full *manora* that keeps the spirits alive. While *manora* is firmly anchored in the life, memory, and history of southern Thailand, it mediates communication between the living and the ancestors, enacts and displays the drama of society on its stage, and thus contributes to the reconstitution of society.

Notes

1. This chapter is based on ethnographic research carried out in the provinces of Nakhon-srithammarat, Patthalung, and Songkhla during regular visits between 2004 and 2009. I would like to thank Phittaya Butsararat of the Institute of Southern Thai Studies in Songkhla for sharing his work and insights with me. In addition, I would also like to acknowledge Christine Hemmet, who has worked on *manora* and organized museum exhibitions on it, and Marlane Guelden, whose work on *manora* has taught me much.
2. See Kitiarsa (2005a) for a thoughtful and critical essay on modern Thai popular culture.
3. Another example for revitalization of spirit possession in southern Thailand is the Chinese vegetarian festival analyzed by Cohen (2001).
4. See Gesick (1995) for a historical account of the Lake Songkhla region, which draws on manuscripts and oral history. The creation myth was told to Lorraine Gesick in different versions, depending on the locality. The play and performance of the *manora rongkru* ceremony has been standardized. The play and skits have also been commodified and now include elements from popular music (*luuk tung*) and TV soap opera.
5. See Muecke (1979) for similar healing practices in northern Thailand.
6. There is as yet no detailed study of the revolutionary impact of different media on *manora* performance—e.g., the impact of radio, newspapers, audio and video recordings, etc. These media have taken *manora* out of the local context and made it an object of the Thai national imagination.
7. For an account of curing practices that bridge ethnic and religious boundaries, see Golomb (1985).
8. The hunter (*phran*) who wants to catch the bird-winged maiden is one of the important figures in the performance of the creation myth and one of the narrators (together with the *nairong*). The hunter's mask has become a popular item for dancers.
9. See Kitiarsa (2008) for a general perspective on the commodification of religion in Southeast Asia.

References

Butsararat, Phittaya. 1992. "Manora Rongkru, Tha Khae Village, Phatthalung Municipal District, Patthalung Province," M.A. dissertation. Songkhla: Srinakharinwirot University.

———. 2003. "The Change and Relations between Society and Culture in the Low Lying Areas of Songkhla Lake: The Case Study of Nang Talung and Manora after the Government Reformation in the Period of King Rama the Fifth to the Present Day," paper presented at the conference "The Tendency of Changes of Songkhla Lake: History, Culture, and Developing Vision," Institute for Southern Thai Studies, Songkhla, Thailand.

Chau, Adam Yuet. 2006. *Miraculous Response: Doing Popular Religion in Contemporary China*. Stanford, CA: Stanford University Press.

Cohen, Erik. 2001. *The Chinese Vegetarian Festival in Phuket: Religion, Ethnicity and Tourism on a Southern Thai Island*. Bangkok: White Lotus.

Gesick, Lorraine. 1995. *In the Land of Lady White Blood: Southern Thailand and the Meaning of History*. Ithaca, NY: Cornell University Press.

Ginsburg, Henry D. 1972. "The Manora Dance-drama: An Introduction," *Journal of Siam Society* 60: 169–81.

Golomb, Louis. 1978. *Brokers of Morality: Thai Ethnic Adaptation in a Rural Malaysian Setting*. Honolulu: University of Hawaii Press.

———. 1985. *An Anthropology of Curing in Multiethnic Thailand*. Urbana: University of Illinois Press.

Guelden, Marlane. 2005a. "Spirit Mediumship in Southern Thailand: The Feminization of Manora Ancestral Possession," in *Dynamic Diversity in Southern Thailand*, ed. W. Sugunnasil. Chiang Mai: Silkworm Press, pp.179–212.

———. 2005b. "Ancestral Spirit Mediumship in Southern Thailand: The Nora Performance as a Symbol of the South on the Periphery of a Buddhist Nation-State," dissertation. Manoa: University of Hawaii.

———. 2007[1995]. *Spirits Among Us*. Singapore: Marshall Cavendish.

Hemmet, Christine. 1992. "Le Manora du Sud de la Thailande: un culte aux ancetres," *Bulletin de l'École française d'Extrême-Orient* 79(2): 261–82.

Horstmann, Alexander. 2004. "Ethnohistorical Perspectives on Buddhist–Muslim Relations and Coexistence in Southern Thailand: From Shared Cosmos to the Emergence of Hatred?" *Sojourn* 19(1): 76–99.

———. 2007. "The Tablighi Jama'at, Transnational Islam, and the Transformation of the Self between Southern Thailand and South Asia," *Comparative Studies of South Asia, Africa and the Middle East* 27(1): 26–41.

Isaradej, Thienchai. 1999. "Social Implications of Manora Rongkru: A Case Study of Ban Bo-Dang," M.A. dissertation. Bangkok: Silapakorn University.

Jackson, Peter. 1999. "Royal Spirits, Chinese Gods, and Magic Monks: Thailand's Boomtime Religions of Prosperity," *South East Asia Research* 7(3): 245–320.

Jungwiwattanaporn, Parichat. 2006. "In Contact with the Dead: Manora Rong Khru Cha Ban Ritual of Thailand," *Asian Theatre Journal* 23(2): 374–95.

Keyes, Charles. 1995 *The Golden Peninsula: Culture and Adaptation in Mainland Southeast Asia*. Honolulu: University of Hawaii Press.

Kitiarsa, Pattana. 2005a. "Beyond Syncretism: Hybridization of Popular Religion in Contemporary Thailand," *Journal of Southeast Asian Studies* 36(3): 461–87.

———. 2005b. "Magic Monks and Spirit Mediums in the Politics of Thai Popular Religion," *Inter-Asia Cultural Studies* 6(2): 209–26.

———. ed. 2008. *Religious Commodifications in Asia: Marketing Gods*. London: Routledge.

Lambek, Michael. 2000. "Localizing Islamic Performance in Mayotte," in *Islamic Prayer across the Indian Ocean: Inside and Outside the Mosque*, eds. D. Parkin and S.C. Headley. Richmond: Curzon, pp.63–98.

Meyer, Birgit, and Annelies Moors, eds. 2009. *Aesthetic Formations: Media, Religion and the Senses*. New York: Palgrave.

Morris, Rosalind C. 2000. *In the Place of Origins: Modernity and its Mediums in Northern Thailand*. Durham, NC: Duke University Press.

Muecke, Marjorie. 1979. "An Explication of 'Wind Illness' in Northern Thailand," *Culture, Medicine and Psychiatry* 3: 267–300.

Nunsuk, Preecha. 1980. "Khun Uppatham Narakon: The Light of Thai Dancing Art and the Great Manora Teachers of the South," *Sinlapa-Watthanatham* 12: 10–19.

Tanabe, Shigeharu. 2002. "The Person in Transformation: Body, Mind and Cultural Appropriation," in *Cultural Crisis and Social Memory: Politics of the Past in the Thai World*, eds. S. Tanabe and C.F. Keyes. London: Routledge Curzon, pp.43–67.

Taylor, J.L. 1999. "Postmodernity, Remaking Tradition and the Hybridization of Thai Buddhism," *Anthropological Forum* 9(2): 163–87.

———. 2008. *Buddhism and Postmodern Imaginings in Thailand: The Religiosity of Urban Space*. Burlington: Ashgate.

Van De Port, Mattijs. 2006. "Visualizing the Sacred: Video Technology, 'Televisual' Style, and the Religious Imagination in Bahian Candomblé," *American Ethnologist* 33(3): 444–61.

10

The Horror of the Modern: Violation, Violence, and Rampaging Urban Youths in Contemporary Thai Ghost Films

Pattana Kitiarsa

Introduction

The uncanny haunting by spirits of socially marginalized figures, the excessive display of violation and violence, and the rampaging of urban youth have emerged as notable features in Thai horror films over the past ten years.[1] Take the following three short films as examples.[2] The first, *Yan Sang Tai/Tit for Tat* (2008), portrays the chaotic phenomenon of inter-school quarrels and fights among vocational college students in cosmopolitan Bangkok and other urban centers around the country. Resulting violence and death are regularly reported by the national media. This filmic story reveals how a young, socially marginalized technical-college student, whose father works as an undertaker (*sapparoe*) at a local temple crematorium, uses a deadly black-magic formula to get even with his gangster classmates. He is badly bullied by his more affluent but violent classmates, who accuse him of reporting them to the school disciplinarian for possessing and using drugs. He barely survives being tortured and lynched by the gang. His old bicycle, perhaps his sole possession of value, is destroyed. He seeks the help of a supernatural and deadly charm to avenge these crimes, which later gets out of control. The result is terror attacks by vengeful ghosts and indiscriminately brutal deaths for each gang member.

In *Lao Cha-on/Novice* (2009), Pey, a troubled teenage gangster from a broken home, is stoned to death by a hungry ghost (*pret*) while temporarily serving as a Buddhist novice and living in a sacred forest monastery. However, he is uncer-

---

Endnotes for this chapter begin on page 217

emoniously disrobed and furiously exposed to the sinful burden of his past acts, and Buddhism fails to protect or salvage him from the cruel karmic consequences. After death, he becomes a hungry demon. Pey has committed a series of sins throughout his young life. He joins a youth gang, whose members throw stones at passing motorists with the aim of causing highway accidents, and they steal valuables from ill-fated drivers and passengers. His aggressive and arrogant behavior leads to the worst possible crime in Buddhist cosmology: he kills his own father in one of his night-time, windshield-smashing sprees. In addition, he hates his mother, who has since remarried. His mother and stepfather hide him away in a remote temple in order to save him from being punished for his juvenile crimes. Pey verbally abuses his mother, calling her a slut who has abandoned her own son and run off with a lover. Youthful, angry, and stubborn-headed, once at the temple Pey violates monastic rules and local taboos. He shows disrespect to the sacred Buddhist monastery, disobeys the instructions of the abbot and a senior monk, consumes food offerings intended for hungry demons at night, and hurts one of the mysterious demons with his impulsive stone-throwing habit. By committing these sinful acts, Pey's life is destined to lead nowhere but to suffering for the severe karmic consequences of his actions.

Finally, *Khon Klang/In the Middle* (2008) shows another tragic death and the haunting of a group of young urban men intruding into the uninhabited natural space of the forest. A group of four college students go camping deep in the rainforest, where they violate the taboo of telling ghost stories. They also carelessly challenge natural and supernatural forces while they venture into the forest and row a boat down a river. One of them is killed when the inflatable boat capsizes during a white-water descent, and the remaining members of the group are terrorized by the ghostly presence of their dead friend.

These three ghost stories come from the multiple award-winning film collections *Si Phraeng/Phobia* (2008) and *Ha Phraeng/Phobia 2* (2009).[3] The first collection contains four thematically-related short horror stories, while the second one features five. I have deliberately chosen these films to open my discussion of the persistent tension and rupture between ghosts and modernity in contemporary Thailand. What do the ghost and its uncanny haunting mean in contemporary Thailand? In what ways are ghost haunting and attacks constructed and represented in filmic stories? How can we read them in connection to the prominence of Western-style modernization and urbanization processes?

In this chapter, I argue that ghosts and their ghostly presence are the products of modern social marginalization, made in and through the modernization process. Ghosts appear and make their presence felt at the various margins of both real and imagined modern social worlds. Thai horror films of late show emotional and intimate sides of modernity, suggesting that modernity has produced a marginalizing dark side that is arrogant, overtly self-confident, indifferent, and, at times, destructive of existing tradition. This dark side of modernity is well represented in the rise of social violation and violence among urban youths. I further suggest that the current generation of Thai horror films contains powerful ethnographic materials with which one can rethink not only the now classic issue in the sociology of religion of the persistence of magic and spirits in an age of post- or late-modernity, but also "the subtle and complex interconnections among everyday forms of relatedness in the present, memories of the past, and the wider [historical and] political context in which they occur" (Carsten 2007: 1).

Taking as my focus a selection of Thai horror films, my intention in this chapter is to investigate the socio-cultural meanings of the presence of ghosts and their uncanny haunting in connection with the encompassing forces and processes of urban modernity. I concur with Pels (2003) that magic and ghosts must not be viewed as backward or premodern remnants in opposition to modernity. They are more supplementary and closely related to one another than appears in anthropological and sociological discourses of religious secularization. Magic and ghosts are indeed "reinvented in modernity" (ibid.: 32) and offer a powerful venue in which "to trace the histories [and changes] through which spirits become critical players" (Langford 2005: 162). By de-emphasizing its premodern root and route, I contend that ghosts are made and remade as a key modern social character and cultural institution.

The sociologist Avery Gordon argues that "the ghost is not simply a dead or a missing person, but a social figure, and investigating it can lead to that dense site where history and subjectivity make social life" (Gordon 2008: 8). I take Gordon's persuasive argument as the starting point of my reading of contemporary Thai horror films and the complex representation of ghosts' haunting in contemporary Thailand. As an analytical position, taking the ghost as a marginal "social figure" and analyzing it as a "dense site where history and subjectivity make social life" is valid for two reasons. First, it reaffirms the idea that ghosts must be taken seriously as an analytic category of modernity. Forms of storytelling and emotional interactions pertinent to ghosts have emerged as legitimate subjects in the study of human religious and everyday experience. Second, in and through the dense site of ghost-haunting phenomena, there are always multiple dimensions to ghosts as socially marginal figures and institutions awaiting some further critical interpretation of modern social life and change. I intend to study ghost films and their implications for contemporary Thai society not only because the cinematic representation of ghosts and haunting are understudied in the literature, but also because they have recently staged a very powerful claim as indispensable socio-cultural subjects. As Gordon reminds us: "haunting is a constituent element of social life. It is neither premodern superstition nor individual psychosis; it is a generalizable social phenomenon of great importance. To study social life one must confront the ghostly aspects of it" (ibid.: 7). As in other modern societies (e.g., Meyer 2003; Tan 2010), the ghostly aspects of modern social life in Thailand are most vividly displayed and critically unveiled through horror films, perhaps the country's most powerful popular-entertainment media.

Studies of Spirits and Modernity in the Thai Context

I begin my discussion by making a distinction between spirit and ghost. Although both have been used as translations of the Thai word *phi*, I use them differently, not interchangeably. Both terms offer closely related meanings regarding supernatural beliefs in the soul or a person's animated force after death. I prefer using the term "spirit" to refer to general religious and cultural beliefs in the force or figure of the dead or nature. I reserve the term "ghost," meanwhile, for the angry, vengeful, or malevolent spirit of a dead person. Instead of more complicated terminologies and categories—like spirit (*phut, phi, winyan*), demon (*pisat*), ever-hungry ghoul (*pret*), malevolent, internal-organ-consuming spirit (*phi pop*), and monster/zombie (*phi dip*)—I employ the generic term ghost (*phi*) in its broad and inclusive sense because it specifically implies vernacular perceptions of ghostly presence and uncanny haunting (see Rajadhon 1972; So 2009). Many ghosts appear in the form of terrorizing and attacking demons or monsters. Dealing with ghosts as well as spirits is the practice of those with specialized ritual knowledge and skills, such as magic, charms, and other forms of supernatural, quasi-Buddhist, or magical Buddhist means (Kirsch 1977; Golomb 1985; Hayashi 2003). In particular, I take ghosts and ghostly presence as key figures and features in horror films. Citing the work of Rosalind Morris, Birgit Meyer, in her description of magic and superstition in Ghanaian films, argues that cinema has a curative magic which brings together the primitive and the modern because "the camera is our one magical tool flush with animistic power to possess, enchant, travel through time and space, and bewitch" (Moore 2000, cited in Meyer 2003: 220).

Magic and spirit, by definition and convention, seem to oppose modernity. By modernity, I mean a post-Enlightenment social process and "a progressive force promising to liberate humankind from ignorance and irrationality" (Rosenau 1992: 5). Modernity was first developed in Europe before "it steamroll[ered] over the entire Earth" (Heller 1999: 4). For Pels, modernity refers to "the global (but not hegemonic) spread of consciousness of radical temporal rupture" (Pels 2003: 30). Wherever modernity penetrates, it always creates moments of tension and schism between tradition and the self-conscious sense of being in a present that is trapped between the past and the future. Living in modern conditions, people constantly feel the pressure of having to keep themselves up to date. A sense of being left behind by ever-changing places and times plays a pivotal part in the modern psyche.

In most sociological definitions of modernity, spirit and magic have no place in the modern world of industrial civilization, which is characterized by: firstly, "a certain set of attitudes towards the world, the idea of the world as open to transformation by human intervention; [second], a complex of economic institutions, especially industrial production and a market economy; [and third], a certain range of political institutions, including the nation-state and mass democracy" (Giddens

1998: 94). However, as many studies of magic and modernity have shown, magic and spirit cults have outlasted the modernist discourse of secularization (see, e.g., Keyes, Kendall, and Hardacre 1994; Tanabe and Keyes 2002b; Meyer and Pels 2003; Kitiarsa 2008). They have persisted and prowled above and beyond technological interventions. Not only have magic and spirit cults reinvented themselves in modernity, but they have also posted fundamental questions pertinent to the modernization process itself. They have challenged our understandings of the seemingly opposed categories of tradition and modernity in different socio-cultural and historical contexts.

Tradition and modernity are not necessarily opposites; the two categories must be carefully examined in particular historical and social contexts. Meyer reminds us that "the claim that magic has been superseded by modernity is ideological rather than real" (Meyer 2003: 221), a scholarly invention rather than an actual social phenomenon. Pels suggests that "the temporal distancing of magic by classifying it as premodern could only take place in the anthropologist's own time and language" (Pels 2003: 5). In the Thai context, Rhum (1996) argues that tradition (*prapheni*) and modernity (*khwam than samai*) are indeed interconnected and complementary to one another. Both are politically and culturally constructed in the process of nation-building. When modernity traveled from the West to other parts of the world, it was imported "with great enthusiasm by Third World elites" (ibid.: 329). However, it was also subtly transformed in the process. The mobility of "modernity" implies an unequal power relationship between the West and the Rest, an Us and Them. Rhum remarks: "we [Westerners] sold modernization as a natural process leading to a natural state, 'modernity'. They imported it as a prescriptive model … for achieving a certain desirable condition, without entirely abandoning its teleological aspects" (ibid.: 329). In Thailand, such a process of importing and transforming Western-style modernity is widely known as top-down, selective modernization, largely initiated and controlled by rulers and elites, who "selectively adopted only good things from the West [e.g., science and technology] for the country while preserving the traditional values [e.g., Buddhism] at their best" (Winichakul 1994: 3).

How have Thais perceived and interpreted modernity over the two centuries of encountering modernization and development? What is the place of spirits and ghosts in the process of modernization in Thailand? Like much of the Third World, Thailand is a country that perceives and treats modernity with caution and doubt. Thais may have embraced Western-style modernity at least since the second half of the nineteenth century, but they have always been conscious of growing tensions and ruptures created by the conditions of being modern. Modernity in the Thai context constantly implies something imported and foreign, as well as the radical break-up of characteristics of social life. Tanabe and Keyes (2002a) argue that modernization always entails dilemmas, having both positive and negative sides. Following Simmel (1978), they show that contemporary Thailand and

Laos "have come to face crises that have made people insecure in the present and anxious about the future" (Tanabe and Keyes 2002a: 1). Social life has been increasingly embedded in the crisis of modernity, resulting from the intrinsic tensions "of the rupture of the present from the past" (ibid.: 6). Thailand nowadays has to make sense of a series of contradictions "between the desire for abstract rationality and the resistant desire to retain particular values and elements previously assured" (ibid: 6).

With regard to Thai modernity, ghosts have attracted less scholarly attention than state-sponsored Theravada Buddhism (see, e.g., Kirsch 1977; Smith 1978; Swearer 1995). Early studies of ghosts and spirit cults in Thailand were carried out as part of folkloric, evolutionist, and functionalist studies, in which it was argued that spirits helped assure agricultural fertility, maintain family and communal cohesion, and ease social anxiety and tension (see Rajadhon 1961; Klausner 1987). The connection between spirit cults and modern economic development was picked up in the 1980s by scholars focusing on Marxist political economy and the impact of modernization. Scholars such as Ganjanapan (1984), Ramitanon (1984), and Tanabe (1986) depict northern Thai spirit cults as a site of the resistance of local peasants to the penetration of the Bangkok-centered Thai state and market economy. Ancestral ghosts are indeed socio-political figures. Through ritual processes they are shown to be the core of traditional institutions, moral agents functioning to safeguard female sexuality and oversee the transference and distribution of land at both family and community levels. In the 1990s, studies of spirit cults shifted significantly from a focus on agrarian communities to the cults' importance among rural migrants and urban populations who have struggled to make a living as well as weave gendered identities during a time when the country has undergone radical socio-economic transformation (Tanabe 1991, 2002). The notion of the crisis of modernity proposed by Keyes, Kendall, and Hardacre (1994) and Tanabe and Keyes (2002a) has gained in analytic momentum. Smutkupt et al. (1996) adopt this conceptual line of thinking and show how the phenomenal spread of urban spirit-medium cults in northeast Thailand is symptomatic of the anxiety felt by people attempting to make sense of the radical socio-economic and cultural changes around them. Similarly, Mills points out that attacks by widow ghosts (*phi mae mai*) in northeastern Thai villages, which since the early 1980s have come to contain large numbers of foreign male labor migrants, reveal "on the one hand, an explicit critique of the transformation of household and gender relations by capitalist modes of production, and, on the other hand, more fundamental … sources of tension and ambivalence in popular experiences of modernity" (Mills 1995: 268).

Ghostly presence, particularly in the form of magic, supernatural beliefs, and popular religion, could be seen as religious and cultural parameters that gauge how deeply and to what extent modernity has penetrated the texture of everyday life. Studies by Morris (2000) and Klima (2002) reveal the links between ghostly presences and their semiotic representations. Ghost stories reveal intimate, emotional, and unconscious aspects of modernity and power struggles. Klima, through his complex philosophical ethnography, takes a critical look at Buddhist meditations on corpses and funerary exchange. He shows that death and dead bodies always have roles to play, especially in political resistance to a regime of radical democracy and in the "fast-paced market of images" (Klima 2002: 5). Morris suggests that while the resurgence of spirit-medium cults in urban Chiang Mai represents the return of the past (Morris 2000: 12), it also "testifie[s] to the ironies of modernity" (ibid.: 88). More recently, Morris has situated ghosts at the juncture between the dead and the living. According to her: "the ghost is not simply a generic mark of any kind of occurrence. It is death that causes death to appear as the effect of death and that calls the living back to itself. And it is death that then permits the living to be conscious of themselves as such" (Morris 2008: 230).

The Proliferation of Modern Ghost Films in Thailand

Meyer argues that "films visualize imaginations" (Meyer 2003: 221). This comment holds true in the world of Thai horror films as it does elsewhere. Cinema also heightens collective ghostly experience. In Thailand, cinema is by far the prime modern media which popularizes and commercializes horror based on scripted stories of haunting. No media could ever convey or tell ghost stories as powerfully and emotionally effectively as film. Known as *nang phi*, literally "ghost" or "horror film," this genre includes a wide range of supernatural and superstitious phenomena, such as the haunting of the unnatural dead, angry guardian spirits, rampant zombies, and mythical supernatural figures. As part of the cinema industry, Thai ghost films have evolved over time. In perhaps the most detailed study of Thai horror films to date, Nueng Diew (2009: 17f.) traces the history of this film genre and situates it in the long march of Thai film. *Nangsao Suwan/Suvarna of Siam* (1923) is recognized as the first feature film about Siam (as Thailand was known before 1939). It was shot by an American film-maker, Henry A. Macrae. In 1927, the first Thai film-makers, the Wasuwat brothers, produced *Chok Songchan/Dubious Luck* (1927). According to Barmé (2002: 55), *Waen Wiset/The Magic Ring* (1929), a forty-minute silent production shot by the Wasuwat brothers on Ko Pha-ngan in southern Thailand in 1929, is the earliest complete Thai film known to exist.

The Thai horror film genre owes its existence to two famous ghost stories: *Nang Nak* (or *Mae Nak*) and *Pu Som Fao Sap* (literally, Grandfather Som, a guardian spirit of ancient treasure and a gnome). The latter was produced in 1934 and is credited as the first Thai ghost film with a Thai language soundtrack. It is reported that the musical score is on a par with international musicals during the 1930s (Nueng Diew 2009). The film *Nang Nak Phra Khanong/The Female Ghost of Phra Khanong District* (1935) was released to extraordinary box office success, with major cinemas in Bangkok flooded with enthusiastic audiences. People were excited to witness the most popular ghost story in the country on the screen. The audience seemed to appreciate and relate to the horror of this legendary Thai ghost more than the Hollywood horror figures of the 1930s, such as Frankenstein and Dracula. The legendary ghost of *Nang Nak* is the most famous and most filmed ghost in Thailand's cinema history, with twenty-nine cinematic versions of *Nang Nak* produced between 1933 and 2005; in addition there have also been portrayals of *Nang Nak* in pulp novels, comic strips, stage plays, and TV dramas. This traditional female ghost has deeply ingrained herself in Thai social memory and imagination over the years (ibid.: 23–47; see also Wong 2000; Knee 2005; Diamond 2006; Ingawanij 2007; So 2009).

With the disruption of the Second World War and its aftermath, Thai horror films endured a slow expansion in terms of annual output. They were not as popular as other film genres—such as romance, comedy, and action—and, like the rest of Thai cinema, horror films had to live behind the shadow of popular Hong Kong, Hollywood, and Indian films, which dominated the market during the 1940s and 1950s. However, with restrictions subsequently placed on foreign film imports, Thai horror films gained in popularity and reached their heyday in the late 1960s and 1970s (Boonyaketmala 1992; Chaiworaporn 2002). Numerous films based on myth, the supernatural, and various kinds of spirits were shown in the growing number of cinema houses both in Bangkok and urban centers around the country. The provincial heartland, where national television networks had limited penetration due to the lack of electricity in the countryside, supplied the main portion of the audiences for the ghost films. Ghost films during this period diversified in terms of plot and content, no longer relying on haunting alone but adding elements from erotic, comedy, and action genres. The popular *phi pop* ("the ogre") films of the 1980s and 1990s are testimony to the popular perception of Thai ghost films as B-movies (Nueng Diew 2009). They were made with low budgets, poor plots, rough scripts, and always featuring sexy actresses and troops of well-known comedians and personalities. Most B-grade ghost films were based on myth, legend, and superstition. Buddhist monks are often used as moral authorities to ward off rampant female ghosts, who were tortured by some crooked exorcists or greedy bad guys with black magic formulas.

Though Thai horror film is indeed an established genre in the world of Thai cinema, it has always existed as a hybrid form. One can never uncover a pure or authentic style of ghost film in the country, where the internationalization as much as the localization of film ideas, techniques, and markets has influenced the genre. Film-makers have been willing to bring in fashionable and marketable ghosts and ideas, regardless of their origin. It is quite common to see Thai horror films featuring Western horror figures (most notably Dracula, zombies, and some sci-fi figures), ghosts from Hong Kong, Japan, or Taiwan, as well as ghosts from legends from neighboring countries such as Cambodia, Laos, and Burma. However, since the economic crisis of the late 1990s, which hit Thai cinema as well as other parts of the economy, the landscape of Thai film has changed. Production quality has vastly improved in terms of acting, budget, plot, film-making techniques, and marketing.[4] Knee's summary of the rejuvenated Thai horror films of the late 1990s and early 2000s is worth quoting at length:

> These films mark a retrieval of the past, a return to a genre quite popular in the heyday of Thai cinema. They do, to some extent, engage modern global (read Hollywood) conventions of the horror genre, but also very specifically refer back to the local genre tradition, itself deeply rooted in local folklore … [They] return to past tradition as a source for narratives explicitly dealing with the return of the past in supernatural form. (Knee 2005: 141f.)

Thai horror films of the 2000s exhibit some distinctive features, which Harrison (2005) describes in terms of the rise of Thai film. First, film-makers are young and talented, and have been deeply exposed to the world of international cinema. Though most are products of film schools in Bangkok, some of them have studied or worked abroad, and a few of them are based outside Thailand. Second, they have a clear understanding of the national, historical, and cultural depth of Thai cinema, and they are keen to (re)present the products of Thai cinema internationally (Jirattikorn 2003; Kitiarsa 2007). Thai identity, or Thai style, has loomed large, if not stood out, in most recently released horror films from Thailand. Third, they have expanded their market to cover international audiences, assisted by favorable factors such as online technology, international marketing networks, and joint financial investment. Finally, the horror films of the 2000s have benefited from the influence of short film, documentary film, and low-budget art-house movies. The business of film-making is no longer confined to big budget studios. With advances in computer and post-production technologies, serious horror films with an emphasis on production values, marketing, and the consumption of fear have started to gain ground commercially and aesthetically. To date, domestic and international markets have responded enthusiastically.

Violation, Violence, and Rampaging Urban Youths

In her study of narrative experience in Karoland, Sumatra, anthropologist Mary Steedly defines the quality of a "good story" as the "one that surprises its audience, transgressing or temporarily exceeding the givenness of its form" (Steedly 1993: 29). She reminds us of the power of narratives of spirit encounters as a form and method for dissecting and countering the official discourse of displacement. I follow Steedly's suggestion of taking stories as narrative experiences, which I use to view the "good stories" in *Phobia* and *Phobia 2*. I suggest that meaningful narrative experience can be grounded in and harnessed by viewing and reading good filmic stories. It is a way of thinking about ghostly experience in the context of contemporary Thai society.

Phobia and *Phobia 2* represent major contributions to the world of Thai horror film. They display the influence of international horror films, both from Hollywood and other Asian cinemas, notably those of Japan, Hong Kong, Korea, and Taiwan. These titles are basically collections of several thematically related shorts, and can be read like a collection of short stories. With limitations of time and space, shorts are an ideal vehicle for telling ghost stories. Extreme emotional expressions, such as fear, shock, and suspense, are effectively conveyed in this mode of cinematic presentation. All the films contained in both collections last between twenty and twenty-five minutes. In addition, most ghost stories in *Phobia* and *Phobia 2* speak critically about contemporary Thai society. They are short films with a conscious aim of social commentary, yet they firmly place ghosts at "a unique juncture of personal, social and mythic structure[s]" (Kawin 1981, cited in Waller 2000: 264) in contemporary Thailand. Terror and fear in both collections are not purely fictional, nor are they the products of an intended horror fantasy that valorizes a return to the past in supernatural form. Horror and terror are portrayed as real because the plots are based on social scenarios as well as cultural beliefs that are part of contemporary Thai society and culture. They are therefore cinematic representations of a reality and imagination about which Thais are anxious and frustrated in their everyday lives. They serve as a perfect platform for representing everyday forms of related-ness and social reality in contemporary Thailand.

Violation, violence, and rampaging urban youths are central themes of the filmic narratives of *Phobia* and *Phobia 2*. These two film collections "offer some insight into the processes by which experience is narratively produced and en-meshed in the practices of everyday social discourse" (Steedly 1993: 8). These themes form the basis of my interpretation of how ghost stories and ghost figures can be analyzed as representations of the dilemmas of modernity and its social marginalization process, which entices ghostly matters into the place where they have always belonged: multiple socio-economic and subaltern worlds.

Violation

The short films in *Phobia* and *Phobia 2* reveal a detailed common process of how persons become ghosts and why ghosts of the dead return to haunt the living. This process starts with violation, violence, death, ghostly haunting, or a return of the dead to wreak revenge. Violation means acts of transgressing or rebelling against rules, restrictions, taboos, or conventions. Lines of authoritative prohibition are crossed or blurred. People for various reasons have committed wrongdoings. Many violations involve insulting or invoking the uncontrollable and unpredictable. Either carelessly or intentionally, violation begins the process of ghostly presence that leads to the loss of life. The life of Pey in *Lao Cha-on/*

Novice (discussed above) typifies most kinds of social and moral violation found in these films. As a teenage boy, he was a gangster and listened to no one. He killed, stole, and showed no respect to his parents. He violates moral restrictions in both worldly and religious realms. In *Khon Klang/In the Middle*, a group of young men go camping in the forest and jokingly challenge the supernatural (by telling ghost stories) as well as the natural (by playfully standing up at the front of their inflatable boat and shouting loudly and provocatively while rowing down a river in flood). The urban male vocabularies and behavior of the characters is also offensive. They do not observe the traditional conduct expected of people entering and staying in the forest with respect to guardian and other spirits. They lack respect for nature. These acts of violation claim the life of one young man, who drowns in the river, and later his ghost comes back to haunt the others. In *Rot Mue Song/Salvage* (2009), Nut, a young mother, violates business ethics by lying to her customers. She profits from repairing and reselling previously owned vehicles. The second-hand cars she sells are supposedly in good condition, but in reality she has repair men salvage cars that have been badly damaged in traffic accidents. Toward the end of the film, she has to pay the highest price for her moral violation: haunted by a ghost in her own yard—itself a cemetery for dead vehicles—she accidentally kills her own son who has mysteriously hidden himself in a car's engine compartment.

Buddhist precepts are repeatedly used as moral benchmarks in *Phobia* and *Phobia 2*. As the dominant religious cosmology and social code of conduct in Thailand, Buddhism comprises a set of universal moral rules and regulations, as well as a way of seeing and behaving. Thus, Thais interpret human acts of violation in Buddhist terms. The most common Buddhist concepts and precepts appearing in these films are the law of karma (*kot haeng kam*) and the five precepts for lay persons (*sin ha*). Breaking or violating Buddhist moral benchmarks is repeatedly a cause of suffering and death. In *Thiawbin 224/Last Fright* (2008), Phim, a young and beautiful flight attendant, is killed by the ghost of a foreign princess while performing her duties while on board a plane. The princess knew that Phim had had an affair with her husband. *Backpackers* (2009), meanwhile, features Burmese migrant workers, whose bodies are exploited for labor and used as human transporters for drug trafficking when they are forced to swallow small bags of heroin. They are thus doubly victimized, and they subsequently suffocate to death in a sealed container truck during an ill-fated cross-border smuggling operation. Treated inhumanely in life, they return as zombies and kill a truck driver, a boy, and everybody else they encounter. The dead workers haunt and kill the living because the living have to pay for their bad deeds: exploiting, torturing, taking advantage of, and making a profit from the weaker, the natural, or the marginalized. Many films in these collections reassert and restore the simplistic yet conservative and hegemonic view that obeying or following Buddhist precepts is the rightful path in life, whereas breaking or violating them is wrong and a literally disastrous way of behaving. Failing to follow the right path always leads to suffering or eventual death. The appearance of ghosts is the consequence of wrongdoing or violations of Buddhist moral, social norms and laws.

Beside Buddhist precepts, violating supernatural taboos appears as a central theme in many of the short films in *Phobia* and *Phobia 2*. The key point is that violating a taboo leads to a series of unpredictable, dangerous events, and violators usually subsequently receive punishment. In *Ngao/Happiness* (2008) and *Yan Sang Tai/Tit for Tat*, the taboo is that one must not look into the eyes of the dead because the spirit of the dead will remember you and come back to haunt you. This act is absolutely prohibited. However, Pin in *Ngao/Happiness* does not do it intentionally. She is returning to her rented apartment in a taxi when the taxi hits a young man and overturns. While the young man—who prior to the accident is angry and in a state of despair after reading a text message signaling the break up of his relationship with his girlfriend—is instantly killed in the crash, Pin lives. The moment she opens her eyes after the taxi has crashed, she finds herself returning the gaze of the dead man. Later, alone in her room nurturing a leg injury, the ghost of the young man comes to haunt her through an exchange of spooky text messages. A sudden attack by the ghost leads her to fall from the multistory apartment building. Her grave mistake being to have accidentally looked into the eyes of the dead, her death is both mysterious and unfair. In *Yan Sang Tai/Tit for Tat*, the taboo on eyecontact with the dead is also the critical point of violation. Taking advantage of this taboo, the son of the undertaker uses a deadly charm to avenge members of the school gang that has bullied him. In *Khon Klang/In the Middle*, the taboo concerns the belief that the person sleeping in the middle of a group while camping in the forest is likely to be the target of a ghost attack. Thus everyone tries to avoid sleeping in this position.

Violence

Acts of violation eventually lead to violence, in both the physical and structural sense. In most cases, violation and violence are closely related; it is always difficult to view them separately. By violence, I refer to a wide range of actions that involve force, sometimes but not always deliberate, that result in loss of life, injury, damage to property, or involve forcing someone to do something against their will. Violent acts are key features of these Thai horror films. The sequential logic is that violence causes death, death in turn produces ghosts, and ghosts haunt the living by violent and deadly means. The cycle of violence is apparent and inevitable. Most violent forms of death in *Phobia* and *Phobia 2* involve car accidents, gun shots, stoning, falling from buildings, vampire-style blood sucking, and piercing with sharp objects. There is more than one form of violence and sequence of events leading to violence in each film. Violent death usually creates terror, horror, shock, sorrow, or remorse, and other emotional and moral disorientations. Most importantly, it gives birth to ghosts and their uncanny haunting, which Gordon describes as: "a frightening experience. It always registers the harm inflicted or the loss sustained by a social violence done in the past or in the present" (Gordon 2008: xvi).

Ghost-induced violence in *Phobia* and *Phobia 2* has several components. First, it takes place in a wide range of places and spaces; most of them are part of the familiar modern geography of everyday life. Ghost attacks seem to happen everywhere. There are at least four types of places and spaces with violent ghostly haunting: natural spaces (for example, forests, rivers); liminal spaces between the living and the dead (for example, Buddhist temple grounds); everyday private spaces (for example, home, the neighborhood); everyday public spaces (for example, highways, workplaces, business settings, and government institutions; instances include a second-hand car garage, a hospital, and a vocational school). Place, space, and time are inseparable. These places and spaces are by no means spooky in themselves, but they are inhabited by ghosts because of certain conjunctions of space–time. The places may be crime scenes; they may be a scene of death and therefore host a wandering ghost; and these places become locales of fear at certain times, especially at night and on certain calendrically determined dates. In *Khon Klang/In the Middle*, the forest and the river are natural and, thus, untamed by human intervention. They are dangerous and unpredictable because they are the habitats of ghosts and wild spirits. In *Lao Cha-on/Novice*, the forest monastery is inhabited by both humans and demons. It requires certain sets of rules to regulate proper behavior in accordance with temporality. In *Ngao/Happiness*, Pin's life is in danger exactly one hundred days after the death of the young man, called Ton, who had seen her at the last moment of his life. Her apartment is suddenly turned into a haunted place, its familiarity undone. In *Yan Sang Tai/ Tit for Tat,* the classroom and school building are flooded with blood and become a site of a murderous ghost attack. In *Hong Tieng Ruam/Ward* (2009), a hospital room, where so many deaths take place, becomes a fearful haunting ground for a young, arrogant man. The contrast and tension between modern medicine and traditional spirit mediumship are revealed in supernatural form. The supreme authority of scientific-bureaucratic institutions is challenged by supernatural powers of ghosts and their human mediums. In *Thiawbin 224/Last Fright*, an aircraft on a commercial flight is the site of a ghostly attack and violent death for an air hostess, Phim. Like a hospital, the aircraft is a high-tech and highly male-dominated workplace. As a female flight attendant, Phim is subjected to multiple regimes of power relations. She is under the command of the flight captain, while serving an unusually demanding, high-class customer.

Second, technologies play important roles in inspiring, staging, or shaping violation and violence in these horror films. Technologies can be both assets—such as a bicycle, motorcycle, car, cellphone, CCTV, airplane—and means of initiating violence—such as a truck, gun, or knife. Many of the short films collected in *Pho-*

bia and *Phobia 2* highlight the roles of technologies, especially cellphones and automobiles, in crimes or in generating death. In *Ngao/Happiness*, a cellphone is central to the story as a lonely and immobile Pin communicates with an unknown sender of a text message; the sender turns out to be the ghost of a dead young man whom she has never met before. Her cellphone, an instrument of modern technology, appears to be possessed by a ghost and, at times, seems to have a life of its own. In *Lao Cha-on/Novice*, Pey and his gangster friend ride a motorcycle to throw stones at motorists at night. Their concern is to collect cellphones and other valuables from the victims. In the last moments of his life, his cellphone seems to betray him because he cannot talk to his mother at this critical time. His mother hears only the strange noise of a hungry ghost instead of her son who is fighting for his life while being attacked by a ghost. In *Rot Mue Song/Salvage*, the second-hand vehicles are valuable commodities. However, all the used cars have a history of being involved in road accidents which have caused the deaths of drivers and passengers. The ghosts of the dead are attached to their cars as they were their last abode before their tragic deaths. Nut, the second-hand car dealer, is an immoral trader and has to pay the highest price for dealing with possessed cars salvaged from the debris of traffic accidents. Her CCTV technology seems powerless in dealing with supernatural forces. It mysteriously reconfirms her suspicion in ghostly intervention and diminishes her fragile self-confidence as a single, working mother whose business lies at the borderland between moral and immoral, ethical and unethical.

The complex relationships between humans and their technological possessions are critically portrayed in these films. As human inventions, technologies are tools which can be manipulated and employed to serve people's needs and wishes. Yet ghosts too can transform tools like cellphones to their advantage. They turn technologies into unpredictable vehicles of supernatural power in order to serve their own purposes, such as wreaking revenge. Technologies can be both useful and harmful, but technologies which are associated with some ghostly power are unpredictable and unreliable, and thus rather dangerous. As Heller points out, "everything that is unpredictable is dangerous" (Heller 1999: 167).

Third, many of the short films in these two collections take persons in marginalized, vulnerable, and less powerful positions as the targets and objects of violence. Kirsch observes of traditional spirit cults:

> women, children, and those with weak *khwan* (vital essence) are likely objects of the spirit's attention; and the period around childbirth is especially dangerous for both mother and child. The impoverished are more likely to be involved in animist activities than the well-to-do; and less accessible regions are likely to have a higher incidence of animist elements than more accessible areas. (Kirsch 1977: 259)

Kirsch's observation is highly applicable to the people who feature in these films. Marginal and impoverished persons—foreign migrant workers (*Backpackers*), street and market vendors (*Salvage*), an injured young woman living alone and troubled teenagers from broken families (*Novice* and *Tit for Tat*)—become victims of the violence of either more powerful persons or ghosts. Women are often oppressed or at the receiving end of violation and violence. Pin (*Happiness*), Phim (*Last Fright*), Nut (*Salvage*), Pink (*Tit for Tat*), and Pey's mother (*Novice*) all suffer to a different extent from different forms of violent attack. Innocent children too are killed. Death not only gives birth to ghosts, it also endows them with extraordinary power and personality. In some senses, ghosts are believed to possess supernatural power. They are able to act or create events that go beyond human capabilities because they come from different realms of existence. They are also no longer subject to patriarchal, bureaucratic, or scientific institutions and regimes of power. Wealth, class, and socio-economic standing mean nothing to ghosts. When the person who becomes a ghost was alive, they were oppressed, tortured, sexually abused, or killed, but they are transformed into powerful and rampant ghosts through death. Ghostly presence is, therefore, a leveling force intended for both the living and the dead. Such ghostly power is beyond the creation and intervention of modern forces.

Rampaging Urban Youth

In the films under discussion, violation and violence cause death and give birth to a vengeful ghost bent on haunting and terrorizing the living. I suggest that social violence, which is carried out by or implicates groups of urban youths, has been central to Thai horror films over the past few years. Youth is a transitional period, that portion of human life located between childhood and adulthood, widely determined by age and physical growth. Youths are teenagers and young adults, whose lives are occupied by play, study, and work without much familial and professional responsibility. Young people are mostly frustrated and confused with the ambiguity, contradictions, and dilemmas that they face in their lives. More than any other stage of human development, youths' psychology is dominated by emotions like anxiety, excitement, and confusion. Their bodies are on the way to or have reached their physical peak. They are full of energy and possess the desire to explore as well as conquer the world. On the other hand, they have come to realize that society has sets of rules, regulations, and measurements, which they often run up against with their youthful desires and will for freedom.

Youths are the prime agent of modernity, especially those who are raised and grow up in urban areas. Since their birth, urban youths have been exposed to modern environments and ways of life; their lives are usually defined by the process of urban modernization. Moreover, they have subscribed to modern ways of being in the world, which Tanabe and Keyes comprehensively summarize as:

the use of rationalized and secularized knowledge in place of understandings derived from religion and magic; orientation of economic action with reference to demands generated in a globalised market instead of to subsistence needs; acceptance of the political authority of those representing a nation-state rather than of those whose status is determined by a hierarchy of personal relationships; and construction of one's identity as a person with reference to diverse messages and images transmitted through mass media, in contrast to the highly redundant meaning ascribed to the ancestors transmitted primarily through ritual. (Tanabe and Keyes 2002a: 7)

Urban youths are the product of these complex modernization processes. Their young life always exists as constantly in the making and, for them, urban modernization is "the illumination of concrete processes of social life" (Giddens 1984: xvii).

The key questions of relevance in the present context are: Why are urban youths the prime targets in Thai horror films? What happens to the life of urban youths in contemporary Thailand? Why do they quarrel, fight, or involve themselves in social violation and violence? What are the social conditions surrounding Thai urban youths? I contend that the short films collected in *Phobia* and *Phobia 2* portray urban youths in a rather ambiguous manner. Urban youths—such as student trouble-makers, teenage gangsters, arrogant tourists, drug-trafficking truck boys, and young flight attendants—are active, reflexive human characters when involved in social violation and violent sprees. However, the films also remind their viewers that it is too simplistic to attribute all blame to the youngsters themselves. Serious attention must be paid to socio-economic conditions and urban environments in which the youths portrayed encounter deadly ghost attacks and other mysterious dangers.

Contemporary urban Thai society has experienced problematic relations with its young people, particularly in the decades since 1970. The films illustrate how urban modernization in Thailand has produced growing numbers of aggressive, arrogant, disobedient, and undisciplined people, such as criminal gang members (*Novice*), groups of drug users and violent students (*Tit for Tat*), disrespectful tourists (*In the Middle*), drug and labor traffickers (*Backpackers*), cheating entrepreneurs and single mothers (*Salvage*), and sexually promiscuous young women (*Last Fright*). The traditional authority of social institutions—such as the family, Buddhist temples, schools, and hospitals dealing with urban youths—is in decline, if not in crisis. Law enforcement is very random and discriminates against the impoverished, the poor, and the powerless. With young people being intensively exposed to modern technological change and subscribing to different lifestyles than those of previous generations, contemporary Thai urban society is struggling to keep track of and discipline its youths. Anderson (1998) shows how the youths of the 1960s and 1970s transferred anxiety and frustration regarding the fear of unemployment, as well as anger over the rigid political structure of military dictatorship, into the students' movement of the 1970s. Urban youths of that generation demanded open spaces for democracy and transparent economic development. However, urban youths of the 2000s have had to endure the effects of political and economic hopelessness due to ideological differences between the pro-establishment Yellow and pro-poor Red Shirt movements, which has sometimes resulted in violent conflict. Their growing concerns point to the effects and encompassing power of globalization. In the Thai context, transnational and cross-border forces have tended to leave the young behind or marginalized them rather than empower them in their anxious and conscious attempts at positioning themselves in relation to the fast-paced ways of being in the postmodern world. Ghostly presence in Thai horror films of the past decade speaks critically in the name and in the voice of socially marginalized figures. Carsten rightly suggests that "the presence of ghosts speaks not only of unresolved griefs and excessive losses, but that these manifest themselves in parallel temporalities in which the past takes on a more than usually vivid existence" (Carsten 2007: 13).

Conclusion

In Thai horror films, modernity intensifies violation, violence, and the haunting of the dead. These films have undressed modernity and revealed its naked truth. They mirror modernity's ironies. *Phobia* and *Phobia 2* illustrate that, in addition to its rationalizing tendencies, modernity has marginalizing consequences. Thailand is haunted by the shortcomings of modernity: it seems to promise many things, but cannot always deliver on what it promises; the process of modernization has created as much as it has destroyed. In the Thai context, horror films reveal a dark side of urban modernization: while it has produced modern urban social life, it has also produced a significant number of aggressive, arrogant, disrespectful, and violent young men and women. In addition, urban modernization must also be held responsible for the creation of horrific deaths and the uncanny haunting of marginalized ghosts. Their everyday appearance may be mysterious and they may be invisible; their voice may be hardly heard—but the dead come back to haunt and wreak revenge on the living, demanding justice and getting even on both personal and societal levels.

Experiences of encountering ghosts and ghostly presence are genuine collective social phenomena and must be counted as a "social idea," as Malinowski (1916: 424) pointed out almost a century ago. Ghostly haunting, particularly in horror films, must be taken as a serious category of social analysis, because "the whole essence ... of a ghost is that it has a real presence and demands its due, your attention" (Gordon 2008: xvi). Waller proposes that the horror-film genre "mirrors our changing fashions and tastes, our shifting fears and aspirations, and our sense of what constitutes the prime moral, social, and political problems facing us individually and collectively" (Waller 2000: 264). The horror and terror which impinges on the hearts and minds of viewers of *Phobia* and *Phobia 2* are indeed emotional effects of the dark side of urban modernization in contemporary Thailand. They remind us what modern suffering looks like and how complicated modern social life can be. People living in urban spaces live multidimensional social and spiritual lives, in which modernity always makes its presence felt. In and through horror films, tensions and crises at the juncture of the traditional and the modern are most conspicuously spelt out in the trauma of ghostly haunting. Urban modernity has not reduced belief in nor the relevance of ghosts, and in its cinematic products it registers that belief and relevance in the conscious and unconscious minds of youths, the children of modernization.

Notes

1. An early version of this chapter was presented at the workshop on "Spirits in Modern Southeast Asia: Challenges for Societies and Scientists," organized by Lichtenberg-Kolleg/Historische Sternwarte, Georg-August-Universität Göttingen, Germany, 18–19 September 2010. I wish to thank Peter J. Bräunlein, Andrea Lauser, and Paul Christensen for their kind invitation. I also owe a debt of gratitude to Rungnapa Kitiarsa and Suriya Smutkupt for their assistance and support. For the romanized transcription of Thai-language names and terms, except some given personal names, I follow the Royal Thai General System of Transcription (RTGS), issued by the Royal Institute of Thailand (*Ratchabandittayasathan*).

2. In what follows I give the titles of the films discussed in both Thai and English, except when referring to a previously cited film, when English titles only are sometimes used. For marketing and other reasons, most English-language titles of Thai films are not literal translations of their Thai-language title. Instead, they are given English titles which make sense to an international audience: for example, *Ngao* (literally "loneliness") is given the English title *Happiness*, while *Thiawbin 224* (literally "Flight 224") is titled *Last Fright*.

3. These two collections, *Si Phraeng/Phobia* (also known as *4bia*) and *Ha Phraeng/Phobia 2*, are both released in Bangkok by GTH.

4. Nueng Diew (2009: 205–30) discusses numerous recent Thai ghost films, including *Nang Nak* (1999), *999–9999* (2002), *Three* (2002), *Shutter* (2004), and *The Eye* (2005). Other notable recent films include *Body* (2008), *Dorm* (2008), *Phobia* (2008), and *Phobia 2* (2009). I focus on the latter two below.

References

Anderson, Benedict. 1998. "Withdrawal Symptoms," in *Spectre of Comparisons: Nationalism, Southeast Asia, and the World.* Manila: Ateneo de Manila University Press, pp.139–73.

Barmé, Scot. 2002. *Woman, Man, Bangkok: Love, Sex, and Popular Culture in Thailand.* Chiang Mai: Silkworm Books.

Boonyaketmala, Boonrak. 1992. "The Rise and Fall of the Film Industry in Thailand," *East–West Film Journal* 6(2): 62–98.

Carsten, Janet. 2007. "Introduction: Ghosts of Memory," in *Ghosts of Memory: Essays on Remembrance and Relatedness*, ed. J. Carsten. Oxford: Blackwell, pp.1–35.

Chaiworaporn, Anchalee. 2002. "Endearing Afterglow," in *Being and Becoming: The Cinemas of Asia*, eds. A. Vasudev, L. Padgaonkar, and R. Doraiswamy. New Dehli: Macmillan, pp.441–61.

Diamond, Catherine. 2006. "Mae Naak and Company: The Shifting Duality in Female Representation on the Contemporary Thai Stage," *Asian Theatre Journal* 23(2): 111–48.
Ganjanapan, Anan. 1984. "The Idiom of Phii Ka: Peasant Conception of Class Differentiation in Northern Thailand," *Mankind* 14(4): 325–29.
Giddens, Anthony. 1984. *The Constitution of Society.* Berkeley: University of California Press.
———. 1998. *Conversations with Anthony Giddens: Making Sense of Modernity.* Stanford, CA: Stanford University Press.
Golomb, Louis. 1985. *An Anthropology of Curing in Multethnic Thailand.* Urbana: University of Illinois Press.
Gordon, Avery F. 2008. *Ghostly Matters: Haunting and the Sociological Imagination*, 2nd edn. Minneapolis: University of Minnesota Press.
Harrison, Rachel. 2005. "Amazing Thai Film: The Rise and Rise of Contemporary Thai Cinema on the International Screen," *Asian Affairs* 36(3): 321–38.
Hayashi, Yukio. 2003. *Practical Buddhism among the Thai-Lao: Religion in the Making of a Region.* Kyoto: Kyoto University Press.
Heller, Agnes. 1999. *A Theory of Modernity.* Oxford: Blackwell.
Ingawanij, May Adadol. 2007. "Nang Nak: Thai Bourgeois Heritage Cinema," *Inter-Asia Cultural Studies* 8(2): 180–93.
Jirattikorn, Amporn. 2003. "Suriyothai: Hybridizing Thai National Identity through Film," *Inter-Asia Cultural Studies* 4(2): 296–308.
Kawin, Bruce. 1981. "The Mummy's Pool," *Dreamworks* 1: 72–79.
Keyes, Charles F., Laurel Kendall, and Helen Hardacre, eds. 1994. *Asian Visions of Authority: Religion and the Modern States of East and Southeast Asia.* Honolulu: University of Hawaii Press.
Kirsch, A. Thomas. 1977. "Complexity in the Thai Religious System: An Interpretation," *Journal of Asian Studies* 36(2): 241–66.
Kitiarsa, Pattana. 2007. "Muai Thai Cinemas and the Burdens of Thai Men," *Southeast Asia Research* 15(3): 407–24.
———. ed. 2008. *Religious Commodifications in Asia: Marketing Gods.* London: Routledge.
Klausner, William. 1987. *Reflections on Thai Culture.* Bangkok: Siam Society.
Klima, Alan. 2002. *The Funeral Casino: Meditation, Massacre, and Exchange with the Dead in Thailand.* Princeton, NJ: Princeton University Press.
Knee, Adam. 2005. "Thailand Haunted: The Power of the Past in the Contemporary Thai Horror Film," in *Horror International*, eds. S.J. Schneider and T. Williams. Detroit, MI: Wayne State University Press, pp.141–59.
Langford, Jean M. 2005. "Spirits of Dissent: Southeast Asian Memories and Disciplines of Death," *Comparative Studies of South Asia, Africa and the Middle East* 25(1): 161–76.
Malinowski, Bronislaw. 1916. "Balowa: The Spirit of the Dead in the Trobriand Islands," *Journal of the Royal Anthropological Institute* 46: 353–430.
Meyer, Birgit. 2003. "Ghanaian Popular Cinema and the Magic in and of Film," in *Magic and Modernity: Interfaces of Revelation and Concealment*, eds. B. Meyer and P. Pels. Stanford, CA: Stanford University Press, pp.200–22.
Meyer, Birgit, and Peter Pels, eds. 2003. *Magic and Modernity: Interfaces of Revelation and Concealment.* Stanford, CA: Stanford University Press.
Mills, Mary Beth. 1995. "Attack of the Widow Ghosts: Gender, Death, and Modernity in Northeastern Thailand," in *Bewitching Women, Pious Men: Gender and Body Politics in Southeast Asia*, eds. A. Ong and M.G. Peletz. Berkeley: University of California Press, pp.244–73.
Moore, Rachel O. 2000. *Savage Theory: Cinema as Modern Magic.* Durham, NC: Duke University Press.
Morris, Rosalind. 2000. *In the Place of Origins: Modernity and Its Mediums in Northern Thailand.* Durham, NC: Duke University Press.

———. 2002. "Crises of the Modern in Northern Thailand: Ritual, Tradition, and the New Value of Pastness," in *Cultural Crisis and Social Memory: Modernity and Identity in Thailand and Laos*, eds. S. Tanabe and C.F. Keyes. London: Routledge Curzon, pp.68–94.

———. 2008. "Giving up Ghosts: Notes on Trauma and the Possibility of the Political from Southeast Asia," *Positions* 16(1): 229–58.

Nueng Diew. 2009. *Roi Phut Phan Winyan: Tamnan Nang Phi Thai* [Hundreds of spirits and thousands of ghosts: the legend of Thai ghost films]. Bangkok: Samnakphim Popcorn.

Pels, Peter. 2003. "Introduction: Magic and Modernity," in *Magic and Modernity: Interfaces of Revelation and Concealment*, eds. B. Meyer and P. Pels. Stanford, CA: Stanford University Press, pp.1–38.

Rajadhon, Phya Anuman. 1961. *Life and Ritual in Old Siam: Three Studies of Thai Life and Customs.* New Haven: Human Relations Area Files Press.

———. 1972. *Muang Sawan Lae Phi Sang Thewada* [Heaven and the worlds of spirit and deity]. Bangkok: Bannakhan.

Ramitanon, Shalardchai. 1984. *Phi Chao Nai* [The spirits of the lords]. Bangkok: Phayap Offset.

Rhum, Michael R. 1996. "Modernity and Tradition in Thailand," *Modern Asian Studies* 30(2): 325–55.

Rosenau, Pauline Marie. 1992. *Post-modernism and the Social Sciences: Insights, Inroads, and Intrusions.* Princeton, NJ: Princeton University Press.

Simmel, Georg. 1978. *The Philosophy of Money.* London: Routledge and Kegan Paul.

Smith, Bardwell L., ed. 1978. *Religion and Legitimation of Power in Thailand, Laos, and Burma.* Chambersburg, PA: Anima Books.

Smutkupt, Suriya, Pattana Kitiarsa, Silapakit Teekhantikun, and Chanthana Suraphinit. 1996. *Song Chao Khao Phi* [Spirit-medium cult discourses and crises of modernity in Thailand.] Bangkok: Princess Maha Chakkri Sirindhon Anthropology Center.

So, Phlainoi. 2009. *Tamnam Phi Thai* [The legend of Thai ghosts], 2nd edn. Bangkok: Phim Kham Samnakphim.

Steedly, Mary Margaret. 1993. *Hanging without a Rope: Narrative Experience in Colonial and Postcolonial Karoland.* Princeton, NJ: Princeton University Press.

Swearer, Donald K. 1995. *The Buddhist World of Southeast Asia.* Albany: State University of New York Press.

Tan, Kenneth Paul. 2010. "Pontianaks, Ghosts and the Possessed: Female Monstrosity and National Anxiety in Singapore Cinema," *Asian Studies Review* 34: 151–70.

Tanabe, Shigeharu. 1986. *Nung Laung Nung Dam: Tamnan Khong Phunam Chaona Haeng Lanna Thai* [Wearing yellow robes, wearing black garb: a history of a peasant leader in Lanna Thai]. Bangkok: Sangsan Press.

———. 1991. "Spirits, Power, and the Discourse of Female Gender: The Phi Meng Cult in Northern Thailand," in *Thai Constructions of Knowledge*, eds. M. Chitakasem and A. Turton. London: School of Oriental and African Studies, pp.183–212.

———. 2002. "The Person in Transformation: Body, Mind and Cultural Appropriation," in *Cultural Crisis and Social Memory: Modernity and Identity in Thailand and Laos*, eds S. Tanabe and C.F. Keyes. London: Routledge Curzon, pp.43–67.

Tanabe, Shigeharu, and Charles F. Keyes. 2002a. "Introduction," in *Cultural Crisis and Social Memory: Modernity and Identity in Thailand and Laos*, eds. S. Tanabe and C.F. Keyes. London: Routledge Curzon, pp.1–39.

———. eds. 2002b. *Cultural Crisis and Social Memory: Modernity and Identity in Thailand and Laos.* London: Routledge Curzon.

Waller, Gregory A. 2000. "Introduction to American Horrors," in *The Horror Reader*, ed. K. Gelder. New York: Routledge, pp.257–64.

Winichakul, Thongchai. 1994. *Siam Mapped: A History of the Geo-body of a Nation.* Honolulu: University of Hawaii Press.

Wong, Ka F. 2000. "Nang Nak: The Cult and Myth of a Popular Ghost in Thailand," in *Thai Folklore: Insights into Thai Folk Culture*, ed. S.N. Thalang. Bangkok: Chulalongkorn University Press, pp.123–42.

NOTES ON CONTRIBUTORS

Bénédicte Brac de la Perrière is Senior Researcher at the Centre Asie du Sud-Est, Centre National de la Recherche Scientifique/Ecole des Hautes Etudes en Sciences Sociales (CNRS/EHESS), Paris. She has conducted field research in Myanmar (Burma) since 1981 and obtained a Ph.D. from EHESS. Since 1984, her research has focused on the spirit mediums of the Burmese cult of the thirty-seven *nats*, and she is now coordinating a research program on local traditions and world religions in Southeast Asia and beyond. She is the author of *Les rituels de possession en Birmanie: du culte d'Etat aux ceremonies privées* (1989) as well as numerous papers, and she recently co-edited a special issue of *Asian Ethnology* (2009) on Burmese religion.

Claire Chauvet obtained her Ph.D. from the University Paris X–Nanterre, and is a research associate at the Centre Asie du Sud-Est, Centre National de la Recherche Scientifique/Ecole des Hautes Etudes en Sciences Sociales (CNRS/EHESS), Paris. Her research interests are religion, spirit possession, and rituals on the one hand, and health, disease, and medicine in Vietnam and France on the other. She has published a number of articles resulting from her research and is the author of *Sous le voile rouge: rituels de possession et réseaux cultuels à Ha Nôi, Viêt Nam* (2011).

Kirsten W. Endres heads a research group at the Max Planck Institute for Social Anthropology, Halle/Saale. She has conducted extensive ethnographic research in northern Vietnam since 1996 and published several articles on the dynamics of religious and ritual change since the country's economic reforms. Her recent monograph, *Performing the Divine: Mediums, Markets and Modernity in Urban Vietnam* (2011) examines the flourishing world of urban spirit mediumship as part of the reform-era revival of popular religion in Vietnam.

Beng-Lan Goh is a cultural anthropologist working on issues of modernity and urbanism in Southeast Asia. She is the author of *Modern Dreams: An Inquiry into Power, Cultural Production, and the Cityscape in Contemporary Urban Penang, Malaysia* (2002) and editor of *Decentring and Diversifying Southeast Asian Studies* (2011).

Alexander Horstmann is currently a visiting professor at the College of Religious Studies and a Senior Advisor of the Multicultural Studies Program at Mahidol University in Thailand. He is also Senior Research Partner at the Max Planck Institute for Religious and Ethnic Diversity in Goettingen, Germany. After many years of studying dynamics of religion in Southern Thailand, he began a research project in 2009 on Karen religions and sacred spaces of Karen refugees that took him to the refugee camps in Northwestern Thailand and to Karen state in Burma (Myanmar). Recent publications include "Sacred Networks and Struggles among the Karen Baptists across the Thailand-Burma Border" (2011), *Moussons* 17: 85–104; "Living Together: The Transformation of Multi-religious Coexistence in Southern Thailand" (2011), *Journal of Southeast Asian Studies* 42(3): 487–510.

Laurel Kendall holds a doctorate from Columbia University, and is curator of Asian ethnographic collections at the American Museum of Natural History (AMNH), New York, and chair of the museum's anthropology division; she also teaches at Columbia University. She was project co-curator for "Vietnam: Journeys of Body, Mind, and Spirit," a collaborative project undertaken between AMNH and the Vietnam Museum of Ethnology, for which she was awarded a Friendship Medal by the Vietnamese government in 2004. She has also written extensively about shamanism, gender, and the cultural construction of tradition and modernity in Korea. She is the author of *Shamans, Housewives, and Other Restless Spirits: Women in Korean Ritual Life* (1985) and *Shamans, Nostalgias, and the IMF: South Korean Popular Religion in Motion* (2009), and she recently edited the volume *Consuming Korean Tradition in Early and Late Modernity: Commodities, Tourism, and Performance* (2010).

Pattana Kitiarsa is Assistant Professor in the Department of Southeast Asian Studies, National University of Singapore. He holds a doctorate from the Department of Anthropology, University of Washington, Seattle. A Thai ethnographer in diaspora since January 2004, he has a wide range of research interests, including popular Buddhism, religious commodification, masculinity, popular culture, and transnational labor migration. His publications include the edited volume *Religious Commodification in Asia: Marketing Gods* (2008) and *Monks, Mediums, and Amulets: Thai Popular Buddhism Today* (forthcoming).

Patrice Ladwig obtained his Ph.D. from the University of Cambridge in 2007. He was a research assistant on an AHRC-funded project on Buddhist death rituals at the University of Bristol, and is currently Research Fellow at the Max Planck Institute for Social Anthropology, Halle/Saale. His research interests include the anthropology of Theravada Buddhism, death and funerary cultures, the anthropology of the state, religion and communist movements, and historical anthropology.

His regional focus is Laos and Thailand. He is co-editor of the forthcoming volume *Buddhist Funeral Cultures of Southeast Asia and China* and he has published several papers on history and religion in Laos.

Andrea Lauser is Professor in the Department of Social and Cultural Anthropology, Georg-August-University, Göttingen. Her doctoral and postdoctoral research has focused on Southeast Asia, with a special focus on power, gender, and generation among the Mangyan of Mindoro, the Philippines, and on Filipino marriage migration. Between 2006 and 2007 she was part of a research project at the Max Planck Institute for Social Anthropology, Halle, about pilgrimage and ancestor worship, and she has conducted fieldwork in northern Vietnam. Since 2011 she has been coordinating a research programme on dynamics of religion in Southeast Asia (www.dorisea.net).

Kari Telle is Senior Researcher at the Chr. Michelsen Institute (CMI), Bergen, Norway. Her research in Indonesia covers issues such as popular religion with a focus on Islam and Hinduism, place and landscape, and vigilantism and security politics, on which she has published a number of papers. She also co-edited the recent volume *Contemporary Religiosities: Emergent Socialities and the Post-Nation State* (2010).

Lee Wilson is currently a research associate in the Department of Archaeology and Anthropology at the University of Cambridge. Topics on which he has published include knowledge transmission in Indonesian material arts and indigenous forms of knowledge and power in Indonesia. He co-edited the recent volume *Southeast Asian Perspectives on Power*, and has a forthcoming monograph on the theme of martial arts and nationalism in Indonesia (http://www.stateofanxiety.org).

INDEX